THE GOAL II THE GOAL II THE GOAL II THE GOAL II THE GOAL II THE GOAL

THE GOAL II

It's Not Luck

Other Books by
Eliyahu M. Goldratt

THE GOAL II

It's Not Luck

Eliyahu M. Goldratt

Ω

Productivity & Quality Publishing Private Limited
Madras

© 1994 Eliyahu M. Goldratt

This Indian edition 2005 - Fourth Reprint
ISBN 81-85984-10-7

Originally Published as "It's Not Luck". This Indian edition issued as *The Goal II - It's Not Luck*, by arrangement with the author for sale only in India, Pakistan, Nepal, Bangladesh, Bhutan, Sri Lanka and Maldives.

Published by:

Productivity & Quality Publishing Private Limited
38, Thanikachalam Road
T. Nagar, Madras 600017
India
Phone   :   +91-(044)-2434 4519
Fax   :   +91-(044)-2434 2009
Email   :   service@kkbooks.com
              www.productivityquality.co.in
              www.kkbooks.com
              www.goldratt.gen.in

Printed at:
Sudarsan Graphics
27, Neelakanta Mehta Street
T. Nagar, Madras 600017
India

PRICE : Rs.350.00

1

"As for Alex Rogo's group . . ." At last, Granby has reached my part. I lean back and concentrate. I enjoy every word. No wonder, as the executive VP in charge of the diversified group, I wrote all of it. Well, not exactly all. Granby has changed some superlatives—his prerogative being the CEO, I guess.

It's not just the way he reads it, with his deep baritone voice, it's the music. Who said that numbers can't be a symphony. Now he reaches the crescendo, "In total, the diversified group has finished the year with an operating profit of 1.3 million dollars."

Granby paddles on, but now I barely listen. Not bad, I think to myself. Not bad at all, considering that when I took over one year ago, this group was deep in the red. Each and every one of its three companies. Granby has finished. Now it's the external directors' turn to justify their existence. You see, a board is composed of three groups. The top managers of the company—we do our work before the board meeting. The decoration directors, the ones who are (or were) top guns in other companies—they do their work elsewhere. And the professional sharks, the "representatives" of the shareholders—they don't do any work.

"Well done," says the pompous ex-CEO of an oil company, "you have succeeded in putting UniCo back on track exactly in time for the upcoming market recovery."

Well done, I say to myself, a whole sentence without referring to his own past achievements. He's getting better. Now it's the sharks' turn. Who will be the one to start poking holes in Granby's report, demanding, as they usually do, something more?

"I think that the budget for next year is not aggressive enough," says one of the sharks.

"Yes," says another. "The forecasted performance is all based on the expected recovery in the market. There is nothing in the plan that shows real effort on the part of UniCo."

Exactly as expected. These professional directors are nothing but modern slave drivers; whatever you do is not good enough, they always crack their whip. Granby doesn't bother answering; but now James Doughty speaks up.

"I think that we must constantly remind ourselves that business is not as usual. That we must put in extra effort." And, turning to Granby, "Seven years ago, when you got the position of chief executive officer, the shares were traded for sixty dollars and twenty cents. Now they are oscillating around thirty-two dollars."

Better than the twenty dollars they were two years ago, I think to myself.

"Moreover," Doughty continues, "this company has made so many bad investments that we have drastically eroded our asset base. The credit rating of UniCo has dropped two categories. That is totally unacceptable. I think that the plan for next year should reflect a management commitment to bring UniCo to what it was before."

This is the longest speech I've ever heard Doughty make. He must be serious this time. Actually, he does have a point, of course, if you ignore the overall economy in which we operate. Never before has competition been so fierce. Never before has the market been so demanding.

Personally, knowing very well how difficult this task is, I think that Granby has done a superb job. He inherited a blue chip company, but a company that had eroded its product base. A company that was diving into losses. And he brought it back to profitability.

Trumann raises his hand to quiet the murmur. This is serious. If Trumann backs up Doughty, they have enough power between them to do whatever they want.

It is quiet around the table. Trumann looks at each of us, the managers, and then very slowly says, "If this is the best that management is able to come up with . . . I am afraid we will have to look externally for a successor."

Wow. What a bomb. Granby is retiring in one year, and until now everyone assumed that the race was between Bill Peach and Hilton Smyth, the executive VPs in charge of the two main groups. I personally wanted Bill Peach to win; Hilton is a political snake—nothing more. But now it's a whole new ball game.

"You must have contemplated some more aggressive moves," Trumann says to Granby.

"Yes, we did," Granby admits. "Bill?"

"We have a plan," Bill starts, "a plan that I must emphasize is not finalized yet, and it is very sensitive. It seems it is possible to reengineer the company, enabling us to cut costs by an additional seven percent. But there are many details that have to be hammered out before we can announce it. It's not a trivial task."

Not again. I thought we were over this stage. Every time bottom line improvements are pressed for, the instinctive action is to cut expenses, which actually means laying off people. This is ludicrous. We have already downsized thousands of jobs. We didn't cut just fat. We cut into flesh and blood. As a plant manager, and even more as a division manager, I had to fight Bill all the time to protect my people. If we put the same effort that is constantly drained by reorganizing into figuring out how to get more market, we would be much better off.

Help comes from an unexpected place. Doughty says, "Not good enough."

Trumann immediately follows, "That's not the answer. Wall Street is no longer impressed by such actions. The latest statistics show that more than half the companies that laid off did not improve their bottom line."

It's not just me, everybody is puzzled now. It's obvious that this time the directors are synchronized. They are aiming toward something—but what?

"We must focus our company. We should concentrate more on the core business," Hilton Smyth says in a decisive voice.

Count on Hilton to say some meaningless empty phrase. What is preventing him from concentrating on the core business? That's his job, nothing else.

Trumann asks the same question. "What else do you need to better develop the core business?"

"Many more investments," Hilton replies. And with Granby's permission, he goes to the overhead projector and starts to show some transparencies. Nothing new; it's the same stuff he's been bombarding us with for the past few months. More investments in fancy equipment, more investment in R and D, buying some more companies to "complete our line." Where the hell does he get his certainty that this will help? Isn't it the same way we have buried over a billion dollars in the past few years? "This is definitely the direction," Doughty says.

"Yes, it is," Trumann backs him up, "but we shouldn't ignore what Hilton said at the beginning. We must focus on the core business."

Hilton Smyth, the snake. He was in it with them all along. It's all just a big show. But where are the concrete actions? Where are they going to get the huge sums needed to invest in this fantasy?

"I think that the strategy to diversify was wrong," Trumann says. Turning to Granby he continues, "I understand why you initiated this. You wanted to broaden the base of UniCo, to give it some security. But in hindsight you must agree it was a mistake. We have invested almost three hundred million dollars in diversification. The return-on-investment certainly doesn't justify it. I think we should go back. We should sell these companies, improve our credit base, and re-invest in the core business."

It's the first time I have seen Granby under such an attack. But that's not the point. The point is that this attack on Granby will destroy me. What Trumann is suggesting is to sell all my companies!

What can I do about it?

Granby won't let it pass. His whole long-term strategy was based on diversification.

But from this point on, things move with the speed of an express train. More directors support Trumann's suggestion. The resolution is proposed, seconded and accepted—all within less than five minutes. And Granby doesn't say a word. He even votes for it. He must have something up his sleeve. He must.

"Before we move to the next item on the agenda," Granby says, "I must comment that we should carefully plan how to invest in the core business."

"Agreed," says Trumann. "The investment plans that we have seen so far are too conventional, and much too risky."

I look at Hilton Smyth. He isn't smiling any longer. It is obvious that a double-crossing took place. The CEO position is not in his pocket. Most likely we are going to get a parachuted-in CEO. Anybody is better than Hilton.

2

Some crummy band is giving a loud concert in my house. I go straight up to Dave's room. He is at his desk doing homework. There is no point in saying hello, he won't hear. I close his door; the noise drops fifty decibels. It's a good thing that together with his new stereo, Julie had the wisdom to install a soundproof door to his room.

Sharon is on the phone. I wave at her and go down to the kitchen. Since Julie has opened her office, we've all gotten used to eating late-night dinners. Being a marriage counselor, Julie says that the best working hours are between four and nine in the evening. For her clients it's the best. For us, we take consolation in the tapas that Julie prepares. Being in America doesn't mean that we cannot adopt some European habits.

"Saturday night I'm invited to a very special party."

"How lovely," I reply, and finish the last of the chicken liver pâté. "What's so special about it?"

"It's a sophomore party. Only four of us who are not sophomores have been invited."

"My popular daughter," I wink at her.

"Why not," Sharon twirls around.

The kids have left me only one cream cheese and olive sandwich. I swallow it in two bites.

"So it's okay with you?" she asks.

"I don't see any reason why not." She sends me a kiss and floats out of the kitchen.

"Wait a minute," I call her back. "Is there any reason I shouldn't let you go?"

"Not really," she says. "You know that I'm almost fourteen."

"Yes, big girl. If you can call eight months away almost." Then it dawns on me. "What time is this party supposed to be over?"

"I don't know," she says casually. Too casually. "Late, I suppose."

"How late, Sharon?" I ask, and open the fridge for a beer.

"But, Daddy," her voice becomes more pinched, "I can't leave the party before it ends."

I open the can and head toward the living room. "How late, Sharon?" I repeat.

"Daddy, it's a sophomore party." She still doesn't answer my question. "Don't you understand?"

"I do," I say, and switch on the TV. "And I want you home before ten o'clock."

"But Debbie, Kim and Chris are all going!" Tears start to roll. "How come I have to stay at home?"

"You don't have to stay home. You just have to be home before ten o'clock." I switch aimlessly through the channels. "What did your mom say?"

"She said to ask you," Sharon sniffles.

"So you asked, and you got the answer. That's it, darling."

"I told her you wouldn't understand," she cries, and runs to her room.

I continue to switch channels. It's ten minutes before six. In a little while Julie will call with instructions for dinner. What an idea to send Sharon to me for such a thing.

Julie makes sure that I'll continue to be involved in running our family. That's okay with me, especially when most of the burden is on her shoulders. But I don't like it when I'm called in to be the bad guy. Julie should have known I wouldn't allow Sharon to come home late.

"So, let me check. At seven o'clock I turn the oven on to 350 degrees, and after ten minutes I put in the lasagna."

"Yes, darling," Julie confirms. "Everything okay?"

"Not exactly. I'm afraid that Sharon will not be joining us for dinner tonight."

"Uh-oh. That means you refused her point-blank."

"Point-blank," I firmly say. "What did you expect?"

"I expected that you would use the negotiation technique that Jonah taught us."

"I'm not negotiating with my daughter," I say, irritated.

"Your prerogative," Julie says calmly. "You can dictate the answer, but be ready to suffer the consequences. Until at least Saturday, don't expect to be popular with your little darling."

When I don't answer, she continues, "Alex, will you please reconsider? It is a typical case of negotiating. Just use the technique, write the cloud."

I return to the TV to watch the news. Nothing new. Negotiations. The Serbs and the Muslims, the Israelis and the Arabs, another kidnapping. Everywhere you turn it's negotiations.

At work, I had too many "opportunities" to negotiate with stubborn, obnoxious, illogical people. It was not fun. No wonder I refused to believe Jonah when he claimed that it's not personalities to be blamed, but the situation. The situation where what you want and what the other party wants seem to be mutually exclusive; there is no acceptable compromise.

I agreed that such situations are tough, but insisted

that the other person's nasty personality had a lot to do with it. Then Jonah suggested I check to see that if when I start to feel that the other person is obstinate and illogical, the other person is developing exactly the same opinion of me.

I did check. Since then, in all my work negotiations, when things start to get rough, I use his technique. But at home? With Sharon?

Julie is right. Sharon and I were negotiating, and we did reach the point where each of us thinks that the other is illogical. If I don't want to see a frowning face, I'd better follow Jonah's guidelines.

"Whenever you identify that you are in a negotiation situation that doesn't have an acceptable compromise, take the first step: immediately stop the dialogue." I can hear Jonah's words.

Sharon has already stopped the dialogue (if you can call two monologues going at the same time a dialogue).

I'm now on the second step, setting the right frame of mind; recognizing that in spite of how emotional it seems, it is not the other party who should be blamed for the situation, but rather that we are both captured in a conflict that does not have an amicable compromise.

This is not easy. I wasn't the one who created the problem. But I guess that it's ridiculous to blame Sharon for wanting to go to the party.

Maybe we can compromise? There is nothing holy in the number ten, I can go as far as allowing her to come home at ten-thirty. But that won't be sufficient for her. And midnight is totally out of the question.

I'd better move to the next step, to write the cloud precisely. I go to the study to find the detailed instructions.

I can't find them, but it really doesn't matter—I remember them by heart. Taking a piece of paper and a pen, I start to reconstruct. The first question is: what do I want? In the upper right-hand corner I write, "Sharon home before ten o'clock." Below it I write the answer to the question: what does she want? "Sharon home around twelve." No way!

Okay, I calm myself down. Back to the technique. To satisfy what need, do I insist on what I want? "To protect the reputation of my daughter." Come on, Alex, I say to myself, what harm is there in letting her go to the kids' party? And what will the neighbors say? Probably nothing, but in any case, who cares?

"What I didn't allow one kid to do I cannot, all of a sudden, allow the other to do." I wish I could use this excuse, but with Dave, the issue simply was never raised. Only recently has he shown any tendency to go to parties, and even now he doesn't return much after midnight. Girls! With boys it's much easier.

So, why am I so adamant about ten o'clock? How come I know so clearly what I want, but it's so difficult to verbalize why I want it?

"Disciplined kids," flashes in my mind. Kids must know there are limitations, that they cannot do everything they want to do. Rules are rules.

But wait a minute, rules must have a reason; they must make sense. Otherwise it's not discipline that I'm teaching my kids, it's just showing who is the boss. This approach is dangerous; it will almost guarantee that as soon as they can, they'll flee from the house.

Julie and I are careful not to institute stupid rules. So where is this ten o'clock rule coming from? Just because at her age I was not allowed to stay out past nine? Inertia? Extrapolating from the past? Can't be.

"Her safety." That's it; that's why I insist on what I want. I feel relieved.

At the top of the page, in the middle, I write, "Ensure Sharon's safety." Now I have to figure out what need of hers causes her to insist on what she wants. How the hell do I know? Who can understand a thirteen-year-old girl? But actually, I do know. She has cried it more than once; she wants to be popular. Good enough. I write it down. Now the toughest question of them all. What is our common objective? Frankly, in the mood that I'm in now, I don't think that we have anything in common. Kids. We love them. We certainly do, it's in our genes. But this doesn't mean that we have to like them. What a headache.

Okay, back to the issue. What is our common objective? Why do we bother to negotiate? Why do we care about finding an acceptable resolution; acceptable to both parties? Because we are a family, because we have to continue to live in one house. On the left I write: "Have a good family life."

I check what I have written. In order to have a good family life I must ensure Sharon's safety. Yes, definitely. On the other hand, in order to have a good family life, Sharon must be popular. I don't see exactly why, but as I said, I'm not pretending to understand a young girl's mind.

Next, to the conflict. In order to ensure Sharon's safety, Sharon must be home before ten. But, in order for Sharon to be popular, she must be home around twelve. The conflict is clear. It's also clear that no compromise is possible. I'm concerned about her safety, and frankly couldn't care less if she is not so popular with those noisy friends of hers; while for her it's the exact opposite.

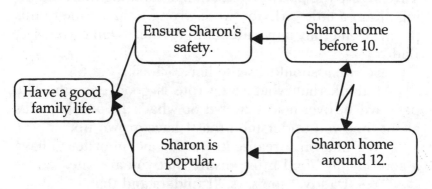

Sighing, I knock on Sharon's door. This won't be fun. She looks at me with red eyes.

"Sharon, let's discuss it."

"What's to discuss," she starts to cry again. "You simply don't understand."

"So help me understand," I say, sitting on her bed. "Look, we have a common objective."

"Do we?"

"I certainly hope so. What about," I start to read the cloud from the paper, "to have a good family life? I want it and you want it. Right?" She doesn't answer.

"I understand that in order for you to have a good family life, you must be popular with your friends."

"No, not at all. It's not a matter of popular or not. Don't you see, Daddy, I have my own friends. I cannot be an exception. Being accepted is very important."

I don't see how what I wrote is wrong, but remembering Jonah's guidelines, I don't argue. I simply cross out what I've written and write "Sharon is accepted by her friends." "Is that what you mean?"

"Roughly."

That's probably the best I can expect at this stage. I keep on. "In order for you to be accepted by your friends, I understand that you must come home from the party around twelve o'clock."

"I must come home when the party ends, I cannot leave before the party's over. It's like standing there shouting, 'I am a little girl. You were wrong to invite me to this party. Don't pay any attention to me.' Don't you see, Daddy?"

"So, what should I write here?" I ask.

"I think that what you wrote is good enough. The party will be over before twelve. So what's the problem? It's about time you understood that I have grown up."

"Yes, Sharon, I realize it. But for me, in order to have a good family life, I must ensure that you are safe."

"Yes, Daddy," she says, "I understand that."

"That's why I want you home before ten."

"But don't you realize . . ."

"I do realize, but let's stop arguing about ten or twelve. That's not the real issue. The real issues are your safety and your need to be accepted by your friends. So why don't we examine the assumptions that lead us to believe that ten o'clock is vital for your safety and twelve is vital for your acceptance."

"I don't see why coming home late has anything to do with my safety," she starts to argue.

"Don't you?"

"No. I'm sure that one of the guys will give us a ride."

"Oh? Since when are sophomores driving?"

That stops her for a moment. "Daddy, could you give us a ride?" Sharon hesitantly asks.

"Who are these sophomore kids?" I start to question her. When I realize that the sophomores are all from Dave's high school, I relax. This is a good school, good kids. And it's no hassle to bring her back. I don't see any safety issue.

"So you agree? Thank you, Daddy, I knew you'd understand." Sharon jumps up and down, on me, and then on the phone. "I'm going to call Debbie. Now her father will allow her to come, too."

Laughing, I rush downstairs to turn on the oven.

I finish updating Julie about the board meeting.

"It doesn't look too good," she says.

"Nope," I agree. "I'm captured in a real cloud. My objective is to maintain my job. For that I must comply with the board's resolution, which means that I have to collaborate with the selling of my companies."

"But on the other hand," Julie continues, "in order to maintain your job, the job must be there, which means you must do everything to stop the sale of your companies."

"Exactly."

"What are you going to do?"

"I don't know yet. Probably sail with the wind for a

while, at least until the situation becomes somewhat clearer," I say, in a not-too-confident voice.

Julie switches to the sofa near me. "Honey," she brushes my cheek, "you know what happens when you let bad situations naturally develop."

Yes, I know. Left to themselves, things go from bad to worse.

I put my arm around her, "We can always live off your income," I try to avoid the issue.

"Fine with me, but would you be happy about that?"

I kiss her. "You are right. I can't rely on Granby alone. And there is no point in waiting for developments. I'll have to find a way to influence them in the right direction."

3

"This is a bad idea," I try to shout at Don.

I guess, by reading his lips, that he says, "What?"

It's useless. These huge printing presses are worse than Dave's stereo. Monstrous, almost frightening, and the speeds the paper is serpentining through them is disturbing. Look at it for more than a minute or two and you become seasick. At least me. Besides, if you've seen one, unless you are a printing press freak, you've seen them all.

I grab Don, my assistant, with one hand, Pete, the president of this printing company, with the other, and head for the nearest exit. Out here, where shouts can be heard, I explain to Pete that when I said I wanted to see his operations, I didn't mean his beloved machines. They will always look the same to me.

"So, what do you want to see?" Pete asks.

"The finished goods warehouse, for example."

"But there is nothing to see there," he says. "Haven't you read my reports?"

"That's exactly what I want to see with my own eyes," I reply.

The warehouse is three times as big as the rest of the complex, and twice as tall. The first time I was here, a week after I became the EVP of the diversified group, it was jampacked with all sorts of printed stuff. The first thing that I did was to cancel their appropriation request for another warehouse. Then I went through the long but enjoyable process of teaching Pete and his managers how to run a company without the devastating crutch of mountains of inventory.

"What are you planning to do with this space?" I ask Pete. "Throw parties? Build airplanes?"

"Sell it, I guess," he laughs. I don't reply.

"What's your on-time delivery?" Don asks.

"In the high nineties," he proudly answers.

"And what was it before you emptied this warehouse?"

"Don't ask. You know, at that point, none of us really believed Alex—that reducing finished goods would allow us to fill more orders on-time. That was a little bit hard to swallow. But let me take you to where the real change took place, the prep room."

As we go, Don continues to question Pete on some details. Don is good, and his relentless eagerness to learn guarantees that he'll become even better. I needed someone to take care of the details. Someone who is good enough to understand not just what I'm doing, but why I'm doing it. It has already been one and a half years since I decided to pinch this bright young engineer who was twiddling his thumbs on Bill Peach's staff. Good decision; one of my best.

We enter the prep room.

No, it's not one room, it's almost an entire floor. It's quiet. Here is where the real work is done, converting client's wishes into "art work." From here, once the client is satisfied, the work goes to the printing presses to be mass produced. At first glance I don't see anything different, but then I realize that none of the nervousness, the running around, the tense expressions on people's faces is left.

"No sense of urgency," I say to Pete.

"Yes," he smiles. "No sense of urgency, and nevertheless we are now turning around new designs in less than one week. Compare it to the four-weeks plus that was the accepted standard before."

"This must have an impact on quality, as well," Don says.

"No doubt," Pete agrees, "quality in conjunction with lead time is today our strongest suit."

"Impressive," I say. "Let's go back to your office and talk some numbers."

Pete's printing company is the smallest company in my group, but it is rapidly turning into a beauty. The huge investment that I put into this company—not in money but in time—to teach Pete and his people has certainly paid off. In one year they have turned from a mediocre printing house into one of the best. And in some aspects, they are the best. But the numbers are not so good. The company is profitable, but just barely.

"Pete," I ask, even though I know the answer, "how come you are unable to translate your superior abilities— your high performance in delivering on time, your very fast response, and your quality—into higher prices?"

"Yes, isn't it funny?" he says in a flat tone. "Every client demands shorter lead time and better performance. But when you deliver, they are unwilling to pay higher prices for it. It is as if they take this improved performance as the entry fee for doing business. If you don't have it, you have a hard time getting business; if you do have it, you still can't command higher prices."

"Do you feel pressure to reduce prices?" Don asks.

Pete looks at him. "Yes, definitely. The pressure is immense, and I am afraid that some of my competitors will start to yield to this pressure, which will force us to reduce prices as well. Actually, it has already started. To get the contract for the small cereal boxes, we had to reduce our price by three percent. I sent you a memo about it.

"Yes, you did," I confirm. "So what will be the impact on this year's forecast?"

"It's already factored in," Pete replies. "But let's face

it, this anticipated reduction in prices has wiped out almost all the impact of our increase in sales. This year we are going to increase our market share, but not our profit."

"This is a problem," I say to Pete. "A real problem. What can you do to substantially increase profits?"

"As I see it, there is only one way. Look at the breakdown of the numbers. Our box business is doing very well. The problem is with the candy wrappers. Last year wrapper department sales were twenty million dollars out of a total of sixty million dollars. But this twenty million dollars caused four million dollars in losses. We have to stop the bleeding on that side of the business; it reduced our overall profit to only nine hundred thousand dollars."

"How do you suggest doing that?" I ask.

"We have to get the high-volume business. Right now almost all our wrapper business is in the low-runners—candies that sell in small quantities. We can't get the work for the really popular candies, the ones selling in the zillions—that's where most of the money is."

"What do you need in order to get those orders?"

"Simple," he answers, "more advanced equipment." And he hands me a thick report. "We have surveyed it in depth, and we have a decisive recommendation."

I flip through the pages for the bottom line number, and find 7.4 million dollars. He is out of his mind. Keeping a straight face, I say, "Pete, don't ask for any investment."

"Alex, we cannot compete with our old machines."

"Old machines? They aren't even five years old!"

"Technology is moving much faster than in the past. Five years ago they were state-of-the-art. But now I have to compete against companies, most of whom have the new generation. It's not offset base, it's rotogravure. Those machines have better resolution in dark colors; they are able to print in silver and gold, which I cannot; they can print on plastic, I can print only on paper. But above all, they are much wider. The width alone gives them three times more output per hour. This difference in output speed gives them a huge advantage when large quantities are concerned."

I look at him. He does have a point. But it doesn't matter, not in light of the board's resolution. I decide to land it on him. In any event, I have to tell all my presidents about it.

"Pete, in the last board meeting the strategy of UniCo turned one hundred and eighty degrees."

"What do you mean?" he asks.

"The board decided," I say slowly, "to switch from diversification to concentrating on the core business."

"So?"

He doesn't get it. I'll have to spell it out. "So, they are unwilling to invest even one more cent in our side of the business. Actually, they have decided to sell all the companies in our group."

"Including me?" he asks.

"Yes, including you."

He is turning white. "Alex, this is a disaster."

"Calm down. It's not a disaster. So you will work for another conglomerate. What's the difference?"

"Alex, what are you talking about? Don't you know the printing business? Do you think that any other company will allow me to operate the way that you have taught us? Do you think they'll allow non-bottlenecks to stay idle from time to time? That they'll allow us to not build finished goods? At every other printer I know the cost mentality is dominant; we will be forced to reverse everything we have done. Do you know what the results will be then?"

Actually, I do. I know it too well, I have seen it in other places. It is one thing to deliver on-time in only seventy percent of the cases—the clients are used to it and protect themselves accordingly. But if they are spoiled by your delivering constantly in the high nineties and then you drop your performance, you have caught your client off guard, when they are not protected by hefty raw material inventory. They will never forgive you for that. Degrading the performance translates almost immediately into lost clients. This will cause more layoffs, even worse performance, and the company spirals down at an incredible speed.

We are not talking here about finding another job for myself. We are talking about the livelihood of my companies. We are talking about almost two thousand jobs.

We sit quietly for a while. Then I pull myself together and say, "Pete, what can you do to increase profits for this year? Substantially?"

Pete doesn't answer.

"Well?" I press.

"I don't know," he says. "I really don't know."

"Pete, let's face it. Our chance of reversing the board's resolution is like the chance of a snowflake in hell."

"And Granby?" he says.

"Yes, Granby might do something about it. But we can't count on him. Pete, the only way left for us is to increase the profits of your company so that when it is sold, it's such a gold mine that the new owner will not interfere in your operations."

"Fat chance," he mutters, but the color is returning to his face.

"One thing is clear," Don says, "Pete must stop the bleeding of the wrapper department."

"Yeah," Pete agrees. "But if you are unwilling to give me the money, the only way I can do it is by closing down the whole department."

It's the same everywhere, it is just a matter of scale. At corporate we are talking about closing plants and at the company level we are talking about closing departments. There must be a better way. "No, it won't do," Pete says. "It will improve the bottom line, but it won't turn the company into a gold mine. It will just reduce the possibilities. I don't see any way out."

I don't know what to say. I don't see it either, but to Pete I say, "Remember what I taught you? There is always a way out. In the last year you and your people have proven it over and over again."

"Yes," says Pete, "but on technical issues, on logistical issues. Not on such a problem."

"Pete, think about it. Use Jonah's techniques. It will come." I wish I felt as confident as I sound.

"Until now, I hadn't realized how devastating the board's decision is," Don says when we're back in the car. "That's the danger of using common sense, when the entire industry is using common nonsense. Things change above you and you are forced back."

I don't answer. I concentrate on finding my way back to the highway. Once we reach it, I say, "Don, you know it's not just Pete's problem, it's ours as well. If Pete's company is sold for peanuts, the black mark is on us. See, that's why closing the wrapper department is out of the question."

After a while, Don says, "I don't see the connection."

"On our books these giant printing presses are depreciated over a ten-year period. If we close the department, the value of the presses drops to their selling value, which is relatively nothing. It will further degrade the asset base of the company. Which could mean that we'd get an even lower price. Don, we are captured in a conflict."

"Yeah, I see. And as you taught me, whenever we face a conflict we should not attempt to avoid it by compromising." Don opens his briefcase, and takes out his folio. "First step is to precisely verbalize the conflict, then we can find how to break it." He starts to write the cloud. "The objective is 'Sell Pete's company for a good price.'"

I don't agree with the objective, but prefer not to comment.

"One requirement is 'Increase profit.' Which means that we have to 'Close the wrapper department.' Another requirement is 'Protect the asset base,' which translates into 'Keep the wrapper department operational.' What a conflict!" I glance over at what he wrote:

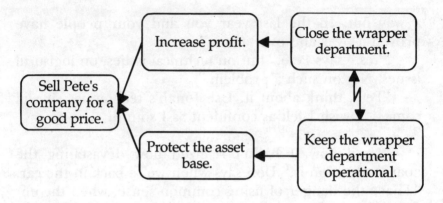

It's a good starting point. "Okay, Don. Surface assumptions, and challenge them."

"In order to get a good price we must increase profit, because . . . ?"

"Because profit of a company determines its value," I surface the assumptions.

"Yes," says Don. "I don't see how to challenge that, especially in Pete's case. He doesn't have any promising new technology, or a new patent that would make the current profits irrelevant."

"Carry on," I say.

"In order to get a good price we must not erode the asset base, because. . . . Once again, because the value of the assets determines the selling price of the company. I don't see how the left side of the cloud can help us."

When I don't comment, he continues.

"In order to increase profit we must close the wrapper department, because . . . because the department is losing money. I have an injection!!" he declares. "Let's turn the wrapper department into a gold mine!"

"Ha, ha." I'm not in the mood for jokes.

"Okay," Don says, "in order to not erode the asset base of the company we must keep the department operational because . . . because the book value of the equipment is bigger than the sales value of the equipment." I don't see any way to challenge that. "One last arrow," he continues.

"Closing the wrapper department is mutually exclusive to keeping the department operational, because . . . because we cannot sell the wrapper department as a stand-alone. Wait a minute, Alex, maybe we can?"

"Of course we can. Get me such a buyer and I have two Brooklyn bridges for him as well."

"I'm stuck," he admits.

"Go over the arrows again. There is usually more than one assumption for each arrow. Concentrate on the arrow that irritates you the most."

"In order to increase profits we must close the wrapper department. This is definitely the one that irritates me the most. Why do we have to close it? Because it is losing money. Why is it losing money? Because we cannot get the big volume business. Wait a minute, Alex. If in the large volumes Pete can't compete against the fast machines, how come he can compete for the small quantities? Something doesn't make sense."

"It's not that something doesn't make sense," I reply. "There must be something we're not aware of. Why don't you call Pete and find out?"

Don places the call. After some "uh-huhs" and "I see's," he disconnects. "The mystery is solved," he says. "Pete's offset presses do have one advantage: they require much less set-up time. This allows him to compete for the small quantities, but in larger quantities, this advantage is wiped out by the speed of the competitors' presses."

We drive the rest of the way in silence. I don't see how to break Pete's cloud. Actually, I do. There is another way to increase the profits of Pete's company. We can rewrite the forecast, ignoring our fear that prices will be reduced. This would probably double the profits. Yuck! No way am I going to use these dirty tricks.

I don't see how to break Pete's cloud. I don't see how to break my cloud. I see only one thing: the need to break them. But how?

4

"Can you come up for a minute?" Granby asks.

"Yes, of course," I answer, and rush up to his office. At last I will find out what he is planning to do about the board's resolution. I knew that the final word was not yet said; I knew that he wasn't just going to lie down and take the punches.

"Hi, Alex," he stands up behind his desk and gestures to the other side of the room. Even better, I think to myself, it's not going to be a formal discussion. I sink into one of the deep couches.

"Coffee, tea?" he asks.

"Coffee will be fine," I respond, guaranteeing that the discussion will last more than five minutes.

"Well, Alex, I have to congratulate you on what you've done with your group. I never thought such big losses could be overcome in just one year. But as a matter of fact, I shouldn't be surprised. You pulled a miracle as a plant manager and even a bigger one as a division manager."

Yes, I think to myself, I pulled miracles, but Hilton Smyth, who didn't pull any miracle, just some strings, became an Executive VP two years before me.

To Granby I say, "That's what we're here to do."

"Tell me, Alex, what can we expect from you this year?

With what miraculous improvements are you going to surprise us this time?"

"I have some plans," I say. "Bob is working on a very interesting distribution system that, if successful, will really change things around."

"Fine, fine," he says, "so what is the actual bottom line forecast that you have. Tell me."

"Here I have to disappoint you. As a matter of fact, I doubt if this year we will even make the forecast."

"What?" he asks, but doesn't seem surprised.

"The market pressure to reduce prices is immense. I've never seen, anything like it. Yes, we factored it into the forecast, but it looks like reality will be even worse. Competition is so fierce that we need to run as fast as we can just to stay in the same place."

If it weren't for the coffee that Granby's secretary is now serving, I'm sure the discussion would end here and now. I wait until the secretary leaves and then say, "Can I ask, what are your plans regarding the board's resolution?"

"What do you mean?"

"Aren't you going to do anything about selling the companies that you yourself bought?"

"Alex," he says, "I have only one year until retirement. If you had some ammunition for me now, maybe I could have done something, but as it stands, I don't have any choice but to collaborate."

In spite of all the mental conditioning that I had tried to go through, I am still deeply surprised. The ace Granby had up his sleeve was me! There is nothing that can be done to stop that devastating decision? Through the fog I hear Granby: "Trumann and Doughty decided to directly supervise selling the companies." When he sees my expression he continues, "Yes, Alex, I still have enough clout to fight it. I could postpone it for one year. But what's the difference. Next year they would do it, and in my absence I would be the prime target for all the mud. No, I'd better bite the bullet now. What a bullet! I hope I won't choke."

"So, what should I do?" I ask. "Business as usual?"

"For your companies it is business as usual. For you it's a lot of work. Trumann and Doughty have already lined up a series of meetings in Europe at the end of the month. You will have to accompany them."

"Why in Europe?"

"Half the investment money comes from there, and besides, it is always a good idea to know what the international market is offering before you begin negotiations with the locals." He stands up. "It's a pity you didn't have another surprise, but I understand. The market is more and more chaotic these days. It's a good thing I'm retiring. I don't think I have left in me what is needed to cope with such a market."

As he accompanies me to the door he adds, "We both don't like to sell the diversified group. Now all the snakes will come out of the closets. I hope that when the sales are over I will be left with some positive reputation."

I leave him and head directly for Bill Peach's office. I must get the full story.

Bill greets me with a big grin. "Did you notice the maneuver our friend Hilton tried? But this time it backfired on him, the creep!"

Bill has his own reasons not to like Hilton Smyth. Not too long ago Hilton reported to him, but now they are on the same level. Hilton is an Executive VP in charge of as big a group as Bill is.

"Yes, I noticed," I say, "but what did you expect from him?"

"He is sharp, very sharp. Granby is not such a good horse anymore, so he tried to switch, he tried to snap up the CEO position. I should have thought of such a move," he says, with a bit of admiration.

"Well, this time he is trying to play against Wall Street sharks," I add. "He's not even in their league."

"Absolutely not in their league," Bill laughs. "They

played him like a violin, and once they got the resolution they wanted, immediately they turned back and put him right where he belongs, throwing all his investment plans in his face. I loved it."

"I never thought that Hilton was a real candidate for becoming the next CEO," I say. "You are senior and you have a better track record."

He slaps me on the back, "A lot of my track record I owe to you, Alex. But no, I don't fool myself. I'm not the CEO type. And after that board meeting, I don't stand a chance."

"What do you mean," I ask, puzzled.

"You know; the decision to sell your companies. I was heavily involved in purchasing them, a lot of the blame will be thrown on me. At least enough to guarantee that I won't be nominated."

Now I am totally baffled. "Why are my companies such political poison? They are not bottomless pits anymore. Last year they even produced some money."

"Alex," Bill smiles, "have you checked how much we paid for these companies?"

"No," I admit. "But how much could we have paid for them?"

"A bloody fortune. Granby was so hot to diversify, and remember we bought them in eighty-nine, when everyone expected a market up-turn—and you know what happened. Rather than going up, the market took a nosedive. I estimate that we paid at least twice what we can hope to get for them now. Alex, everyone involved in these purchases will catch some flack."

"Wait a minute, Bill," I say. "As long as we don't sell the companies, they appear on our books at their purchase value. But the minute that we sell them, we have to write off the entire difference. Maybe Trumann and Doughty haven't paid attention to this?"

"Don't fool yourself," he beams. "They pay attention to any number that is preceded by a dollar sign. They know exactly what they are doing. They will take the bite this year, they will improve the cash position of the company, and then next year—when they bring in some known hot-shot as the new CEO—the shares will jump."

I have to think about it, but one thing I can't figure out. "Why are you so happy about it?" I ask aloud.

"Because now I can relax." Seeing the puzzled look on my face, he continues. "Alex, I knew all along I wasn't going to be the next CEO, but I was terrified that Hilton would be. If there is someone I really don't want to work for, it's Hilton. Any outsider is better. Now, because of his last maneuver, he's lost Granby's support and he definitely didn't win Trumann's or Doughty's. He is doomed."

The minute I return to my office, I ask Don to get me information about the purchases of our companies. We both analyze it. The situation is much worse than Bill said.

According to what we estimate, Pete's company can be sold for a maximum of $20 million. It was purchased for $51.4 million. Stacey Kaufman's company, Pressure-Steam, can currently be sold for no more than $30 million. We paid almost $80 million.

The worst of all is Bob Donovan's company, I Cosmetics. Bearing in mind that even today it is slightly in the red, and taking an optimistic view of their assets, I don't believe that we can sell it for more than $30 million. We paid $124 million. Yes, $124 million.

Now I understand why Granby wants the sales while he is still in control. He personally initiated and authorized the purchases. Almost $255 million. Not to mention the other $30 million or so thrown in since. For all this invest-ment, since the purchases, we have accumulated total addi-tional losses of $86 million. And now, for all this money, the maximum we are going to get back is only about $80 mil-lion. Talk about bad decisions!

"You see, Don," I say to him, "that's what happens when you read the market trend wrongly. Now I understand why everybody, including J. Bartholomew Granby III, is running for shelter. There is enough mud here to drown an elephant."

"What will happen to us?"

"Don't worry, Don. If push comes to shove, I'll have no trouble finding you a good position. No problem at all. But let's put our worries aside. We have something else to take care of right now."

"And I thought that the big gambling was in Las Vegas or on Wall Street," he says in astonishment.

"Yes, but let's put it aside." I tell him about my upcoming trip to Europe.

"Should I schedule a briefing meeting with the presidents of all the companies?" he asks.

"Good idea, but stagger the meetings. I want to spend half a day with each. Now, let's figure out what paperwork I need for the trip."

It takes us almost two hours to compose the long list of papers Don will have to prepare for me. On this trip I will not be traveling light—in any aspect.

5

"In two weeks," I say as casually as I can, "I'm going to Europe."

"Aaawsome!" Sharon jumps in her chair. "You have to bring me 'Hard Rock Cafe' shirts."

"For how long?" Julie asks. She doesn't look too happy.

"About one week," I reply. "I have to meet some prospective buyers for the companies."

"I see," says Julie, looking even more unhappy.

"Daddy, what about my T-shirts?"

"Sharon, decide, coffee-shirts or tea-shirts?" I ask. Only to get a long lecture on these particular shirts. When I was a kid we treasured baseball cards. Now it's funny T-shirts. I guess each generation of kids finds fascination in something useless to collect. The only difference is in the price. The shirts are outrageously expensive. I promise Sharon I'll do my best—subject of course, to my schedule restrictions.

"And what about you?" I ask Dave. "What do you want?"

"I don't need you to bring me anything," he smiles. "I want something you already have. Can I have your car while you're gone?"

I should have guessed it. Dave has a crush on my car, any occasion is a good excuse to ask for it, and when appropriate, I yield. But for a whole week? No way.

"I'll pay for the gas," he hurriedly adds.

"Thank you, very much."

"And the ten-thousand-mile check-up that's due, I'll take care of that, too."

Not really decisive arguments. Since he got his driver's license a little over a year ago, he's become a car freak. I think he spends more time disassembling and assembling his junk car than he spends studying.

In order not to ruin dinner, I say, "Let me think about it." He doesn't press the issue. Dave is a good kid. The rest of dinner we spend talking about the places I am going to visit—Frankfurt and London. Julie and I were there once, before the kids were born, and they—especially Sharon—are interested in hearing about our romantic memories.

After dinner I turn on the TV. There is nothing to see. I give up and turn it off. Julie is humming over her files.

"I'm bored," I say. "Let's go somewhere."

"I've a better idea," she smiles. "Why don't we both work on your commitment?"

"What commitment?"

"The commitment you just gave Dave. You answered him, 'Let me think about it.' "

Count on Julie to turn any potential problem into a win-win situation. What she's referring to is the fact that whenever we answer, "Let me think about it," we are actually giving a commitment. We are committing ourselves to take the time to think about it—whatever the "it" is.

"That's a good idea," I say, knowing that otherwise I'll never give Dave's request a second thought. Until he raises the issue again, that is. And then I'll have to shoot from the hip. One thing I have learned is that I am not John Wayne. Whenever I try to shoot from the hip, I usually hit my own foot.

It's strange. I do take my commitments seriously, and

I do know that if you say to somebody "Let me think about it," usually the person with the crummy idea does come back and demand an answer. Nevertheless, too often I find myself in the embarrassing situation where I haven't devoted any time really thinking about it.

It's not only that it's difficult to clearly verbalize gut feel, it is unpleasant to criticize someone else's idea. We all know that if we criticize the idea of the inventor, the reaction is usually a counterattack and hard feelings. If there is one thing that irritates people more than criticism, it's constructive criticism.

Jonah taught us how to turn these sensitive situations into win-win. It takes some work, and some reexamination, but it certainly pays off. To tell the truth, even though it works like a charm, the effort involved causes me to be more careful with the phrase—"let me think about it." Probably not careful enough.

"Okay, let's start by the book," I say. "What are the positive things about Dave's request to have my car while I'm away? I'm stuck. I can't see any. He's a good driver and relative to his age he's quite responsible. But my new Beamer?" Desperately I write, "The check-up will be done on time."

"Can't you come up with something more convincing?" Julie is amused.

"Frankly, no," I laugh. But there must be something else, or I would have given him a flat "no."

She echoes my thought, "Well, why didn't you tell him 'no' on the spot?"

"Because I was afraid of his reaction. He would have been hurt, and have felt as though I were treating him like a child."

"Yes," Julie replies. "At his age it is very important to feel that his father trusts him."

"I don't know if I trust him to that extent," I say. Nevertheless, I write down, "Strengthening the trust between me and my son."

"What else?"

"That's good enough," I say. "This is a good enough reason. Now, let's go to the easy part, the negatives. I have zillions of them."

Julie smiles. "You know what usually happens, Alex. Before we write them it looks as if there are infinite reasons, but when we put them down, it turns out that there are relatively few, and more embarrassing, most of them are pitiful excuses."

"Okay," I say to Julie, "let's see if it's the case here; I don't think so."

"Start writing."

Without hesitation, I put down the first two reasons that pop into my mind. "One. 'High risk of damage to the car.' Two. 'High risk of Dave injured in an accident.' "

"Wait a minute," Julie says. "I thought you said that Dave is a good driver. You are letting him drive your car from time to time. Besides, if you're so worried about increasing the risk of damage to your cherished toy, why do you drive it downtown?"

I think about it for a second. And what about the alternative, parking it at the airport? "You're right," I agree, and cross off the first item.

I look at the second reason. My car is much safer than Dave's piece of junk, I admit, and cross the second reason out as well.

Julie smiles at me. "Yes, that happens. When you verbalize and examine each negative, often it turns out that they are just unfounded prejudices."

I don't buy it. I don't want to give my car to Dave. I don't want to share it with anybody. It's mine. "Okay, here's a real one," I say. " 'Dave gets used to using my car.' No, that's not strong enough." I cross it out and write instead, "Dave feels he has a right to use my car."

"Yeah, kids do get used to things very quickly," Julie agrees. "He will drive it for one week and you will have a partner for your car."

"That's a big negative," I say.

"There is another one," Julie adds. "You know his dream of driving to Mexico? His spring break is the week you'll be in Europe."

"Take my car to Mexico!" I jump out of my seat. "And then he'll get stuck there and I'll have to come to his rescue." I can vividly see this horrible scenario.

"How are you going to write that down?" Julie asks.

"Having to stop my business in Europe to come and rescue Dave."

"Aren't you exaggerating?"

"Julie, if, God forbid, he is stopped in some village in Mexico, if he needs a parent's signature for whatever reason—remember he is still under age—would you go down there?"

"I prefer not to."

Mexico, my God. What a thought. "What else?"

"Why don't you put what it will all boil down to," Julie suggests. "Deterioration in the relationship between you and Dave."

I examine the list again. It's very short, but it will do. Now we start the enjoyable part, proving with lock-tight cause and effect how giving the car to Dave will actually lead to the predicted negatives. We have fun constructing the "negative branch," as Jonah calls it. And even more so when we rewrite it all, so that it will be less insulting and more convincing when I show it to Dave. A delightful evening, and I'm ready for Dave.

I wish it were as easy to solve my problems at work.

6

"What's on the agenda?" I ask Don.

"You have your briefing with Bob at eight-thirty and at twelve o'clock with Stacey. They are both waiting for you."

"Both?" I ask. "Never mind, call them in."

Bob Donovan and Stacey Kaufman are good friends. They worked for me when I was a plant manager—Bob as production manager, and Stacey as materials manager. Together we learned how to turn a plant around; together we learned from Jonah how to manage a company. They were my key people when I was a division manager. So when I took over the diversified group and saw what a shambles it was, I insisted Bob be nominated as president of I Cosmetics and Stacey as president of Pressure-Steam. They are both very capable and solid people. A little bit older than I, but that has never disturbed our relationship.

Bob lets Stacey precede him, and booms from behind her, "Hey, Alex! Ready for your trip to Europe?"

"Not yet, but with your help I will be," I smile back.

"Just tell us what you need and we'll deliver," Stacey says.

It's good to be with old friends, people whom you can trust. Jokingly I say, "What I really need is a bloody miracle."

"No problem," Bob laughs, "miracle is our middle name." And to Stacey, "I told you he'd find a way to turn it around."

"I didn't doubt it for a minute," she says. "Okay, Alex, let's hear it."

"Hear what?"

"Your plan," they both reply. And Stacey adds, "How we're going to convince the board not to sell our companies. Don refuses to give us even a hint."

I look at them. They have too much confidence in me. Much too much. Not knowing what to say, I ask, "Why are you two so worried about it?"

"Isn't it obvious?" Stacey smiles. "We are conservative people, we don't like any change."

"Yes," Bob joins in. "And besides, where are we going to find a boss like you? Someone who is so dumb as to let us do whatever we like."

"Thank you, Bob. But seriously, why are you worried? You are superb managers, you know Jonah's techniques inside out. Do you think that you'll have a problem convincing any boss, whoever it will be, to leave you alone? To let you manage your companies your way?"

"Is this some type of test?" Stacey says in a flat tone.

"Calm down, Stacey," Bob says. "Don't you see what Alex is doing? Alex is rightfully disappointed. He expected us to find the answer on our own, to figure out his plan." And turning to me, he continues, "So now you are going to ask us pointed questions until we, the dummies, figure it out ourselves? No problem!"

Don leans forward. He has bugged me more than once about my plan, and refuses to believe that I don't have one.

"Can you repeat your question again?" Stacey smiles.

This situation is becoming more and more embarrassing, but now I'm trapped. "What is so unique about working for UniCo?" I ask. "If UniCo decides to sell you to another conglomerate, what do you care?"

That stops them for a moment. "Actually," Stacey hesitantly answers, "as long as you continue being our boss, we don't care."

"Stop the flattery," I say, "be serious."

"No, I am serious. Look, you know our situation. You know we got these companies only a year ago, and what shape they were in. But with someone who doesn't know, and doesn't care, and moreover doesn't understand our mode of doing business, do you think we stand a chance?"

Bob continues in the same vein. "They'll just look at the bottom line numbers and see that my company is still losing money, and Stacey's company is barely making it. Then you know what will happen. The ax will come down. They'll start to cut expenses. They'll start to force us into the cost world. We'll resign and our companies will be destroyed."

Don nods his head in agreement. What do they all want from me? What do they take me for? Why are they so confident that just because I'm the boss, I've got the answers?

"If our companies were very profitable," Stacey adds, "then it would be another ball game, they'd leave us alone. Nobody messes around with a gold mine. But, as Bob said, we're not there—not yet, at least."

She is right. "If we were much more profitable . . ." I echo her words.

"So that's your solution!" Stacey says in astonishment. "You really are asking for miracles."

"How much time do we have?" Bob asks.

"How much time until when?" I ask back.

"Until we switch ownership, until we're sold, until we have to report to another owner?"

"More than three months," I reply.

Stacey laughs dryly, "Déjà vu. We've been here before."

"Yeah, but this time we are better off. Now we have more time, more than three months," Bob adds sarcastically.

What they're referring to is the time we worked together at Bearington, a plant that was a bottomless pit. We
had exactly three months to turn it around, or else. . . .
That's when we met Jonah, and started to learn his Thinking Processes. That's where we did the impossible; we actually turned it around in three months.

"Can we do it?" Don hesitantly asks.

I don't think so. But if Bob and Stacey are willing to
take the challenge, I'll give it my all. In any event, what
other choice do we have?

"Don, you haven't worked with Alex long enough,"
Stacey dismisses him, and then turns back to me. "Okay,
Boss. What is the first step? Do you want a review of where
we stand now?"

"Certainly," I say, and look at Bob. "Go ahead, the
floor is yours."

He starts, "Remember the logical trees we constructed
on how to handle distribution? Well, we have implemented
them. Surprisingly enough we haven't found any real
problems. The central stock is established and we've
started rearranging the regional stocks. So far, so good."

"Good," I say, "very good. So you straightened up
production and now distribution. What's next?"

"Engineering," Bob replies confidently, "but I'm
afraid it will take more than three months. Much more."

"Not sales?" Don asks, sounding surprised.

"Not according to my analysis," Bob says.

"How come?" Don asks. "Isn't the market your constraint? I thought your improvements revealed enough excess capacity to double production. Isn't your problem how
to sell it?"

"Don, you're right," I interject, "Bob's problem is how
to increase sales, the constraint is in the market. But the
fact that the constraint is in the market doesn't mean that
the core problem is in sales. The major reason preventing
more sales might be anywhere in the company."

"Yes, exactly," Bob agrees. "And that's why I think I should address engineering next."

Turning to me he continues, "You see, in our business —cosmetics—if you want to increase sales, as a matter of fact if you want to just protect your sales, you must come up with new product lines. In the past a good product line was sufficient to sustain the company for four or five years. That's not the case anymore. It's become a rat race. I estimate that we will have to come out with a new product line every year."

"To that extreme?" I ask.

"That's on the optimistic side; probably it's going to get worse. Anyhow, we have huge problems coming out with the products fast enough. Research is much too slow, and very unreliable. On top of it, even when they say that a product is complete, and we start to launch it in production, it turns out that what engineering calls complete is not what production calls complete. We start to produce a new product and a whole myriad of problems is immediately exposed.

"Currently, engineering spends more time on the production floor than in their labs. You can imagine this leads to some unpleasant surprises when we get to the market. We have huge problems synchronizing advertising the new lines with what the shops are actually offering."

"So why did you bother with distribution?" Stacey asks.

He turns to her. "Stacey, when your finished goods pipeline has more than three months' inventory, not taking into account what the shops are holding, do you know the meaning of launching a new product that's replacing an existing one? Do you understand the magnitude of the write-offs?"

"I can imagine," she replies. "All the inventory of the replaced product in the pipeline becomes obsolete. You must have a heck of a problem deciding when, and even if, you should launch a new product. Thank God I don't have this chaotic situation to deal with. My products are relatively stable."

"That's what I claimed all along," Bob laughs. "I should have gotten the pressure steam division, it's much more in line with my character."

Not just with his character; Bob even looks like a steam locomotive.

"So, Stacey, want to switch?"

"Bob, I have my own share of problems. Don't offer it so casually, I might take you up on it." We all laugh.

"I'd like to hear more about your distribution system," Stacey says, and when I nod, she continues. "On one hand you have added central stocks, but on the other hand you have done this whole thing to reduce the pipeline. I want to understand it a little better."

"No problem," Bob says. "We are supplying a range of about six hundred and fifty different products to thousands of shops all over the country. In the past, we held about three months' inventory, and it was never enough. Whenever a shop ordered—and remember they don't order one item but a whole spectrum in one shot—we usually were out of some items. Only about thirty percent of the time could we ship a complete order. You can imagine how much it cost to ship the missing items later.

"With the new system, we are now able to respond to a shop within one day, with complete orders more than ninety percent of the time. Inventories are dropping fast; we expect to stabilize at roughly six weeks' stock."

"How did you achieve such a miracle?" Stacey is astonished.

"Simple," Donovan replies, "we used to hold all the inventory in our regional warehouses."

"Why?" I interrupt.

"The same old syndrome of local optima," Bob answers. "The plants were treated as profit centers. From the point of view of a plant manager, once he shipped the inventory, it left his jurisdiction, and it became distribution's headache."

"I bet the formal measurements reflected it," Don says.

"Reflected, and enhanced it," Bob agrees. "The minute that a product was shipped from the plant, on the books of the plant it was recorded as a sale. You can imagine that the minute the plant finished producing a product, that same day it was shipped to one of the regional warehouses."

"Yes, naturally," Don concurs. "So what are you doing differently?"

"Now we keep the stock at the plants themselves. At the regional warehouses we plan to have only what we've forecasted to sell in the next twenty days. That's good enough because we now replenish each regional stock every three days."

"I don't get it at all," Stacey admits. "But first, how do these changes lead to better fulfillment of orders with less stock. I don't see the connection."

"It's simple," I interrupt. "It's all a matter of statistics. Our knowledge of what a shop sells of each item is very rough. One day they can sell ten units of something and the next day zero. Our forecast is based on averages."

"That's clear," Stacey says.

"Now, which forecast will be more accurate?" I ask. "The forecast of the sales of one shop or the aggregated forecast of the sales of one hundred shops?"

"The aggregated forecast," she answers.

"You are right, of course. The larger the number, the more accurate the aggregated forecast. The mathematical rule is that as we aggregate more and more shops the accuracy of the forecast improves in proportion to the square root of the number of shops that we aggregate. You see, when Bob moved the majority of his inventory from twenty-five regions into the plants themselves, his forecast became more accurate by a factor of five."

"Alex, you with your statistics," Bob cuts in. "I never understood them. Let me explain it in my way. Stacey, when you ship to a regional warehouse and you have, on average, three months' inventory in the system, this inventory will be sold, on average, three months after the plant shipped it, right?"

"Provided that you have produced the right stuff in the first place, otherwise it will be even worse," she agrees. "Now I see; as long as the plants have shipped immediately whatever they produced, their shipments to the warehouses were based on the forecast of what will be sold in that region three months down the road. Knowing the accuracy of such forecasts, especially when you are dealing with over six hundred products, I can imagine what was going on."

"Don't forget," Bob adds, "that on top of six hundred and fifty products, I have twenty-five regional warehouses. This considerably adds to the mismatch."

We all nod, and Bob summarizes, "When a regional warehouse goes to fulfill a shop order, some items are always missing. At the same time, we do have these items; we have a lot of them, but in other warehouses. Now the madhouse starts. The warehouse manager is pressing the plants for immediate delivery, and if he can't get it, he starts to call other warehouses. You won't believe the amount of cross shipments between warehouses. It's horrendous."

"I can easily believe it," Stacey says. "What else can you expect when the plants ship the goods three months in advance of consumption? You must end up with too much of one product in one place and too little in another. So I see what you've done; you wiped out local considerations and decided to hold the stock at the origin—at the plant."

"Where the aggregation is the biggest," I add. "Where the forecast is the most accurate."

"But you still need the regional warehouses," Stacey says thoughtfully.

"Yes," Bob agrees, "since we want to respond quickly

to the shops' orders and cut shipping costs. Otherwise I'd have to ship each order to each shop directly from the plant. Federal Express would love it!"

"I see," she says. "So how did you determine how much inventory you need to hold in each regional warehouse?"

"Ah-ha. That was the sixty-four-thousand-dollar question," Bob beams. "Actually, it is quite simple. I just had to extrapolate from what we learned about buffering a physical constraint. Stacey, you're probably as paranoid as I am about building inventory buffers before a bottleneck."

"Yes, of course," Stacey agrees.

"How do you decide on the size of a bottleneck's buffer?"

"We figured that out together already in the Bearington plant," she smiles. "The size of the buffer is determined by two factors: the expected consumption from it, and the expected replenishment time to it."

"You got it," Bob says, "and that is exactly what I've done with my distribution system. I treat the regional warehouses as buffers to the real physical constraint—the shops, the consumers. The size of each regional stock is determined, as you said, according to the consumption from it (by the shops it serves), and the replenishment time to it—which in this case is roughly one and a half times the larger of the shipping time from the plant, or the time interval between the shipments. You see, I use in distribution the rules we developed in production. Of course, with appropriate adjustments."

"Carry on," she says.

"Since I ship every three days, and for most regions the transportation time is about four days, I have to hold enough inventory in a regional warehouse to cover the next week's actual sales. Bearing in mind that I really don't know what exactly will be sold in the next four days, that the shops' consumption is fluctuating all over the map, I have to be wary. Remember, the damage of not having the stock is bigger than the damage of holding more inventory. So, we decided to hold in each regional warehouse the equivalent of twenty days of average sales for the region."

"I understand that you have to be a little paranoid, but it looks to me that inflating one week to three is not paranoia, it's bordering on hysteria," I say.

"You know me," Bob laughs. "Nobody yet accused me of being hysterical."

"So why so much? Why twenty days?"

"It's because of the way the shops are ordering, in big bulk," he answers. "I think that they got used to doing it because, in the past, we and our competitors were extremely unreliable. To guarantee that they don't lose too many sales due to shortages, they don't dare hold only what they need for the very near future. Some of them exaggerate to the extent that they order for the next six months. This, of course, causes spikes in the demand from our regional warehouses. Thank God that in each region there are so many shops that the weekly consumption is not totally erratic, otherwise even twenty days wouldn't be sufficient."

"If the shops would order according to what they actually sold, if they would just replenish," Stacey thoughtfully says, "then your life would be much easier. Did you do anything to convince them to change?"

"Yes, of course," Bob replies. "Our distribution managers sent them a letter, telling them we are willing to replenish to them even on a daily basis, but most are not taking advantage of this service. I guess that every change is slow, especially when we're trying to change purchasing habits that have been in place for decades."

"So how do you know if twenty days will be sufficient?" Stacey asks.

"This number is based not on experience, but on calculation," Bob admits. "According to the current patterns of orders from the shops, twenty days will be sufficient to guarantee over ninety percent immediate response. Right

now we are in transition. We already replenish the regional
stock twice a week, but we haven't yet totally drained the
mountains of inventory that we still carry there. As a result,
the current performance is too good; we can fulfill immediately over ninety-nine percent of the orders.

"There is no need to give such exceptional response. If
in ninety percent of the cases the full order is immediately
filled, we know that in the remaining ten percent of the
cases the shops will wait a week for the residuals.

"This is paradise compared to what we, and our competitors, have given them until now. As a matter of fact, in
order to not spoil them too much, we deliberately deterio-
rated our performance to only ninety percent. Yes," he says
confidently, "we can safely lower the stocks to maximum
twenty days. But in any event we'll know for sure in another four or five months."

"How much do you have now in your regional warehouses?" Don asks.

"It has already dropped to forty days and continues to
rapidly shrink. Of course, as time goes by this rapid decrease will slow down. Remember, we were so much out of
control that in some of our warehouses, for some products,
we had more than nine months of inventory."

"Not bad," I conclude, "not bad at all. So you increased on-time delivery from thirty percent to the nineties, while reducing inventories from ninety to forty days,
and you are still going strong. Nice."

"Forty days is what he currently has in the regional
warehouses," Stacey unnecessarily reminds me. "To guarantee that the replenishment time to the regional warehouses is only dependent on transportation and not on
availability, Bob must also hold additional finished goods in
the plants, his central stocks, as he calls them."

"Yes, of course," Bob laughs. "I wish my total finished
goods inventory would have been only twenty days. As for
the plant stock, I do the same thing. The replenishment
time in this case is determined by the ability of the plant to

produce its full range; the improvements we made last year shrunk this time considerably. I have roughly twenty days' finished goods inventory in the plants. This is sufficient."

"I see," Stacey summarizes. "Before, you were sending products the minute they were produced, relying on a forecast that is three months into the future. No wonder you ended up with the wrong products in wrong places. Now you ship to a specific region only when the shops have actually consumed the product. That's smart. I have to think more about it," Stacey is trying to digest. "Can I get the detailed, logical trees?"

"No problem," he beams, "I'd be delighted."

Don looks totally puzzled. I don't believe that he understood it all. He didn't go over the logical trees with Bob, and he is not a logistical expert like Stacey.

"Do you have any questions, Don?" I ask him.

"Many. But I'm particularly curious as to what happened to the transportation costs?"

"We're now replenishing regional stocks on a constant basis," Bob patiently explains. "This enables us to ship only full truckloads. Moreover, we never need to air freight a small quantity to a regional warehouse; and the warehouses don't have to ship to each other. No wonder transportation costs went down."

"This was heavy stuff," I say, "let's break for lunch. Stacey, after lunch we'll discuss your company, okay?"

"Sure thing, Boss."

7

I don't go to lunch with them. I need the time to think. Bob has already reduced his inventory by thirty days, and he will continue to reduce it. Operationally it makes perfect sense, but there's a problem. A huge problem. Reducing finished goods inventory has a bad short-term impact on the bottom line.

We hold inventory on our books at its cost value—cost as calculated by cost accounting. This means that the finished goods inventory is not registered as raw material cost but rather as raw materials plus added value—the labor and overhead. During the period we reduce finished goods, all the added value in the portion we have reduced hits the bottom line as a loss.

I try to figure out the numbers in Bob's case. He will reduce his inventory by about fifty days of sales. His company is now selling about $180 million a year; so fifty days means approximately $25 million. On the books I won't see the inventory reduced by $25 million, since on the books we carry the finished goods at cost value rather than sales value. I will see the inventory reduced by about $17 million. And the impact on profit? For that I have to subtract from this number the money that we paid for raw materials, let's say about $7 million. My God, his loss will grow by $10 million.

I'm trying not to panic. Of course this is just funny money, cost accounting distortions; and yes, later it will be more than compensated for by real money, by the real savings from less obsolescence and also, hopefully, by increased sales. But how am I going to explain all this to a prospective buyer? Even if he fully understands it, he will pretend that he doesn't. It gives him a trump card to substantially decrease the price for the company.

Are there any positives? Obsolescence will go down. Due to reduction of inventory, introduction of new products will not mandate the write-off of stocks of old ones. How much is it? I flip through Bob's budget. He budgeted $18 million for finished goods obsolescence. Has he factored in the new scenario, when the inventories are reduced? I fish out his last year's performance. No, thank God. Last year it was $18 million, he just copied it from one year to another.

If the inventories are cut by about 50%, obsolescence will be cut even more. Especially as it is much easier to monitor the phasing-in of new products when half of the stocks are held in one place rather than scattered all over the country.

Okay, what does it translate to? Bob will be ahead by the amount he will not have to write-off, by about one million dollars a month; $12 million let's say. The more I succeed to postpone the sale, the better off we are. If I can postpone it to the end of the year. . . . But that's impossible.

When is it likely that the buyers' examiners will start to check us with magnifying glasses? Even if I stand on my head and play every trick I know to procrastinate, it is going to happen in two or three months. Damn it, right at the worst possible time. Exactly when the inventories have been reduced, but the impact of less obsolescence is still in its infancy.

What the hell am I going to do? It's one thing to try to sell a company that is almost breaking even. It's a totally different story to try to sell a company that is losing over $10 million on sales of $180 million. To tell Bob to revert back to the old distribution system? No way. Besides, it won't help. Bob and Stacey are absolutely right, if we don't find a way to make the companies very profitable before they exchange hands, we are all doomed. Me, them and the companies. Everything will go down the drain.

We must find a way to increase sales immediately. It's the only way out. And we cannot do it in the proper way. Pete cannot have the more advanced printing presses that he so desperately needs. Bob cannot afford the time to systematically improve his engineering department. We must move much faster. Damn these Wall Street sharks for putting this devastating pressure on us. Why can't they leave us alone?

They return from lunch.

"Alex," Don starts, "during lunch we discussed the impact Bob's new distribution system will have on his bottom line."

"Pretty devastating," I say in a casual voice.

"So, you noticed it as well," Don says, somewhat disappointed.

"What did you expect, that he wouldn't?" Bob dismisses him, and to me he says, "What should I do? Ignore it, or inflate my central stocks—you know that with my excess capacity I can easily do it."

I think about it for a minute. Inflating the central stocks, not like the regional stocks, will not cause any damage to Bob's ability to quickly respond to the shops' needs. Introduction of new products will be affected, but not by much. On the other hand, he won't suffer from the bad effects that stem from the distortion in the way we currently evaluate inventories on our books. The temptation is big.

"No, Bob. Don't do it," I decide.

"I thought that would be your response. You never wanted to take the easy way, to play the numbers game. But, I thought I should ask."

"Thank you. Okay, Stacey," I say, "your turn."

"Surprisingly, when you look at the general picture, it's not much different," she starts. "I, too, have revealed a lot of excess capacity in the past year—it's going through our ears; we have even more than Bob. Our problem, as you may expect, is sales.

"As you know," she continues, "we don't sell to shops, we sell to industries that need high pressure steam. There are more and more technological improvements in our field, and some new products, but nothing close to what Bob has—some of our designs are ten years old. The problem is that competition is so fierce that often, in order to penetrate, we have to sell the initial equipment for our raw material cost. We make our money more and more on the additions and spare parts. They are still quite lucrative."

"Is your supply of spare parts adequate?" Don asks.

"No," Stacey admits, "not at all. Oh, we have mountains of spare parts, all over the place. But too often it's not the right part in the right place, and then the clients are all over us."

"Could Bob's distribution system help you, as well?"

"It might. That's why I asked for the logical trees of it. We would have to do many adjustments; our situation is quite different. Responding ninety percent of the time is not sufficient. You see, whenever a client needs a spare part from us and we can't deliver immediately, we are shutting down part of his operation. I need to bring my response from what it is now, about ninety-five percent, to almost one hundred percent.

"It's clear we can do a better job. We have to reexamine the levels of inventory that we're holding in our regional stocks. I think by following Bob's concepts I can vastly improve." Turning to me she adds, "Alex, better service on spare parts will not be sufficient to solve my sales problem. I need a real breakthrough idea."

"You said that the prices for spare parts are quite lucrative," Don hesitantly starts.

"Yes, I did," Stacey confirms. When she realizes that Don is reluctant to continue, she encourages him. "Come on, speak up. Many times an outsider can come up with an idea that we, so entrenched in the way things are always done, are too blind to see."

"It's probably nothing," he continues, "but I thought that you sell the basic equipment for only raw material cost, just to get a foot in the door."

"That's also correct."

"Does it mean that the company who sells the basic equipment to a client has, for all practical purposes, a monopoly on the spare parts that client will need?" Don sounds much more confident.

"You are absolutely right," Stacey answers. "Each company has its unique designs. You sell the basic system and the client is locked into buying additions and spare parts from you."

"Well, can you get ahold of your competitors' designs? I assume that technically you can produce them. The differences between theirs and yours cannot be so big."

"So that's what you mean," Stacey sounds disappointed. "To your question, Don, not only can we get hold of their designs, we've already done it. And yes, we can technically and legally produce their spare parts. So what are you suggesting?"

"For you to offer their clients the appropriate spare parts," he says much less confidently. "But it's obvious that you've already thought about it. Why won't it work?"

"Simple, Don," she answers. "Why would their clients buy from us? Because we'll offer it at a slightly lower price?"

"Yes, I see," he breaks in, "and then your competitors

will do the same to you, and the result would be a price war."

"And if there is something," Stacey concludes, "that we have to avoid at all costs, it's a price war."

"Sorry, it was a dumb idea."

"Not so dumb," Stacey smiles at him. "If we'll succeed in properly implementing the equivalent of Bob's distribution system, and we have time to establish an outstanding reputation in spare parts supply, then your idea might work. The problem is that building such a reputation takes years, and we have months."

"Fellows," I slowly say, "we need marketing ideas. Something that will differentiate us, that will make our offers much more attractive than our competitors'. Something that we can implement fast."

"Yes," Stacey agrees, "but we cannot risk doing it by reducing prices."

"Which means," I add, "that those ideas must only take advantage of the products that we already produce. Maybe with slight changes, nothing major."

"Right," Bob joins in, "we need real breakthrough ideas."

"Yes," and to myself I add, "three of them; one for each of the companies."

8

We are about to finish dinner when the unavoidable occurs. "What about the car, Dad?" Dave asks.

Not bad, the kid has patience. I was expecting the attack would start as soon as I entered the house. Julie probably advised him to wait until I was relaxed and fed. Somehow it provokes me. "What about it?" I reply.

"Can I use your car while you have fun in Europe?"

"Fun?" I say.

"Sorry, not fun, hard work. Can I have your car while you are away?"

I don't like his tone of voice, he is not requesting, he's practically demanding. "Give me one good reason why I should?"

He doesn't answer.

"Well?" I press.

"If you don't want to give me the car, don't give it," he mutters into his plate.

I can leave it at that. I actually don't want to give him my car, and now I don't have to. It's okay.

Julie and Sharon are talking about something. Dave and I continue to eat in silence. No, it's not okay. The negative effect that caused me to hesitate in the first place is now reality. Dave is frowning, he's hurt, but worst of all he

is convinced that it's impossible to communicate with me.
Teen-agers.

"You said that you will pay for your own gas and take
the car in for the check-up?" I finally say.

Dave raises his eyes from his plate and looks at me.

"Yes, that's right," he says tentatively. And then, pick-
ing up steam, he continues, "And during that week, whenever Mom has to drive Sharon, I'll do it instead."

"Smart move," I laugh. "Continue in this way, Dave,
maneuvering your mother and sister to your side, and I'm
pushed into a corner."

"That's not what I meant." He's blushing.

"Wait a minute." Sharon is not a girl to overlook such
an opportunity. It doesn't take long, and Sharon summarizes: "Hooray, wait until I tell Debbie, she won't believe
it."

"Neither do I," Dave cools her down. "Dad hasn't yet
agreed to give me his car."

"Daddy, please, pretty please?" Sharon does what
Dave expects her to.

"I don't know," I say. "I haven't decided yet."

"But you promised to think about it," Dave moans.

"Yes, I did."

"And . . ."

"And I have some open concerns."

"Yeah, sure." Dave is visibly irritated.

"Son," I say in a firm voice, "I promised to think about
it, and I did think about it. Not surprisingly I have some
concerns. If you put my mind to rest about them, you can
use my car while I'm in Europe. Ignore them, as if they are
my problems and not yours, and I'll refuse you point-
blank. Is that understood?"

"Yes, Dad," he quiets down. "What are the problems?"

"Let me show you," I answer, and go to the study to
get my papers. Returning, I hand him the first page. "To
the list of positives here I have to add another one," I say.
"Your promise to be the chauffeur for your sister."

"Not exactly what I would call positive," he mutters, and then he reads aloud the last point: " 'Strengthening the trust between me and my son.' " He thinks for a second, and then says, "That means that whatever I promise, I'll have to make bloody sure I deliver." With a sigh he concludes, "What's fair is fair. Okay Dad, what are the problems?"

"The first one, I think, is already solved. Nevertheless, let's go over it. I'm going to Europe exactly when you have your spring break, and we all know that you want to tour Mexico. . . ."

"Daddy, don't worry about Mexico," Sharon immediately interrupts, "Dave promised to drive me every day, and trust me, I'm not going to let him off the hook."

"I had hoped that we could strike a deal," Dave says. "But, okay Dad, no long journeys. Promise."

Relaxed, I turn to the next page. "You read," I say to Dave. "Start from the statements at the bottom."

" 'When I'm away,' " he starts reading, " 'the car is at your disposal.' "

Puzzled, Sharon asks, "Does that mean Daddy's decided to give you the car?"

"I wish," he says, "but unfortunately it only means that he is trying to figure out what will be the negative outcomes if he does."

"Ah."

"Carry on," I encourage him.

" 'I'm away for a lengthy period of time,' " Dave continues to read, and then adds his own interpretation—"one week is not so long."

"Speak for yourself," Julie says.

"Okay, Mom, no more of these remarks. I'm now reading the next level: 'For a lengthy period you can use the car whenever you want.' "

"No," I say. "You are not reading a list of statements, you are reading a logical tree. Read according to the arrows." And to demonstrate, I point to the first statement

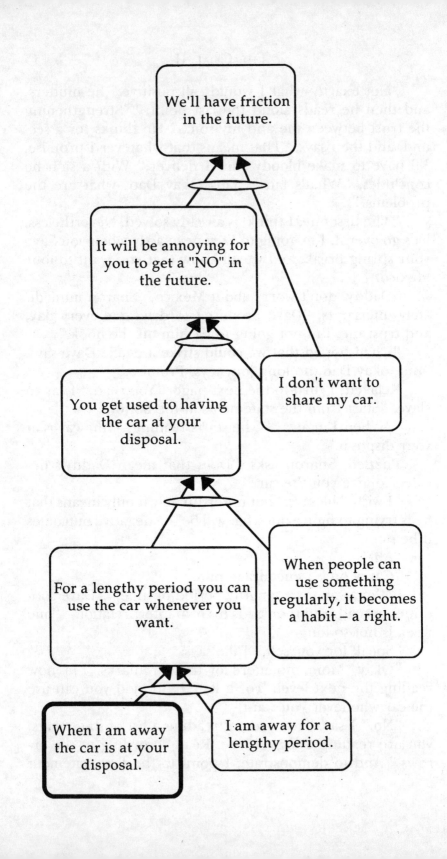

and start to read it properly: " 'If, when I'm away, the car is at your disposal, and . . .' " I shift my finger to the second statement, "and 'I'm away for a lengthy period,' then . . ." and I point to the higher statement, "then 'for a lengthy period you can use the car whenever you want.' "

"Obvious," is Dave's only comment.

"Now read the next entry," I say, and smile at Julie. She smiles back. We both remember what Jonah said: "When the reply is 'obvious' or 'it's only common sense,' it means that you are communicating."

Dave continues to read: " 'When people can use something regularly, it becomes a habit—a right.' "

"Right?" I ask.

"Yes, that's usually the case. Now can I read the next level?"

"Yes, but try to read the cause and effect relationship. Use if . . . then . . ."

"If 'for a lengthy period of time,' " he reads slowly, " 'you can use the car whenever you want,' and 'when people can use something regularly it becomes a habit—a right,' then 'you get used to having the car at your disposal.' Now I see what you're concerned about, but . . ."

"Dave," I interrupt him, "before you start to dismiss it by some rash promises, I'd prefer that you realize how important this concern is. Please read it to the end."

"Okay, I'm reading. The additional entry first: 'I don't want to share my car.' "

"Now the unavoidable derivative. If . . . and . . . then . . . please."

"If 'you get used to having the car at your disposal,' " he reads without much enthusiasm, "and 'I don't want to share my car', then 'it will be annoying for you to get a "NO" in the future.' "

"Correct?" I ask.

"Yes," he admits, "I can see how it could lead to friction."

"Well?" I ask.

"I don't know," he replies. "Whatever I say now can be interpreted as if I just want to ignore the problem."

I sure am glad I took the trouble to write it in such detail. I'm about to suggest a resolution when Julie sends me, just in time, a look. I swallow my words, and instead say, "Take your time, Dave. My trip is not until next week."

Dave gives a convincing demonstration of a fish, opening his mouth to say something and regretting it. At last he says, "Maybe, if I promise not to ask for the Beamer for . . . two months?"

That's too much. Moreover, I don't think that Dave could keep such a promise—he's too much in love with my car.

"Why do you think that would work?" Julie asks him.

"Simple," Dave answers. "If a week is enough to get spoiled, then two months must be enough to reverse it."

"What do you say?" Julie asks me.

"I say that two months is too long, one month will be sufficient."

Julie is working on her files, constructing trees to better understand and solve her clients' problems. In this way she can restore shaky bonds in three or four meetings rather than allowing problems to flounder for months on end. When I mention that she is getting paid by the hour and not by results, she just laughs and points to her long waiting list.

She is very involved in her work but it doesn't put her under stress. You always find her busy but never without time.

I like these peaceful nights, when Julie murmurs over her cases while I try to catch up on my paperwork. In the background Simon and Garfunkel are telling us once again their problems with Cecilia. The kids are in their rooms, probably fast asleep.

"I'm happy with the way you handled Dave," Julie smiles at me.

"Back at UniCo, we called it 'Buying industrial peace,'" I smile back.

"What do you mean?" she is puzzled.

"Julie," I try to explain, "don't get me wrong. I'm at peace with my decision, but frankly, look objectively at what happened: Dave asked for my car, I gave him the car, end of story."

"Darling, do you really feel badly about your decision?" she softly inquires.

"No, not at all. I feel good about it."

She kisses me on the cheek. "Then saying that what happened is just that Dave got what he asked for is, at best, a partial description."

I think about it. It's not that I didn't want my son to get what he so badly wants. It's that I didn't want some other interrelated things to happen, like Dave feeling that he is entitled to my car. The way we've arranged it now, I'm certain that will not happen. Also, some good side benefits emerged. Julie will have fewer demands on her time, and Sharon, rather than being envious, is all for the idea.

"You're right," I hug her. "Who would have imagined that Dave would agree not to ask for the car for even two weeks! You know, Jonah's advice of just clearly presenting the negative branch without trying to suggest a solution is right on the mark. If I had suggested it, he would have treated my suggestion as an insulting unfair demand, at best."

Smiling, Julie nods her head in agreement. "Jonah's methods do work. They always lead to win-win solutions."

"I wish I had your confidence," I say quietly. "Julie, I've so many important clouds now at work. . . . I'm skeptical if there is any good win-win solution for even one of them."

"Tell me more," she says, in the same quiet voice.

I don't know what to say. There is no point in whining about my personal cloud. It will just upset Julie and put me in a devastating, self-pitying mood.

"Have you figured out how to protect your companies?" she asks.

"Not really," I sigh. I tell her about the "plan" that was discussed today with Stacey and Bob. "It's really grasping at straws," I conclude.

"Why?"

"Julie, what do you think is the chance of finding a marketing breakthrough that will enable us to jump sales within a few months?"

"Such things do happen," she tries to cheer me up.

"Yes," I admit, "rarely. But we have to do it without new products and without any advertising budget to speak of." After a pause, I add, "And we don't need just one such miraculous solution. We need three of them. It's totally impossible."

"No, it's not totally impossible," she firmly says. "It may be difficult, but not impossible."

"Oh, come on."

"Alex, listen to me. Jonah taught us his method especially for such situations—where it seems that there is no way out; when it seems that the only thing left is to give up.

"Honey," she keeps on, "I know what I'm talking about. Almost every week I face such situations."

"I haven't noticed." I raise my eyebrows to indicate the extent to which she is exaggerating.

"No, not personally, silly. I'm talking about my clients. Some of them have brought their marriage to such an impasse that it really seems beyond repair." And then, in a thoughtful voice she says, "You know the difference between us? You almost never use Jonah's methods."

I start to protest, but she continues, "Yes, I know that you use parts of them daily—in negotiations, in team building, even when you need to plan an important meeting. But Alex, when is the last time that you tried to use them in full? To analyze a tough situation and construct a win-win solution that will turn it around?"

I want to say that I did it just last month, on the distribution problem. But I didn't do it. It was Bob Donovan and his people.

"In my work," she continues to hammer, "I'm constantly facing new situations; I have to constantly use all the Thinking Processes. No wonder that I'm confident about the results of using them. It's tough. It requires a lot of hard work, but it's working. You know it."

When she realizes that I don't intend to reply, she lays it on me. "Alex, you are living off the generic solutions that you developed in the past. You cannot afford it anymore. You must develop a solution to your current situation."

"What do you mean?" I'm irritated. "You think that I can develop a generic process to find marketing solutions?!"

"Yes, that's exactly what I mean."

I don't bother to answer.

9

"I think we found a way to make the wrapper department even more profitable than the box department." Pete
is excited, and so am I.

Last year, the wrapper department caused four million dollars in losses, reducing the overall profit of the company to less than one million dollars. If Pete is right, if he
found a marketing breakthrough that turns the wrappers
into being as profitable as the rest of the business,
then. . . . Jesus, if they just break even the profit will be
five million dollars!

I can't believe it. It's too good to be true. Could it be
that Pete, in his eagerness to stop the sale of his company,
has come up with some farfetched, risky approach?

"Start at the beginning. Take your time," I say to him.
"And prepare yourself for in-depth scrutiny."

"That's what I want," he smiles broadly. "It all fell in
place after Don's phone call."

"My phone call?" Don says surprised. "I don't remember giving you any new ideas."

"Yes, you did," Pete insists. "A big one."

"It's very nice of you to say so," Don is clearly confused, "especially in front of my boss. But, sorry Pete, what
I recall is that I asked how come you can't compete against

the fast printing presses on large quantities, and you can on small ones."

"Exactly!" Pete is clearly amused by Don's expression. "You caused us to stop feeling sorry about our apparent disadvantages, and start concentrating on the advantages that we do have."

"I see," Don says. But after a moment he adds, "No, I don't see. I don't see how your ability to do quick set-ups can help you compete on large quantities."

"Don, you miss the point," I say. "Pete didn't say he is going after the large quantities, he just said that they decided to concentrate on the markets where they have an advantage. Congratulations, Pete. I knew that if you overcame your obsession that big money can only be found in the large quantities, you would find that there are enough additional lucrative markets that require small quantities. So tell me, what are those markets?" I ask, pleased.

Pete doesn't answer, he just clears his throat in embarrassment. I burst out laughing. It looks like it's not Don, but me, who missed the mark, and by a mile. "Okay, Pete, tell us your brilliant idea. How can quick set-up help you win the large-quantity market in spite of the speed of your competitors' presses?"

"Simple," he says. "Actually, not so simple. Let me start by describing the cloud of our customers."

"Please do."

Pete goes to the white board and starts to unfold the cloud. "The objective of a buyer is to be in line with his corporate directives. In order to be in line with his corporate directives, the buyer must try to get the best financial deal from the vendors. In our industry, where set-up is large, the only way to get a price break is to order large quantities. So, in order to get the best financial deal from the vendor, the buyer must order large quantities."

"This is clear."

"On the other hand," Pete continues, "in order to be in line with his corporate directives, the buyer must strive to reduce inventories. I don't have to tell you to what extent corporate culture has changed in regard to its tolerance for holding large inventories."

"No, you don't have to tell us," I full-heartedly agree.

"This means," Pete completes the cloud, "that in order to strive to reduce inventories, the buyer must order in small quantities more frequently."

"The conflict is clear," Don says, "but the pressure to get low price is dominant, isn't it?"

"Yes," Pete agrees.

"Do you see any reason for that to change?" Don continues to ask.

"Maybe," Pete answers. "As competition in the market becomes more fierce, and I'm talking about the market of my clients, their forecast becomes less accurate. This makes ordering large quantities more hazardous for the buyer. Government regulations are also a big help to us, the printers; every so often they refine the regulations of how the listings of the miniscule ingredients in the food have to appear on the wrapper. Any change, and the entire stock is obsolete. But the real point is that because of the fierce competition, our customers surprise their buyers with more frequent marketing campaigns, which almost always involve some printing change on the wrapper."

"Their internal communication is so bad? They don't inform the buyer about the upcoming marketing campaign?" Don asks.

"It's not so much a problem of internal communication. In the current market, our customers have to react much faster than ever before. Many times they have to launch a new specific marketing campaign within two or three months."

"So," Don concludes, "you hope that as time goes by, the buyers will be more receptive to buying smaller quantities?"

"Yes and no. This tendency has already started, and

will probably accelerate, but we don't have time to wait for this gradual process. We have to help it."

"How?" I inquire.

"By helping our buyers break their cloud," Pete answers.

That's certainly the right approach. "Which arrow do you intend to break?" I ask.

"The one that states that in order to get the best financial deal from the vendor, the buyer must order large quantities," he says.

"Carry on," I encourage him.

"Wait a minute," Don interrupts. "If we want to thoroughly scrutinize Pete's solution, why don't we try to break the cloud?"

"Good idea," Pete grins. "The more solutions proposed and knocked down, the more you will be impressed with my solution."

He sure is confident about his solution. That's promising.

"The assumption under this arrow," Don follows the guidelines of breaking a cloud, "is that due to long set-ups, a buyer can get lower prices only if he orders in large quantities. How can we challenge this assumption? You have relatively quick set-up. . . . Wait a minute, why do we have to think like everybody else, why do you have to price according to the time it takes to print? You have a lot of excess capacity, any price that is higher than your raw-material price is better than letting the resources stay idle."

"Don, are you recommending a price war?" Pete cannot believe his ears.

"No, not at all." Don is getting excited. "What I'm suggesting is that you match your competitors' prices for the large quantities."

Pete tries to say something, but Don is on a roll. "You can do it in spite of the fact that your printing presses are slower, since you have so much excess capacity. It will work. The increased pressure on the buyers to reduce the size of the batches they order will guarantee it. Have you calculated how much more profit you can do? Remember the amount of excess capacity that you have is limited."

"No, Don, this can't be the answer," I say.

"Why not?"

"First of all, I don't see how matching the competitors' prices for large quantities will enable the buyer to order in small quantities. The price-per-unit for a large order will still be lower than for a small order."

"My mistake," Don agrees. "But, nevertheless, my solution still holds. Pete will be able to compete on those orders, and the fact that he is cheaper for small quantities will give him an advantage. Buyers prefer to work with fewer vendors whenever possible."

"Don," I patiently say, "your solution doesn't break the buyers' cloud, so it is obvious that it's not Pete's solution. Besides, Pete would not come here, all excited, to present a solution based on utilizing the fact that he has excess capacity to lower prices. He must have a much better solution. Isn't it so, Pete?"

"Yes, of course." And turning to Don, he adds, "Not only is lowering prices to match competition very risky, the amount of excess capacity we have wouldn't be sufficient to swing the wrapper section into profitability."

"Why is it risky to match the competitors' prices?"

Grinning, Pete answers: "Don, have you considered that the same clients who order large quantities of wrappers for the popular candies are ordering smaller quantities for the less popular candies. It's the same buyers."

Don thinks for a minute. Pete and I wait for him.

Finally he says, "Let me see. The buyers expect that the larger the volume, the lower the price per unit.

"Correct," Pete encourages him, "this is the key."

"That means," Don continues somewhat more confidently, "that the buyer not only compares your prices to the competitors, he compares your price per unit for larger orders to your price per unit on smaller orders. Now I see the problem. If you reduce your price per unit on the large quantities, the buyer will demand a proportional reduction on the small quantities, even if for those quantities you currently offer lower prices than the competition."

"You got it," Pete smiles. "The habits of the buyers would cause pressure to lower prices across the board. This would ruin the business."

"That's clear," Don agrees. "I don't see another solution. Alex, do you?"

"Let me try," I start. "The arrow we are examining is 'in order to get the best financial deal from the vendor, the buyer must order large quantities,' because large quantities enable lower prices, which improves profitability. How can I challenge that?"

For a moment I don't see any way, but then I find the soft spot, the words "financial performance" and "profitability." Profit is only one of the financial performances a company is concerned about. There is another one, which sometimes is even more important than profit-cash flow.

"Pete," I ask, "do some of your clients have severe cash flow problems?"

"Some," Pete answers. "Cash flow is a major concern for a few of my clients, certainly not all. But I don't see how I can use it to cause them to pay higher prices."

"Don't you see? Ordering more frequently in small quantities ties up less cash in inventory. Even if the buyer has to pay higher prices for small orders, he is much better off on his cash flow."

"But only for the short term." Pete doesn't fully agree.

"Pete," I say, "don't you know that when cash flow is pressing, only short-term considerations exist."

Pete thinks about it. "Yes, it might work . . . sometimes . . . for some of my clients. I don't think I can base my business on it. But in any event, it will strengthen the arguments for my proposal to the buyers. Thank you."

"You're welcome."

"Want to try another idea?" he asks.

"No, Pete," I laugh, "even if I had one, which I don't, I'm too eager to hear yours."

"Our solution," Pete begins, "is based on a direct attack on the assumption that ordering in large quantities gives the buyer a cheaper price-per-unit."

"Isn't that the case in your industry?" Don asks.

"No, it is not," is Pete's surprising answer.

"How come?" I'm baffled.

Pete is apparently delighted. "Let's take a recent case where we lost a sale to one of our competitors." He takes out a bunch of pages from his folder, and pointing to the top page he says: "This is what we quoted. The first column is the quantity and the second is the price." Turning to the next page, "And here is what the competition quoted."

We compare the two pages. At the top, where the quantities are small, Pete's prices are significantly lower, but as the quantities grow, it gradually changes. Toward the bottom of the pages, Pete's prices are almost 15% higher. No wonder. Due to Pete's quicker set-up, we are cheaper for small quantities, but due to the competitor's faster printing press, he is cheaper for larger quantities.

"I don't understand you at all," Don says. "You just claimed that large quantity doesn't give a lower price-per-unit, and now you give us real price lists that prove the exact opposite. Your list and your competitor's list have only one thing in common: in both quotes, price-per-unit goes down when the size of the order increases."

"Continue," I say to Pete.

"The client elected to order this quantity;" Pete is pointing to a number near the bottom of the page. "And, of course, since for this quantity the competitor is much cheaper than us, we lost the order. But," he adds in a triumphant voice, "what you don't know is that for this client this quantity represents his needs for the next six months."

"So now we know, so what?" My impatient Don.

"I told you, so what," Pete takes pleasure in teasing

Don. "I told you that our client's forecast is rapidly becoming more unreliable, that their own push for more and more marketing campaigns causes them to change, much more frequently, some of the printing on the wrappers."

"Yes, you told us, but I still don't see the relevancy."

"What is the chance that the client will actually use all of what he ordered?" Pete asks. "Remember his order is theoretically sufficient for the next six months. Do you know how many changes can happen by then?"

"No, I don't," Don answers. "But you don't know either."

"Maybe you don't know, but everybody in the industry has a pretty damn good idea," Pete continues to tease him. "Our industry journals are full of statistics; look at these."

And he gives us another page. It's a copy from some magazine. Pointing to a somewhat fuzzy graph he says, "On average, the chance that you'll use up a six month quantity is only thirty percent."

I examine the graph. I've seen such stuff before, but it's still surprising. I glance at my watch. In a little less than an hour I have another meeting. Did Pete find a real solution to his marketing problem or not? His confidence indicates that he did. At the snail's pace that we are moving there is a good chance that I'll have to postpone my next meeting. Should I do it now?

"I'm coming to it," Pete assures me. "Our solution is based on the fact that the chance of not using the entire ordered quantity is much less when the order is supposed to cover only the next two months. According to this graph it's only ten percent. You see, what we have to do is to convince the client that if he considers obsolescence, as he should, then ordering in batches of two months, from us, is giving him a cheaper price-per-unit than ordering in batches of six months from the competitors."

"In other words," I'm trying to digest the concept that Pete has introduced to us, "what you are suggesting is that the buyer will not consider the price-per-unit that he purchases, but rather the price that he pays per unit that he is likely to use. Makes sense."

I examine the first two pages again. Pete didn't choose two months out of the blue. For this relatively small quantity (one third of what actually was ordered), we are cheaper than the competitor. That's smart.

"I have a big problem with this." Don is more than skeptical. "Not with the concept—that I agree is sensible—but with the impact. I'll accept that in thirty percent of the cases the entire order is not used, but how much of it is not used? I guess that it all depends on the numbers."

"What do you mean, it all depends on the numbers? Of course it all depends on the numbers," Pete rises to defend his solution.

"My gut feel is," now it's Don's turn to tease, "that in almost all cases, I'm afraid, you won't be able to demonstrate clear savings."

Usually I enjoy seeing Don and Pete's friendly arm wrestling. But today I don't have time, and besides, the issue is much too important. "Don, compare the two cases," I somewhat impatiently say. "It's obvious that when the order is for six months, in ten percent of the cases more than two thirds of it is obsolete."

True to his nature, Pete doesn't proceed, but rather explains it to Don. "The fact that in two months there is a ten percent chance that something unexpected will make the wrapper obsolete, shows that in ten percent of the cases the additional quantity ordered for the next four months would be scrapped."

"I see," Don says. "So, based on this logic you computed the price-per-unit for the usable portion of an order?"

"Yes."

"By how much was your competitor's offer more expensive than yours?" I ask.

"Mine was still slightly more expensive, by about half a percent," Pete answers.

"So why the big celebration?" Don asks.

"Considering the pressure on the buyer to reduce raw-material inventories, and the fact that no buyer likes to get stuck with obsolescence, I think I have a good chance of winning against a price difference of half a percent. But my idea is to do better than that. My plan is to offer a client the option of ordering in two-month quantities while I ship to him on a two-weeks basis."

"You mean," I try to understand, "that the price will be based on two-month quantities, but the client will not get the entire amount in one shipment; for two months he will receive smaller quantities every two weeks."

"Exactly," Pete confirms. "And after the first shipment, he can cancel the rest, without any penalties, whenever he wants."

"That's generous," Don says. "Too generous."

"No," I say, "that's smart. The client is paying the price for quantities of two months, but suffers obsolescence as if he ordered for only two weeks. That will bring the price-per-usable-unit to be the absolute lowest."

"And on top of it," Pete beams, "the buyer will have very low inventories, less than five percent compared to what he currently holds."

"A perfect breaking of the buyer's cloud," I conclude. "Actual price is lower than what he currently pays for even large quantities, and at the same time, he will have lower inventories than what he currently can expect when he orders in what he perceives to be small quantities. From the buyer's perspective it's like having his cake and eating it."

Pete is pleased. "Do you see any negative effects?" he inquires.

"Only the obvious ones," I answer. "Those you probably already considered."

"Don't be too sure," Pete says. "Let's hear them."

"I have one," Don says. "If I understood you correctly, you are going to hold the remainder of the order in your possession, at your risk. Does it pay? Remember, in ten percent of the cases you are going to be stuck with some of it."

"Don, this is not a big concern," I say.

"Why?"

"First of all, do you agree that Pete's offer would not lead to a price war?"

"Yes. The competition cannot really compete against it. To lower the prices they must go to large quantities, but then the risk of holding the client inventories is too high." Don starts to get excited about Pete's idea. "This actually means that Pete gets the large quantity market for medium quantity prices.

"No wonder he can afford to swallow the damage from a little bit of obsolescence. And actually the damage is very small; let's not forget that the risk of obsolescence for us is much smaller than for our clients. For them it costs the selling price, for us, as long as we have excess capacity, it costs only the raw material. Good solution, I really like it."

"I've calculated the risk." Pete is visibly flattered, but tries to hide it. "For such orders, it will cost us, on average, less than two percent."

"Aren't you afraid that some buyers will abuse your offer?" I ask.

"What do you mean?"

"How are you going to make sure that a client who needs a relatively small, one-shot run, will not put in a large order to get lower prices, and after the first shipment cancel the rest? According to your suggestion they can do it without any penalty or even an explanation."

"I haven't thought about it," Pete says, and after a short while he adds, "I think that we can come up with a good way to close this loophole without insulting our buyers."

"Yes, I'm sure," I say. "So you are going to offer the market the best price, relief on cash, the lowest inventories and almost no obsolescence. Coupled with your excellent on-time reliability and high quality, it's a buyer's dream. What will be the impact on your bottom line?"

"As I said in the beginning, if I can sell all my excess capacity at those prices, the wrapper department is going to be more profitable than the rest of the operation. It means roughly nine million dollars profit. Big bucks. So, you like it Alex? Do you see any problem with it?"

"I like it. Sure I like it. But I see one problem. So big that it can turn your brilliant solution into nothing but a heartbreak."

"What is it?" Pete is concerned.

"Your solution is too good and too complicated to explain. I'm afraid you'll have a hard time convincing a buyer that your offer is real, that he will really get all these benefits. And even if he will see the benefits, don't forget that a buyer faced with what he perceives to be a seller's generosity becomes suspicious. It's going to be a problem."

"That's all?" Pete sounds relieved.

"Yes."

"Don't worry, Alex. I think that we can sell it. It might be that I have more trust in our buyers than you do, but I really think we won't have any problems selling it."

"I'll take your word for it. It sounds good, very good. Go ahead with it."

"Sure thing, Boss. We'll have a much clearer idea of how well it works very soon." As I accompany him to the door he adds, "Tomorrow we are going to submit two such quotes, and then my sales manager and I will meet with those buyers next week."

"Super job." I shake his hand. He has done a super job, his solution is a true win-win solution, but I have my doubts if he can sell it. Until I see the orders rolling in, I'm not going to revise the forecast.

A minute later he sticks his head back in to tell Don, "By the way, as long as we have a lot of excess capacity, we don't have any intention of printing batches of two months and storing them."

10

It's the first time I'm crossing the Atlantic in first class. I'm entitled to fly first class, being an executive vice president, but in the last year I simply haven't needed to go to Europe. Actually, I don't think that I need to go now, and if it were my choice, I wouldn't. I don't think that we should sell my companies. I think it's a mistake. The only reason for the sale, in my opinion, is that the board wants to show Wall Street that they are doing something, that they have a decisive plan of action. Baloney. They don't even know what they are going to do with the money they'll get.

And the man who stands behind this big empty show, Trumann, is sitting beside me. In the big leather first class couch, big enough to sit two tourists, the most expensive seat in the world. The going rate is over three thousand dollars for seven hours.

They start to serve dinner. You should see the choice of appetizers. Goose liver pâte, lobster's kastanietas, Caspian Sea caviar. Have you ever ordered Caspian Sea caviar for an appetizer? I haven't. Not until now, that is. These little black balls cost fifty dollars an ounce. It's like eating pure silver.

It tastes like shit. Now I understand why they serve it with vodka. Frankly, I prefer pizza and beer.

Trumann sure knows how to handle the caviar. You should see how quickly he spreads it on this small toasted triangle with egg yolk and thin chopped onion. A real pro, I tell you. Why is it that a person who produces nothing, who doesn't contribute anything, lives in such luxury? I guess that was always the case; slave drivers always lived in better conditions than the slaves.

"How many boards do you sit on?" I ask.

"Right now, only twelve."

Right now only twelve, I think to myself. Probably last month they closed one company and sold another two.

"Why do you ask?" Trumann raises his eyes from the consommé.

Bad mistake. The way that the plane is shaking now, and with these shallow spoons, he's bound to spill soup on his silk tie. He doesn't.

"Just wondering," I say.

"Wondering about what? Do I have enough time to know what is really going on in the companies I serve? Or wondering in general what my job is?"

"Both, actually."

"Alex," he smiles at me, "you are relatively new at this game, aren't you? I don't recall having heard you speak in the board meetings."

Trumann is a powerful man. When my companies are sold and I lose my job, I'll need him. You can't find an executive position through answering an ad in the papers. You need connections. You need to know and be known by the right people. Thanks to Granby, I now have that opportunity. A whole week is enough time; I have to impress Trumann, to make him know me better.

"Not like some others," I say, thinking of Hilton Smyth. "I prefer to do, not to speak."

"Oh," his smile widens, "so that's how you see my job —just talk, no deeds." Before I have a chance to correct his accurate impression, he continues, "I guess a production worker chained to his machine for eight hours a day says the same about you."

I force myself to smile back. But in spite of all the warning bells, I cannot play the game. "I don't think so," I answer flatly.

"Why? What's the difference?"

There is a difference, a huge difference, but for some reason I can't find the words to clearly demonstrate it. What is this leech thinking to himself? That sitting in board meetings can be compared to having the responsibility of running a company? Does he know how hard and demanding it is to turn around a losing business?

"Do you know that in the last year I've turned three companies around?"

"Alex, don't get me wrong. In spite of the fact that you never show off in the board meetings, Doughty and I are quite aware of your achievements. We do read the reports carefully, including what is written between the lines."

"So?"

"So, you didn't answer my question. What is the difference between your job and mine? Do you produce something with your own hands? Isn't it true that all your work is done through talking?"

"Yes, of course." I'm starting to get irritated at my inability to express myself. "I think, I talk, I decide. That's how the work is done."

"Why do you think it is different for me?" Trumann continues to be calm and gentle. "I also think, talk and decide."

He does—at least the latter two. He talks and decides. He talked in the board meeting, and he decides. He decided to sell my companies. The only thing I don't know is whether he thinks. Selling my companies makes no sense at all. Then it dawns on me. There is a difference, a major one. How can I express it without offending him?

"I guess," I begin slowly, "that I don't know enough about your job."

"Apparently."

"I have responsibility for managing companies. What are you responsible for?"

"I manage money," he answers.

I think about it. I guess he's right. But how does a person go about managing money? Probably through investing in companies, and then . . .

"So your job is to be a watchdog, observing the companies you have invested in?" I think I could have chosen my words more carefully.

He bursts out laughing. "Yes, I guess you could describe it like that. My job is to determine which companies to invest in, and then to be the watchdog. Watching out for local optima."

This piques my curiosity. "Local optima?" I echo.

"Alex, do you know how many top execs forget that the goal of their company is to make money? They concentrate on production, on costs, on strategies, and so often they forget that those are only the means—not the goal. Take UniCo, for example. Do you know how long the top executives have behaved as if the goal of UniCo is to provide them with fat jobs? Sometimes I get the impression that top executives forget that it's not their company; it is the shareholders' company."

I don't answer.

"Take your group as an example. We invested almost three hundred million dollars in it. What we've gotten back so far is zilch. And now we will be lucky if we can sell it for half. Whose money is it, do you think? Who paid for it?"

"My group is not losing money anymore," I say. "Give me some more time and I will make it really profitable. Why sell now?"

"Alex, how profitable can you make the diversified group? I've seen your forecast for this year. Do you realize inflation exists? In order to protect the value of the money, and bearing in mind how risky it is, we must invest only in companies that have a real chance of making more than inflation."

I see where he is coming from. I cannot guarantee that my companies will bring more than inflation. Still . . .

"That's the most unpleasant part of my work," he continues. "Sometimes management makes a bad decision; it is unavoidable. But when they insist on protecting their bad decision, we have to step in. That's our job. Remember, the goal is to make money. Your companies have to go Alex, it is unavoidable."

Trumann doesn't have to tell me that the goal of my company is to make money. That has been my motto since I became a plant manager. But at the same time, I was careful not to do it at the expense of my people. I never thought that the way to make more money was through slashing parts of the organization. That is Hilton Smyth's way. To save some pennies he will cut anyone.

"I don't think that in my case," I try to choose my words carefully, "it's a matter of protecting a bad decision. I have nothing to protect. I wasn't involved in making the decision to diversify. Still, I'm not sure that it is correct to sell my companies."

"Why?"

"Because we are not dealing only with money. We are also dealing with people. Top executives, I think, have responsibility not only to our shareholders, but also to our employees."

Maybe I just signed my death sentence, but what the heck, there is a limit to the extent I'm willing to play their money game. Let me give it to him in full. "Sometimes, from where I stand, it seems unfair to put the squeeze on the employees, who have invested their lives in the company, just so that some rich people will become even richer. . . . The goal of our company is make more money, but that's not the whole story."

Trumann doesn't seem surprised. He has heard such

things before, even though I wonder if he has heard it from one of his executives. Maybe from an ex-executive.

"Some rich people become even richer." He repeats my words. "Alex, where do you think the money that I invest comes from? Rich investors? Banks? Don't you know that most of the money invested in the market belongs to pension funds?"

I feel myself blush. Of course I know it.

"People save all their lives for old age." Trumann explains the obvious to me. "They are saving now so that in twenty or thirty years they can retire peacefully. It is our job to make sure that when they retire the money will be there for them. Not dollar for dollar, but buying power for buying power. It's not the rich peoples' interest we are watching out for, it is the same people you are worried about—the employees."

"Interesting cloud," I totally agree.

Trumann looks disappointed. "Don't dismiss what I'm saying. I'm not talking about clouds, I'm talking about facts of life."

Rather than trying to explain, I take out my pen and start to draw the cloud. "The objective is to serve the stakeholders. Do you have any problem with that?"

"No. I only have problems with people who forget it."

"To achieve it, we must make sure to satisfy two different necessary conditions. One is to protect the interests of our shareholders, and the other is to protect the interests of our employees." I wait for him to object, but he nods his head in agreement.

"In order to protect the interest of our shareholders, you insist on selling the diversified companies."

"Don't you agree?" he asks.

"I agree that under the current circumstances, to protect the interests of the shareholders we should sell the companies. But that doesn't mean that I agree we should sell them."

"Alex, you sound like a politician. Do you agree or don't you?"

"There is another side to this question; bear with me. We also said that we must protect the interests of our employees. But in order to do that we must not sell the companies."

I am expecting that he will not agree, that he will claim that selling the companies has nothing to do with the interests of the employees. But he doesn't say a word. He takes the napkin and examines the cloud.

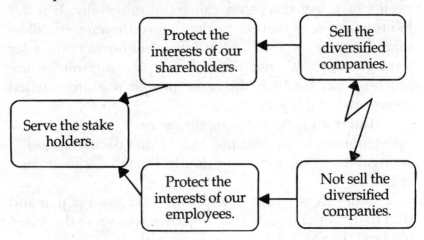

"You have it easy," I say. "To you it's obvious that we should sell the diversified group. You look at the bottom line numbers, you look at the forecast, and they tell you the answer. Not enough money now as well as in the future—sell. No wonder, you look only at one side of the equation, as you should. That's okay, it's compensated for by the employees and the unions who also look at only one side. Only we, the executives, are torn. We are in the middle. We have to satisfy both sides. Put yourself in my shoes and try to answer your question, to sell or not to sell the companies. You see, it's not so easy to answer."

Still looking at the cloud he says, "We do look at both sides of the equation. Maybe we didn't do it in the past, but

now we definitely do. No prudent investor is in'
just looking at the numbers. We learned, the har(
the key factor is the people. If they are not pleaseu ..
their jobs, if they are not proud of their company, it's just a
matter of time until losses will start to show up."

"I guess that the same is true for the unions. They
know that there is no job security in a company that loses
money, no matter what we, the executives, promise them.
More and more they start to demand to see our investment
plan before they'll even consider giving any concession."

He raises his eyes from the cloud and looks at me. "In
our case I think that it is."

"What is?"

"I think it is easy to answer that we should sell your
companies. No, don't get excited, let me finish. Look, you
know our credit rating. You know that it's almost at rock
bottom."

I know. We pay two percent above prime.

"Everybody is trying to cheer me up by the market
upturn. But markets oscillate, the downturn will follow.
The last downturn almost brought UniCo to its knees. We
don't have the reserves anymore to carry us through another down period, and I don't think that we can count on
gathering enough reserves in the current good period. Nobody knows how long it will last, and everybody is telling
me that it won't be easy to make money in this upturn, that
pressure to reduce prices continues."

I start to see his point.

"Alex, even if I forget my bosses for a minute, even if I
concentrate on the interests of the employees of UniCo, I
come to the same conclusion: we must sell some portion in
order to protect the others. And the diversified group is the
only choice; we have to protect the core business."

"But why by selling it now? Why not accumulate profits as long as the market is good?"

"The timing has very little to do with Granby's retirement," Trumann answers my unspoken concerns. "It is the

time that we can probably get the best price, when every-body is looking hopefully into the future."

"We bought my companies under similar circum-stances, in 1989 when everybody was expecting an upturn. And we definitely paid exaggerated prices."

"Exactly my point," he sighs.

"This is interesting," he says after a while. "Where did you learn this presentation technique?"

"It is neat. On half a page you see the entire picture."

"Right. The conflict hits you right between the eyes. You can't ignore the real issue. It's a powerful way to pre-sent."

"It's not just a presentation technique," I comment. "This technique claims that you should not attempt to strive for a compromise. It advocates examining the as-sumptions under the arrows in order to break the conflict."

"What do you mean?"

Jonah claims that any cloud can be broken, but he is wrong. If I could find a way to break this conflict, I wouldn't have to sell my companies. Now, because of my big mouth, I have to defend his technique.

"Look, for example, at this arrow," I say to Trumann. " 'In order to protect the interest of the shareholders, we must sell the companies.' The assumption here is that the companies are not profitable enough. If we can find a way to make them more profitable, a way that will guarantee that they can sell many more products without increasing their operating expense, then the cloud is broken. We don't have to sell the companies. We simultaneously pro-tect the interests of the shareholders and the employees alike."

"Do you know how to do it? Do you have an idea how to increase their product sales without increasing their op-erating expense?"

"No," I admit. "I don't see any way to do it."

He smiles. "So even though in theory the conflict can

be eliminated, in practice we have to live with it. I guess that there is quite a distance between nice theories and harsh realities."

I must agree with him.

11

At first sight the cabs in London look strange, but when you enter one, it looks even stranger. In the back there is one seat, big enough for only two people. Two more shelves for sitting can be folded down from the wall separating the driver from the passengers. Even in a train I hate to sit with my back to the driving direction. In a cab, facing Trumann and Doughty, I like it even less.

We are returning from a meeting where we negotiated the sale of Pete's company. Actually, this is not an accurate description. We didn't negotiate anything, we just talked—mainly me. Four people asked questions, and because of the nature of the questions, Trumann and Doughty let me answer. Most of the questions honed in on the reasons for the exceptional operational performance (not to be confused with exceptional financial performance, of which Pete's company is innocent).

It took me quite a while to explain how come on-time delivery is so high, while inventories are so low. It's not easy to explain to people whose starting point is so different. People who think that managers must concentrate on squeezing the maximum from each link, when by doing so they unintentionally jeopardize the performance of the chain. I had to prove why efforts such as trying to save set-up on the presses, or optimizing the work load of each technician in the prep room, lead to the exact opposite—to pockets of disguised idleness and to degradation in the overall performance.

I must say they followed with interest, asked a lot of questions, and listened attentively to my more and more elaborate explanations. Not just the Brits; Trumann and Doughty were no less attentive. I think I scored some points with them.

After five hours of grilling, we left, leaving behind homework—about three inches of financial reports. Only in the next meeting will the battle about terms and conditions start. But that is Trumann and Doughty's headache. I will not have to participate. If they are successful at bringing the prospect to agree on the framework of the deal, the prospect will send his examiners to the company. That is when Pete's headache will start.

"Shall we meet in half an hour in the bar?" Trumann suggests as we reach the hotel.

Good idea. I certainly can use a quick pint. Or two. Reaching my room, I try to call Don. Since European hotels are taking four hundred percent markup on telephone calls, I use my calling card. Three long strings of numbers, two mistakes and finally Don is on the line.

"Anything new?" I ask.

"What do you want to hear first?" Don is cheerful. "The good news or the bad?"

"Start with the bad."

"The bad news is that you were wrong in assuming that Pete would have problems presenting his new offer to his customers."

"I didn't think that Pete would have problems presenting his offer," I laugh. "I thought that his customers would have problems accepting it. So the bad news is that I was wrong, and the good news is that Pete was right?"

"Precisely. Pete claims that they were quite enthusiastic. He can't wait to tell you how well it went. Why don't you give him a call?"

I forgot to use the pound key, so five minutes and more than thirty digits later, I reach an enthused Pete.

"No, I don't have the purchase orders in hand. I've something even better."

"The only thing that is better than a purchase order," I say sarcastically, "is the customer's money in our bank account. Pete, I understand that you had two good sales calls, but could you be a little more specific?"

"I started by presenting the 'buyer's cloud.' Do you remember: the conflict between the need to get lower prices and the need to have lower inventories?"

I'm anxious to know what business deal he struck; to find out the reaction of the buyers to his unconventional offer, but my impatience has just caused Pete to swing all the way to minute details. Realizing that the quickest way is to let Pete tell it in his own way, I assure him that I do remember the buyer's cloud.

"Then I established the difference between price-per-unit and price-per-usable-unit. You know, I used the graph of the chance for obsolescence as a function of the horizon of the order . . ."

He goes on like this for a while, giving me, blow-by-blow, what he presented, how it was presented, why he presented in the way he did, etc. I look at my watch. In five minutes I have to be in the bar; not to mention that we are on a trans-Atlantic call.

Finally he reaches it. "In each sales call, the buyer liked my offer so much that he asked for a proposal for their entire wrapper needs. Did you hear that—their entire wrapper needs."

"What does that mean, Pete, in dollars?"

"We are still in the process of preparing the quotes; it will take us at least until late tomorrow. But in each case we are talking big deals, over half a million a year."

"What are your realistic chances of winning?" I try to cool him down.

"Very good. Extremely good."

I make some sounds to indicate my skepticism.

"Alex, don't you see? Now the buyer has a tangible reference. He can compare my quote to what he is actually paying per year. There is no better way to demonstrate to him the concept of price-per-usable-unit. I'm bound to win."

He has a point, but . . .

"Alex, I have meetings scheduled with both of these customers later this week. There will be enough time to go over our quotes in detail."

That's a good idea. Not to send it by mail but to discuss it face to face with the buyers. It can avoid a lot of misunderstanding, especially in this case, where the offer is so unconventional. "So we'll know by the end of the week?"

"We'll have a better idea, but I don't expect to get the purchase order then; they need some time to digest it. They will also ask for a counter-offer from their existing vendors; at least that's what I would do. Nevertheless, I think that we'll have them before the end of the month. Our offer is simply too good, and I'm going to continue to sit on top of them."

I tell him how pleased I am with the work he's doing, and hurry to the bar. In the elevator I realize I have a new problem. Right from the start I liked Pete's solution. My only problem was if the buyers would fall for it. Now that he's tried it on two tough cookies, and in both cases they understood it to the extent that they are contemplating giving him their entire business, my reservation is over. Yes, we still have to wait and see if the buyers will go through with the deal, but now it's a matter of refining the presentation, not whether or not the solution will work.

So what is my problem? It's credibility. Today, when I explained the performance of Pete's plant, I emphasized that the wrapper department will need heavy investments in order to make it profitable. How am I going to explain that this bottomless pit is, all of a sudden, a gold mine? I have to plan some tap dancing.

It's not a bar, it's a typical English pub, jammed with people stopping on their way home from work.

"Here comes my savior." Trumann waves at me, "What will you have?"

"A pint of lager, please." I try to adjust to the environment.

"I'll have a refill," Doughty calls after Trumann, now winding his way to the bar.

"What savior? What is he talking about?"

Doughty just gives me a napkin. It's scribbled all over. I barely recognize the cloud I drew on the airplane. So, that's what Trumann wants. That I'll explain the dilemma of protect the shareholders—protect the employees to Doughty. I start to do it. Trumann arrives with three large mugs and places them silently in front of us. When I finish, Trumann is beaming over the cloud. "Well, what do you think now?"

"It's a nice impractical game." Doughty is unimpressed.

"Yeah, I know what you mean." Trumann pats him quite hard on the back. "I, too, have such cynical moods, when everything seems no more than a game. Brutal, many times unfair, and whatever we do, the game will continue to be played, with or without us. Cheer up, lad, drink your beer."

Doughty smiles, wraps the napkin around his glass, and raises it high, "To the game." We join the toast.

"And I still claim," he winks at me, "that all the diagrams, concise as this one or as elaborate as the financial reports, do not help us to play any better. At the end it all boils down to intuition, to the hunch."

"You and your hunches," Trumann lowers his mug. "But one thing I'll admit, this 'cloud' as Alex calls it, has very few practical ramifications, if any." Seeing my expression, he asks, surprised, "Don't you agree?"

I see a golden opportunity to break the good but embarrassing news about Pete's company, and decide to move on it. "No, I don't agree."

As expected, they grab the bait. "What can you do with such a diagram except use it to pass the time in a bar?" Doughty says in a doubting voice.

"Actually," I decide to be somewhat arrogant, "you bother to write a cloud only if you intend to use it. Of course, if after stating the problem precisely, after writing the cloud, no attempt to solve the problem is made, then I must agree that it is impractical. The real value of the cloud is that it provides a straightforward way to solve the problem, to evaporate the conflict."

"Do you claim that this diagram," Doughty carefully peels the napkin from his glass, "can be used to give us tangible results?"

"Yes, that's precisely what I claim."

"It can be used to help us win the game?" Trumann sticks to their metaphor.

"The game and even the set."

"Prove it," Doughty says firmly.

In an instant I feel like I'm under the microscope, passing through some type of important test. But not to worry. I'm well prepared.

"Let's take, as an example, the subject we worked on all day—my printing company." I carefully straighten the napkin. "In order to protect our shareholders we are trying to sell this company, because it is not profitable enough to justify the investment."

"It is not profitable enough now, and according to your reports, it will be only marginally profitable in the foreseeable future," Trumann corrects me.

"Yes," I agree, "that is our assumption. We've examined the situation carefully. As you know, the key to substantially increasing profits is to do something about the losses of the wrapper department."

"If you intend to persuade us to invest in new printing . . ." Trumann cuts into my explanation.

I don't hesitate to do the same to him, "And since we know that additional investments are out of the question, we have to figure out how to compose a new offering to the market. An offer based on the existing equipment, very attractive to the market and very profitable for us."

"In short," Doughty says, "mission impossible."

"So it seems." Smiling, I slowly sip the tasty lager from my mug.

They both look at me. After a while Trumann asks, "Do you mean that you found such a way?"

"So it seems." I celebrate the moment.

"Alex, I'm going to bring you another pint, but God be with you if you're pulling our legs."

Trumann waits until Doughty goes to the bar. "What's going on? Alex, you told me on the way to Europe that you don't have a clue how to increase the sales of your companies without increasing expenses. Did something change in the past two days? Or are you trying a kamikaze move to sabotage the sales of your companies?"

"Nothing of the sort," I assure him. "I know how strange the last five minutes must sound to you, but I'm not playing any tricks. I admit I still don't know what to do with the other two companies, but as for the printing company, I just got confirmation on the phone that our innovative idea does work."

"I want to hear all about it." Trumann is as firm as Doughty.

I wait for Doughty to settle down, and then begin to explain Pete's solution to them, giving of course the credit to whom it's due. "So you see," I end a fifteen minute explanation, "why I couldn't possibly tell you about it before. I couldn't expect you to take it seriously. Frankly, until an hour ago, I'm not sure I took it seriously myself."

"We'll have to wait and see if the two large deals actually go through, but I'll admit, it is encouraging."

"We'll have to procrastinate with our negotiation on the printing company," Doughty slowly says, "At least until the situation becomes clearer."

"Yes," Trumann agrees, "and we better prepare some more prospects. If what Alex told us becomes reality, this is a totally different ball game. And we cannot go back to the existing prospects with such a change in our story. As much as we explain it, our credibility will suffer. No, Alex, don't worry about it, we'll be happy if your solution will actually work. It's much more fun to sell a company that makes fifteen percent profit on sales than a company that barely breaks even." They start to calculate how much they should ask for Pete's company.

Yes. They intend to continue with their plan to sell the company. No wonder; their major concern is the credit rating of UniCo. But if Pete's idea does work, and I'm becoming more and more convinced that it will, then his future is secure. No one will mess around with a goose that lays golden eggs. And to think that our starting point was to invest a small fortune to replace our fast set-up presses. How stupid could we be?

Doughty breaks into my thoughts. "Alex, were the diagrams used to construct this nice solution."

"Yes, definitely. Without them we didn't have a chance. With them we barely made it."

"Hmm," is the only response.

12

Many travelers complain about English cooking, but in my opinion English restaurants have one thing that compensates for everything: the way they serve coffee. For the coffee they direct us to another room, furnished with big leather sofas, low tables and a real wood fire.

I'm easily persuaded to try a 1956 brandy. Brandon and Jim are persuaded just as easily. I stare at the fire, trying to digest what I've learned in the last two days. If you noticed, it's not Trumann and Doughty anymore. After two pints of beer and two bottles of red wine, it's only natural for me to switch to using their first names.

Trumann gained my respect on the flight when I came to better understand his motives. This evening I learned to appreciate the other side of his personality, the "Brandon side," as I think of it. He is a warm, caring human being. So different from the stereotype of a heartless shark that I glued on him. But the big surprise is Jim. He is not a cold fish. After-hours Jim is quite different from the Doughty at work. Not that he's very talkative or optimistic, but he is friendly and has a charming but rather cynical sense of humor.

When Brandon notices that I have returned to reality he says, "Alex, there is one thing bothering us. You said

es, that is the true answer
 sure it would just be a

," I explain. "You must
nt all his life in the print-
tion to draw from. That's
rocesses he succeeded in
or his company. But Bob
e relatively new to their

 Brandon sounds disap-
 is the big advantage of

w important the Think-
 verbalize your gut feel,
g of your intuition, and
heck. If I do it, they will
 stion of why haven't I
    division? So

that this breakthrough marketing solution that you are testing in the printing company was not invented by fluke, but by systematically using logical diagrams. But you have two other companies, bigger and more in trouble. How come you haven't succeeded in coming up with marketing solutions for them?"

They are starting to sound like Julie. But what can I tell them? That I haven't tried? Y —but why haven't I? Because I' waste of time.

"Logic by itself is not enougl have intuition as well. Pete has spe ing business; he had enough intui why working with the Thinking P finding a breakthrough solution f Donovan and Stacey Kaufman ar companies."

"So we are back to intuition." pointed. "If that's the case, what using these logical diagrams?"

I can demonstrate to them h ing Processes are. They force you t and by that enable true unleashin the ability to check it. But what the turn back on me with their heavy q done it for I Cosmetics and the pre rather than answering, I just finish

Jim takes my lack of response marizes, "If you don't have intuitic you. If you do have intuition, you

This provokes me. That is total have intuition," I reply, "no metho But if you do have intuition, you ition is a necessary condition for fi my experience it is far from being s a method to unleash, focus and cr you want to arrive at practical, sim

"Maybe," Jim Doughty says.

"No, not maybe. Definitely. Have you ever been in a situation where you felt that you were in a swimming pool filled with ping-pong balls and your job was to hold all of them under water? The feeling that you are spending almost all your time fighting fires?"

"Have I?" he laughs. "That's the story of my life, especially in the past five years."

"You see, in such situations, the mere fact that you know how to fight the local fires clearly indicates that you have intuition. Nevertheless, you don't have even the beginning of the thread to help untie the knot."

"I agree," says Brandon, "but if I don't have the beginning of the thread, how can I write the relevant cloud?"

"Oh, sorry. I gave you the wrong impression. The cloud is not always the first step. You are supposed to use the cloud only after the existing situation is well organized in your mind."

"What do you mean?"

"If you are constantly fire-fighting, you have the impression that you are surrounded by many, many problems."

"I am," says Jim.

"The Thinking Processes claim that these problems are not independent of each other, but there are strong links of cause and effect between them."

"Yeah, I believed so too, when I went to Sunday school. What life has taught me since then is that problems are linked by excuses."

I ignore his joke. "Until these cause and effect connections are established, we don't have a clear enough picture of the situation. The first step, then, is to use a very systematic way to build what is called a Current Reality Tree, diagramming the cause and effect relationships that connect all the problems prevailing in a situation. Once you do this, you realize that you don't have to deal with many problems because at the core there are always only one or two causes."

"What you are telling us is that underlying any given situation there are actually only one or two core problems?" Brandon finds it hard to believe.

"Precisely. Only one or two core problems that are the cause for all the others. That's why I don't call the symptoms problems, I call them undesirable effects. They are unavoidable derivatives of the core problem."

"This is important," Brandon says thoughtfully. "If what you say is possible, which I doubt, then we have the key to direct our efforts toward the core reason, not to the symptoms."

"You got it!" I smile. "And the Thinking Processes give us a step-by-step recipe of how to do it. You start with a list of undesirable effects, between five and ten of them. Then you follow the recipe, and you end up with a clear identification of the core problems. Moreover, it intensifies your intuition, which is vital for the next step, which is directing your attention to finding a solution to the core problem."

"It sounds much too simple," Jim says.

Why do I do it to myself? I repeat Jonah's claims as if they are mine, but if I truly believed in them I would use his methods more frequently. For example, since the last board meeting I have had the feeling that I'm floundering, that I'm clutching at straws, and God knows how much I need a solid solution. But the truth is that I don't believe enough in Jonah's theory to give it a try now.

"Have you ever tried it yourself?" Brandon asks me. "I mean in situations that looked hopeless?"

I think about it for a while. As a plant manager I didn't use Jonah's methods. I used his conclusions. No wonder, at that time I was not aware of the Thinking Processes, the hard core of Jonah's Theory Of Constraints. When I became a divisional manager, Jonah insisted that I learn his methods so I'd stop being dependent on him, and be able to help myself. Since then I've used sections of them a lot, mostly to empower my people, to solve conflicts and to build team spirit. But in at least three situations I used the Thinking Processes in full.

"Yes, I did," I must admit, "more than once."

"And?"

"And it worked. . . . Surprisingly well." To justify to myself I add, "What you need is intuition about the subject and the will power to do the meticulous work."

"How much time does it take?" Jim asks.

"It depends. Five hours, or so."

"Five hours?" Jim laughs. "That's less than the sleep that I'm losing in one night over such problems."

He doesn't understand the difficulty. It's not the time. It's bringing yourself to do it.

"Let's try it," Brandon Trumann suggests. "Why don't we pick a subject we all have intuition about, and then you demonstrate it to us."

I glance at my watch. It's almost eleven o'clock. "I don't think it's practical. It's late, and we have two important meetings tomorrow. And besides, what subject can we pick? I don't think there is one subject that each of us has enough intuition about."

"Yes, there is," Trumann says. "You have a lot of experience in running companies and turning them around. We have a lot of experience in controlling companies. And if there is one thing that drives us all nuts, it is the subject of how to increase sales."

"Yes," Jim Doughty agrees. "And we don't have to do it all tonight. We'll just do the first step; provide you with a list of problems—undesirable effects, to use your terminology. Later you can show us how to connect them to each other, if it is at all possible."

What can I do? I'm trapped. Brandon Trumann takes out his pen, searches for another napkin, settles on the doily under the chocolates, and announces his undesirable effect.

" 'Competition is fiercer than ever.' I am sick and tired

of hearing about it from every company I'm involved with."

"Yes," says Jim, "and add to that, 'There is increasing market pressure to reduce prices.'"

"That's a good one," Brandon agrees. "No matter how high the demand, you still hear the same excuse. It's reached the point that we, as external directors, are afraid to ask for more sales. They usually achieve it, but by lowering the prices."

It's interesting to see how it looks from their side of the table. "Keep on," I say. "We need between five and ten undesirable effects."

"What other excuses do we hear all the time?" Brandon is really into the game. "Ah, I've got one, listen: 'In more and more cases the price that the market is willing to pay doesn't leave enough margin.'"

"You call that an excuse?" I cannot hide my surprise.

"Definitely. I think that the real problem, if you can call it a problem, is that more than ever the market punishes suppliers that don't perform according to its expectations."

"Fine," I say desperately. "Add it to the list."

"I think that the real problem," Jim says, "is lack of an overall vision. What I see is ad hoc solutions, fire-fighting, but not a sound overall strategy backed up by a reasonable, detailed, tactical plan."

"Can I write a whole speech as an undesirable effect?" Brandon asks.

"Okay," says Jim. "I'll give it to you as concisely as possible. I think that the real problem is that managers are trying to run their companies by striving to achieve local optima."

"Yes, that's a good one." Brandon is busy writing. "That's what they are trying to do, and as a result, what we see as outside observers is that the various functions inside the companies are blaming each other for lack of performance. It is always the other departments' fault."

"Write that down as well," I say. "This behavior is definitely a problem."

"I'm writing," says Brandon. "Alex, do you want to donate a problem from your perspective?"

"Okay. I'll give you one, and you know the source of this problem very well. There is unprecedented pressure to take actions to increase sales."

They laugh, and Jim says, "And judging from the results, not enough pressure."

"But seriously," Brandon continues, "we have neglected something that is really troubling. I'm talking about the need to launch new products at an unprecedented rate. Remember the time when products had life spans of more than ten years? Those days are gone. In more and more industries that I am involved in the lifetime of a product in the market is not more than three years, and in some it is already less than one year."

Remembering what Bob Donovan said about his cosmetics products, I agree completely. "There is another problem because of it. This constant introduction of new products confuses and spoils the markets."

When Brandon finishes writing he asks, "Jim, do you have anything to add on this topic?"

"You know I have," Jim says. "You've heard my skepticism regarding the positive impact of new products. Many of them fail. Most don't justify the investment in their development, but even when the new or improved product is successful, it almost always eats into the sales of the existing products. In fact, it's not just with new products; the same holds true for new outlets."

I wonder if I should tell him my opinion on what he just said when Brandon backs him up. "Just last week I heard a story you won't believe. Unfortunately it was in a company we are heavily invested in. Six months ago they reported on a big success—they had signed a very large deal with a club chain. Last week I found out that the drop in sales we saw in the last quarter is due to the fact that the club sales substantially ate into the sales of the shops."

Since exactly the same thing happened to us in UniCo recently, I prefer to close this issue as fast as possible. I say, "Why don't you write 'Most new outlets and most new or improved products eat into the sales of existing outlets or products.'"

"Good."

I do a quick count of Brandon's list. "Okay, we have ten. That will be enough."

"No, no," says Jim. "You are not going to get away with this list. This list puts too much blame on the market and too little on the companies. Let me add some more."

Turning to Brandon he says, "Write that 'a large percent of the existing sales force lacks sufficient sales skills.'"

Before he continues I interrupt, trying to somewhat balance the picture. "Salespeople are overloaded." I make sure it gets listed.

Jim continues, "'Production and distribution do not improve fast enough or significantly enough.'"

"Wait, wait," says Brandon. "Let me catch up. . . . Okay, continue."

"Engineering," says Jim.

"What about them?" I ask, as if I don't know.

They both smile at me and Brandon writes, "'Engineering is unable to deliver new products fast enough.'"

"And reliably enough," adds Jim.

"Okay, I have enough," I say. "There's really no need to go on."

Jim smiles at me. "Let me close the list with one last problem that will remind you what we are talking about. Write it carefully," he says to Brandon. "Companies don't come up with sufficient innovative ideas in marketing."

Jim Doughty waits for the reminder to sink in, and then says, "Alex, do you really believe you will be able to connect all the entries on this list with rigorous cause and effect relationships?"

"And remember," Brandon Trumann says, "according to what you said, this recipe of yours is supposed to lead us to the identification of only one or two core problems that cause this list. It looks hopeless. Alex, maybe we should just drop the idea and forget about it? You have a lot of things to concentrate on this week."

"No," my pride forces me to refuse. "Let me have it."

"Okay," says Doughty, all business. "But before we return to the States we'd like to see what you've done with it."

"Sure," I say, feeling that I am once again facing an important test. Why didn't I drop the whole thing when I had the chance?

13

We are in a meeting discussing the sale of Pressure-Steam. It's a strange meeting. It's not with a company (like the meeting yesterday), or with investors (like the meeting this morning). I have the distinct impression that we are talking with a wheeler-dealer. It makes me nervous.

"Okay," Mr. Smooth-Talker says after a while, "let's discuss the real issue, the assets of the company." He opens the balance sheet.

"The real assets of the company are its people," I can't help myself from reminding this person of the obvious.

He looks at my card and then smiles at me. "Are you in charge of this company?"

"Yes, I am," I firmly say.

"And your company is doing less than a quarter of a million dollars net profit on sales of, let's see . . ." He looks at his notes, "of 91.6 million dollars? Not too good. What I'm trying to figure out now is how much profit you do on net assets."

Mr. Snake-Oil smiles at me, "If you can put a dollar value on your people, I'm afraid that it will reduce your return on net assets. Shall we proceed to determine the realistic value of the company's assets?"

I like it less and less.

Mr. Snake looks again at my card. "Mister Rogo, on your balance sheet the company equipment is reported at a value of 7.21 million dollars. What is the real value?"

"What do you mean?" I'm puzzled and irritated. "At UniCo, we don't play games with our books."

"I know." He gives me another look at his teeth. "I'm sure that your books are kept according to all the accounting regulations. But that is exactly the reason for my question. On your books," he patiently explains, "the equipment is recorded at its purchase value minus the depreciation since the time of purchase."

"For the purpose of depreciation we are using a ten-year period," I explain. "It's written in one of the footnotes."

"Footnote number twenty-one, to be exact." He demonstrates that he knows my balance sheet better than me. "But that is not the point." He looks at Brandon and Jim for help, but they don't say a word.

"Mister Rogo," he tries again. "A machine that your company bought ten years ago now appears on your balance sheet as having zero value."

"Of course, by now it is fully depreciated."

"Yes, but it still might have value. When we come to sell it, we might get a nice price for it."

Before I can comment, he continues. "On the other hand, a machine that you bought only a year ago, which therefore appears at almost its full purchase value, often can be sold for only a song. You see, the balance sheet doesn't give me a clue to the realistic value of your equipment."

"I don't see the relevancy," I say, "but hypothetically, if we put the machines alone on sale, we are not going to get much. Many of them are quite old and most are built according to our special needs. There are few manufacturers that can use our equipment."

"So how much can we get?"

"I don't know." Under the pressure I add, "Less than 7.21 million dollars, that's for sure."

The cobra probably realizes that I don't intend to give him a better answer, so when Brandon and Jim don't show any sign that they are going to clarify it further, he scribbles something on his pad and moves to the next item.

"What should we estimate the value of the inventory to be?" he asks.

"Why don't you use the book value?"

"Because, Mister Rogo, your books are handled according to the proper regulations."

I bet yours aren't, I think to myself. No, I don't like this person one bit. Aloud, I say, "What's bad about it?"

"Nothing, except for the fact that it gives useless information. You evaluate inventory according to what it costs you to have it. I'm interested in its value if you try to sell it. Do you agree that the two numbers are vastly different?"

"No, I don't. At least not in our case."

He throws a desperate look at Brandon and Jim.

"Why?" Brandon asks me.

"Because we have very little work-in-process," I explain. "Most of our inventory is finished spare parts, whose selling price is minimum our cost, even if we sell at wholesale. The rest is common raw materials."

Brandon looks at him.

"Makes sense," he replies. "What about the land?"

I know what he means. Usually the number appearing on the books is some historic number that has nothing to do with the current value.

"No surprises here," Brandon says. "The land was appraised when we purchased the company four years ago. Since then, real estate values in that region have stayed about the same."

"I prefer to get an up-to-date appraisal."

"Certainly," Brandon agrees.

I don't understand what is going on. This person is approaching it all wrong. The company is profitable, it is a going concern. Why do Trumann and Doughty let him value the company through its components? This way we are bound to get a very low value. I get the answer right away.

Brandon says, "Shall we discuss the real asset of the company? Its market share? We have about 23 percent of the North American market and our share is very stable."

The snake turns to me, "How difficult is it to penetrate into this market?"

"Very." I give him my sincere evaluation. "The market is dominated by four companies, all about the same size, all in this business for over forty years."

"I see." He chews on his pencil. I hate it when people chew their pencils. "Why is it so?" he asks.

"Several reasons," I calmly answer. "There is customer loyalty. This business is actually a spare parts business. You sell the basic equipment to the client and he is locked into buying additions and spare parts from you."

"That will do it," he agrees.

"And," I continue, "it's not so simple to build this equipment. Every order is different; you have to tailor everything to the client's specific needs. It's more craftsmanship than anything. It takes a long time to grow the expertise." I barely control myself from adding, "The real assets of the company are its people."

"Is there a lot of excess capacity in this industry?" he asks.

Where is this question coming from? Then I understand. "Yes, there is," I answer. "All the pressure steam companies took advantage of CNC and CAD technology, so it's no wonder that a lot of excess capacity exists. But everyone is very careful not to start a price war. Extremely careful. As I said, they are all in the business for many years, they are all in it for the long run. I don't see any danger of a price war."

"Good," he says. Turning to Brandon and Jim he asks, "How much?"

To my surprise they answer, "One hundred million dollars."

This is a very high number. Unbelievably higher than the real value of Stacey's company. Maybe this slick person is not as shrewd as I thought, because his only response is, "Let me check around. I'll get back to you next month."

No, this inflated number is just a starting position. I'd better remember that the market of buying and selling companies has a remarkable resemblance to an eastern bazaar.

On the way down we don't talk. I don't like this type of meeting. I don't like this person. I'm disgusted with the whole situation. Analyzing the value of companies as if they are just a collection of machines, inventory, land and market share. It's so wrong. It's so distorted.

And the cherished balance sheet, what a joke! Until now I hadn't realized to what extent it's useless. The real assets, like people's expertise, market share, reputation, etc., don't appear at all. And the numbers that do appear— the value of machines, inventory and land—have only a remote resemblance to their real value.

I want to leave this artificial number world. I want to go back home.

14

This day didn't start well, and as it stands now, it's going to end up even worse. Two meetings were scheduled to negotiate the sale of Bob's cosmetics company. My problem was that I hadn't yet decided what to do about Bob's new distribution system. His system represents a remarkable improvement in service and inventory levels, but the reduction in inventory leads to a short-term loss of about ten million dollars.

The financial reports that we sent to the prospects are from last quarter, so the impact of the new system doesn't appear in them. Can I afford not to mention it? What's the best way to reveal it?

On the way to our first meeting I consulted with Brandon Trumann and Jim Doughty. I can tell you, they were not too happy with the new surprise I landed in their laps.

"A new distribution system? Inventory down by seventeen million dollars? The expected loss is ten million dollars larger than is currently presented? Alex, we should be used to you by now. But, next time, give us a little bit more warning."

Thank God that it was a relatively short taxi ride. Otherwise I suspect that they would have elaborated more about how much they like facing such news at the last minute. Pressed for time, they didn't have the opportunity to tell me what they really would like to do to me. Rather, they made sure that I understood how important it is to raise the issue in full.

"If there is one thing that can ruin a deal," Brandon said, "it is a last minute surprise. This is our first meeting with prospective buyers for I Cosmetics. Give it to them in full, don't hide a thing."

Even in the elevator they kept on telling me to emphasize the benefits, but to be very explicit about the expected negative outcome from the one-shot decrease in inventories.

I followed their instructions and my explanation was well received. It seems that most investors are aware of the fictitious profits and losses associated with a change in inventory levels.

The prospects were not concerned with the short-term drop in profits. On the contrary, they were impressed with the changes we implemented, and the speed in which we did it.

They received it so well that Trumann insisted the expected one-time negative impact should not be a factor in determining the price. To my surprise, in both meetings the prospects agreed.

Of course they questioned me, in depth. But the concepts of our new distribution system are so logical, and make so much sense, that I didn't have any problem convincing them of the validity of what we are doing. The only question that I couldn't answer was, "Why didn't you do it before?"

I guess that is always the question with a new, common sense solution.

Maybe I'm too paranoid about selling my companies? Maybe the world has changed and it's not as short-term numbers driven as it was? If everybody is like the people I've spoken with today, I think Bob and Stacey will be allowed to run their companies their way.

No, that is not correct. It's just my attempt to persuade myself that it's okay to collaborate in the sale of my companies. I know, too well, the distortions coming from the pressure to meet the budget. This quarter-to-quarter, month-to-month pressure that forces even prudent top executives to interfere. If the sale of the companies goes through, Bob and Stacey don't stand a chance. I must find a way to stop the sale.

But now I can't even think about it. I have something urgent to do. In an hour I have to be in Trumann's suite.

I throw my clothes on the bed and get in the shower. It is hot here in London. Very hot. In more than one way.

No, it's not what you think. They don't intend to hang me for what seems to be my blatant attempt to sabotage the sale. There is another issue. Alex Rogo, the world champion at putting himself in impossible situations, has done it again.

You see, when the last meeting was over, Doughty and Trumann came down really hard on me: "Alex," Brandon started, "I want to ask you more about this new system for distribution."

"It's just common sense, nothing more to it." I tried to avoid what was rightfully coming to me.

"Just common sense, nothing more to it," Brandon sarcastically repeated. "Have you noticed that your solution is very awkward? In your solution, plants are no longer judged by what they are traditionally responsible for, their production."

"But this doesn't mean," I hurried to correct his impression, "that they are not measured on something that is essentially under their control. It is their responsibility to have, at the plant, enough inventory of each item."

"Which only brings me to the next point," Brandon continued. "In the name of reducing inventory, you increased inventory in the plants from less than a day to twenty days. On top of that, in the name of quick response to the shops, you now delay shipments until almost the last possible minute. Alex, if you don't mind, all of this, every aspect, flies in the face of common practice."

I didn't know how to answer this line of attack. I thought they had understood the distribution solution. My problem, I thought, was that they also understood why I hadn't told them about it until the last minute.

Should I start explaining the distribution solution from the beginning? No. Their remarks in the meetings clearly indicated that they did understand it completely. So what's going on?

Cautiously I said, "Yes, our approach to distribution does fly in the face of common practice. But it is common sense."

"That's exactly what bothers us," Doughty interjected.

Now I was totally confused.

"How did you do it?" Brandon Trumann asked. "What enabled you to ignore tradition so blatantly? Changing what was always done to the extent that you were capable of developing such a simple and powerful system?"

So they did like our solution!

"I didn't develop it." I put the credit where it belonged. "It was Bob Donovan and his people."

"And the sales solution for your printing company? The one that enables you to compete against the fast printers, commanding higher prices for large quantities. That's not yours either, but Pete and his teams'?"

"Yes, it was developed by them," I insisted.

Brandon didn't let go. "And the turn-around in the pressure steam division, bringing it, in just one year, from a bottomless pit to small profits. This, I suppose, was done not by you, but by Stacey and her people?"

"That's a fact."

"And to whom are you going to attribute the phenomenal achievements in your previous division?"

I would have been flattered if not for his tone of voice. It came out as if they had something against me.

"What do you want?" I finally say.

"Isn't it obvious?" Jim Doughty was not less aggressive. "It seems as if you and your people have a method, a system enabling you to break free from the common practices."

"Thinking Processes that enable constructing and communicating common sense," I heard myself repeat Jonah's words.

"That's what we find so hard to believe."

"And the alternative," I started to laugh, "is that I'm some type of management genius. That is even harder to believe."

It was amusing. Really amusing.

They didn't seem amused.

"We find it hard to believe that you do have a system, but we cannot afford to drop it." Jim was serious.

I shrugged my shoulders.

He looked straight into my eyes and said, "Alex, you'll have to take us through such an exercise."

And Brandon added, "Frankly, I didn't believe that you could make any sense out of that pile of problems we dumped on you two days ago. I didn't take your claims seriously you know, the claim that you can find only one core problem that is the cause of all the problems that we listed. But now I'm not too sure. Maybe you do have a system, as awkward as it sounds."

So in less than an hour I have to go to Trumann's suite and show them how to find a core problem. For that I'll have to build the Current Reality Tree of the most involved subject I ever faced. I don't stand a chance.

I dress in a hurry. When did I last construct a Current Reality Tree? I have used all other Thinking Processes extensively, and I helped Bob with the work on distribution, but the last time I struggled with constructing a Current Reality Tree myself was more than two years ago. I'm not sure if I even remember Jonah's guidelines to do it. Me and my big mouth. How do I manage to land myself in such impossible corners?

I take the doily with Brandon's scribbles. Judging from his handwriting he should be a physician. I can barely decipher what he wrote. First, I'll have to copy it so that it's legible. While deciphering, I start to see some connections. Maybe I can do something with it.

UNDESIRABLE EFFECTS

1. Competition is fiercer than ever.
2. There is increasing pressure to reduce prices.
3. In more and more cases the price the market is willing to pay doesn't leave enough margin.
4. More than ever the market punishes suppliers who don't perform according to expectation.
5. Managers are trying to run their companies by striving to achieve local optima.
6. Various functions inside the company blame each other for lack of performance.
7. There is unprecedented pressure to take actions that will increase sales.
8. There is the need to launch new products at an unprecedented rate.
9. The constant introduction of new products confuses and spoils the market.
10. Most new outlets and most new/improved products eat into the sales of existing outlets/products.
11. A large percent of the existing sales force lacks sufficient sales skills.
12. Salespeople are overloaded.
13. Production and distribution do not improve fast/significantly enough.
14. Engineering is unable to deliver new products fast and reliably enough.
15. Companies don't come up with sufficient innovative ideas in marketing.

15

"The next step," I confidently say, "is to find a cause and effect relationship between at least two of the undesirable effects that we listed." I wish I were as confident as I sound, but at least I remember the next step.

"Does it matter which two?" Jim asks.

"No. Not like in other methods, prioritizing the undesirable effects is not part of the process."

"That's good," he says. "Brandon and I would never agree which of the undesirable effects is more devastating. By the way, saying undesirable-effects is quite a mouthful, wouldn't it be easier to call them problems?"

"I prefer to call UnDesirable Effects, UDEs, like cooties. Somehow it describes them better."

They smile politely and bend over the list.

I am in trouble. It's not a matter of remembering the steps, I think I remember all of them. It's a matter of meticulously performing them. It's very difficult to convert intuition into precise verbalization. I've never succeeded in constructing a Current Reality Tree without going through a long period of floundering. Now I have to do it under the scrutiny of Trumann and Doughty. I hope that they will be patient, otherwise I'll come out looking like a complete fool. In any event, trying to construct a Current Reality

Tree in front of them is not the best way to impress them—
and impress them I must.

"How should we do it?" Brandon asks.

"How should you do what?"

"How are we supposed to go about finding a cause and
effect relationship between two undesirable effects?"

"Just review the list and use your intuition. Connections will jump into your mind."

Then it dawns on me. I'm saved. They are willing to
do the job; I'll be the teacher. This way any floundering
will appear to be theirs, not mine. Up to a point, that is. As
long as they still feel they are making some progress, that
they are not just aimlessly floundering.

"God help me," I whisper, and dive into my new role.
"Well, did either of you find at least two undesirable effects,
UDEs, that you can connect?"

"Yes, more than one pair," Brandon says.

"So, what's the problem? Give it to me."

"I don't feel really comfortable with any connection.
It's too riffraff," he says.

I know the feeling very well. You examine the list and
many connections pop up in your mind. You try to put
them down on paper, and none is substantiated. But for
that, Jonah taught me the categories of legitimate reservations. That means converting an intuitive connection into
something so solid that everyone will refer to it as common
sense.

"Don't worry," I say encouragingly to Brandon, "give
me one pair, any pair."

"It looks to me," he hesitantly starts, "that the fact that
'There is unprecedented pressure to take actions that will
increase sales,' leads to the fact that 'There is a need to
launch new products at an unprecedented rate.' But I
don't feel comfortable with it. Not that it's not correct,
but . . ."

I take two yellow Post-it-notes. On one I write his first

UDE, UDE number seven, the one about pressure to increase sales, and on the other I write his second, the one
dealing with the need to launch new products. I stick them
on a large piece of white paper and connect them with an
arrow.

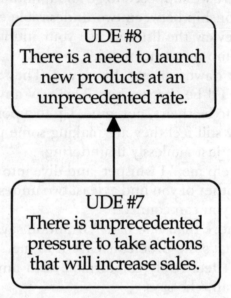

UDE #8
There is a need to launch
new products at an
unprecedented rate.

UDE #7
There is unprecedented
pressure to take actions
that will increase sales.

"Some clarity is needed," I agree. "These two effects
seem to be connected by a very long arrow."

"A trans-Atlantic arrow," Doughty laughs.

"Try to clarify the cause-effect connection by inserting
an intermediate step," I advise Brandon. When it doesn't
help, I try again. "What is the connection between pressure
to increase sales and launching new products?"

"Isn't it obvious?" he seems surprised. "Pressure to
increase sales translates into pressure to develop new
products, which then have to be launched into the market."

"Makes sense," I say, and on a third post-it I write,
"There is unprecedented pressure to promptly develop
new products." I stick this new post-it on the white sheet
between the other two. We all examine it.

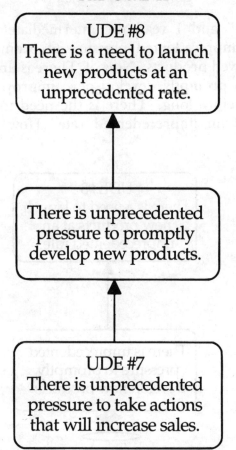

"It makes more sense," Doughty agrees, "but something is still missing."

"Yes; we call it 'insufficiency.' So let me add what I think is missing." They wait for me while I scribble another note and stick it alongside the bottom one. I read the note that I've just added, " 'One of the most effective ways to increase sales is to develop new, improved products.' Agree?"

They do.

"So, if 'There is unprecedented pressure to take actions that will increase sales' and 'One of the most effective ways to increase sales is to develop new, improved, products,' then," and I read the intermediate note, "then, 'There is unprecedented pressure to promptly develop new, improved products.' Now, if 'There is unprecedented pressure to promptly develop new, improved products,' then, not before long, 'There is the need to launch new products at an unprecedented rate.' How does it look now?"

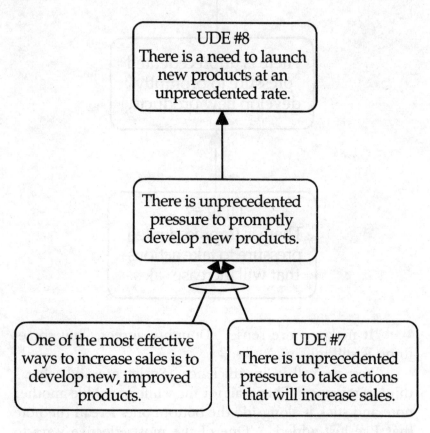

They like it.

I don't.

"Fellows," I say, "something is still wrong. In almost all industries there is unprecedented pressure to take actions to increase sales, but only some industries are launching new products at unprecedented rates."

"I don't agree," says Brandon. "Almost every industry is launching new products at a higher frequency than ever before. Even banks are constantly coming up with new programs."

"There is a difference," Jim says. "Can you really compare what is happening in industries like cosmetics, golf clubs or anything related to electronics to what happens in banks? In those industries the average lifetime of a product is less than two, or even less than one, year. They have to replace almost all their products every two years. That is what I call at an unprecedented rate."

"I guess you are right," Brandon agrees.

"You see the problem?" I say. "At the bottom of the tree, we have statements that are correct for all industries. At the top, we have a conclusion that is correct for only some industries. Something is missing from the bottom," I conclude. "So if we want the tree to be correct, we must add to the bottom the entity that exists for only some industries, which enables those same industries to develop new products at such a frantic pace."

Finally, I say, "Let me suggest something," and I add another post-it to the bottom. " 'There are industries where fast development of new materials enables the development of new products.' "

"He has a point," Jim thoughtfully says. "A mediocre electronic engineer working with today's components will produce a much better product than the best engineer ten years ago. So, what are we going to do with it? How are we going to correct our tree?"

"Like porcupines making love," I say. "Very carefully. First we have to decide on a name for these special industries. Let's call industries where fast development of new materials enables the development of new products 'advanced material industries,' for short.

"Now we have to reread what we've written and do any necessary corrections. If 'There are industries where fast development of new materials enables the development of new products—advanced material industries,' and 'One of the most effective ways to increase sales is to develop new products,' and 'There is unprecedented pressure to take actions that will increase sales,' then, 'In advanced material industries there is unprecedented pressure to promptly develop new, improved products.'"

"It's long, but it makes perfect sense." Brandon is satisfied. "Let's correct the top statement accordingly."

Since I already know how clear his handwriting is, I prefer to do it myself. Now the upper statement reads, "In advanced material industries there is a need to launch new products at an unprecedented rate."

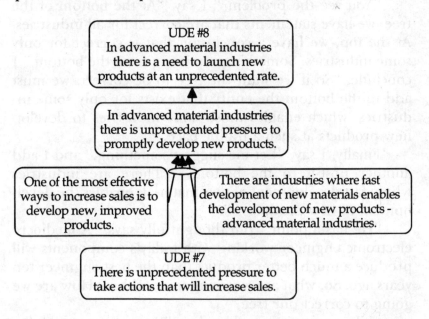

UDE #8
In advanced material industries there is a need to launch new products at an unprecedented rate.

In advanced material industries there is unprecedented pressure to promptly develop new products.

One of the most effective ways to increase sales is to develop new, improved products.

There are industries where fast development of new materials enables the development of new products - advanced material industries.

UDE #7
There is unprecedented pressure to take actions that will increase sales.

"So far, it's common sense, nothing more," Doughty says.

I restrain myself from reminding him that just a few minutes ago we had a lot of reservations regarding this "common sense."

"Common sense, my foot," Brandon is less forgiving. "If it were just common sense, how come I didn't agree with the way we initially wrote the first arrow and it has taken us almost half an hour to reach this stage?"

"Okay, okay," Jim apologizes, "I didn't say that to construct common sense was easy. But Alex, what's the next step? So far we have connected only two of the UDEs, we have thirteen more to go."

"That is exactly the next step," I say. "We have a solid nucleus, we have to connect all the other UDEs to it. But slowly, this process cannot be rushed. What other UDE can we easily connect?"

"The next one on the list," Brandon says. " 'The constant introduction of new products confuses and spoils the market.' "

I check it. "If 'In advanced material industries there is the need to launch new products at an unprecedented rate,' then, 'In advanced material industries the constant introduction of new products confuses and spoils the market.' It fits." I add it to the tree.

"What about UDE number twelve," Jim suggests. " 'Salespeople are overloaded.' It seems like we should be able to connect it pretty easily."

Well, it wasn't so easy. After several trials and errors we found out why. This UDE didn't stem from one place in our tree but from a combination of two reasons. When we finally finished, it was connected in the following way: If "There is unprecedented pressure to take actions that will increase sales," then, "There is pressure on salespeople to bring in more sales." This by itself is not enough to justify an overload, but on top of it there is something else demanding their time. If "In advanced material industries there is unprecedented pressure to promptly develop new products," then, "In advanced material industries salespeople have to learn about new products at an unprecedented rate." Now we could put it together. Now it's clear, why "In advanced material industries salespeople are overloaded."

"And what about regular industries, industries where

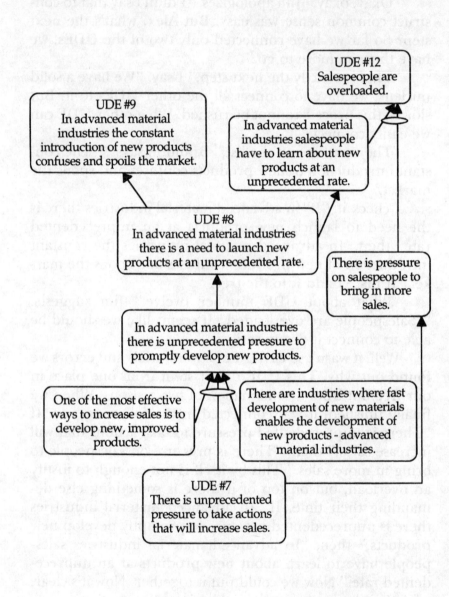

UDE #12
Salespeople are overloaded.

UDE #9
In advanced material industries the constant introduction of new products confuses and spoils the market.

In advanced material industries salespeople have to learn about new products at an unprecedented rate.

UDE #8
In advanced material industries there is a need to launch new products at an unprecedented rate.

There is pressure on salespeople to bring in more sales.

In advanced material industries there is unprecedented pressure to promptly develop new products.

One of the most effective ways to increase sales is to develop new, improved products.

There are industries where fast development of new materials enables the development of new products - advanced material industries.

UDE #7
There is unprecedented pressure to take actions that will increase sales.

advanced materials don't push them into the rapid race for new products?" I wonder aloud. "We cannot neglect them."

"As I pointed out," Brandon says, "even for these industries the starting point is still valid. They too are under unprecedented pressure to increase sales."

"We know the immediate result of such a pressure," Jim picks up the ball, "we know it too well. Let's not forget that a desperate traditional 'method' to get an order is to reduce price. Alex, what should we do with it? I thought that we should concentrate only on connecting additional UDEs to our tree."

"Yes, and there is no contradiction." Two more post-its and I read the result: "If 'There is unprecedented pressure to take actions that will increase sales,' and 'A desperate traditional method to get sales is to reduce prices,' then, 'There is increasing pressure to reduce prices.' Hello UDE number two, welcome to the party."

"And this UDE is, unfortunately, correct for almost every industry," Brandon sighs.

"I think," Jim is into it, "that we just reached UDE number one; 'Competition is fiercer than ever.' What fuels competition more than a price war? Put on top of it the technological war, the launching of new products at an unprecedented rate, and you get the real thing. That is what we see all around us, that's it."

I don't hurry to add it to the tree. Brandon also looks skeptical. "What's the matter?" Jim pushes us. "Don't you think that pressure to reduce prices, especially when it is often enhanced by the rat race to introduce new products, is the cause for the fierce competition that we face everywhere?"

"Yes, we do," Brandon reluctantly admits. "But . . ."

"But what?"

"But, I thought that the fact that competition is fiercer than ever is the cause for the fact that 'There is unprecedented pressure to take actions to increase sales.'"

"Yup, I see your point." Jim turns to me. "What are we supposed to do now?"

"What's the problem?" I pretend not to understand.

"The problem is," Brandon explains to me patiently, "that according to Jim, UDE number one is the result of what we wrote, so it's supposed to be at the top of the tree. But according to what I say, UDE number one is the cause of our starting point, and it should be at the very bottom of the tree."

"Brandon, do you agree with Jim's reasoning?"

He takes his time to rethink it, and then he agrees.

"Jim, do you agree with Brandon's reasoning?"

"Yes, I do."

"So, what is the problem? UDE number one should appear both at the top and the bottom. It's in a loop where it feeds itself," I calmly say.

"But if something feeds itself," Brandon tries to digest the idea, "if there is a loop, then the effects should become bigger and bigger."

"Precisely. Isn't that what we see in reality? Look at the wording that we used in the UDEs: 'unprecedented pressure,' 'unprecedented rate,' 'fiercer than ever.' They express to what extent these effects are already ballooning. Moreover, examine the last UDE that we connected, 'There is increasing pressure to reduce prices.' Doesn't it clearly imply a process that is still going on? As a matter of fact, because of the choice of words, I expected, right from the start, that a loop is involved. It's not so rare. On the contrary, in any involved subject I have always found at least one devastating loop."

They add the loop to the tree and reread it. It probably gives them a deeper understanding of the current situation, since before long Jim and Brandon are busy discussing the plausible outcome in the future.

I'm much slower. I'm still examining the tree. When I finish, I start again, and realize that there is an insufficiency in what they added. Competition by itself is not sufficient to

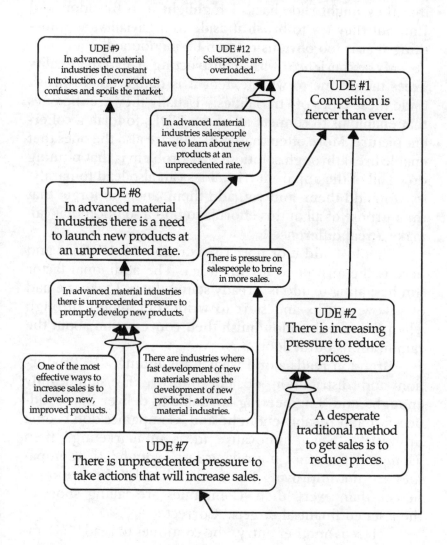

cause the unprecedented pressure to increase sales. There must be an additional factor. Something to state that companies are finding it hard to compete, and most are afraid that they might slide back. I highlight it to Brandon and Jim, but they try to brush it aside as a triviality, as something that is too obvious to even be mentioned.

My experience with constructing Current Reality Trees taught me to what extent it is dangerous to brush aside these types of "trivialities." Usually they are the ones that enable us to connect all of the UDEs to form a coherent picture. More often than not, they are also the ones that enable breakthrough solutions. My problem is that pinning down all of the apparent trivialities can also lead to paralysis. You add them, and you add them, and you forget that the purpose of all of this effort is to find a solution that can make a real difference.

Should I add it or not? I reexamine the UDE list and here is the answer to my dilemma. The additional factor I'm hesitating to add is already stated there. I take the pad of yellow post-its and start to write. I'm almost through when Jim and Brandon finish their conversation about the ramifications of the loop.

Brandon reads aloud what I am adding: "If 'Production and distribution do not improve fast/significantly enough,' and 'Engineering is unable to deliver new products fast and reliably enough,' and 'Companies don't come up with sufficient innovative ideas in marketing,' then 'Companies are not improving fast enough.' If, 'Companies are not improving fast enough,' and 'Competition is fiercer than ever,' then 'Companies are falling short of their stated financial targets.' Correct.

"Here is another entry," he continues to read, " 'Companies have already cut all costs they know how to cut.' I'm not sure, but let's see where you are going to take it. If, 'Companies are falling short of their stated financial targets,' and 'Companies have already cut all costs they know how to cut,' then 'There is unprecedented pressure to take actions to increase sales.' It's on the nose. Jim, don't you think so?"

Rather than answering, Jim says, "At the bottom of the tree, there are three UDEs, all indicating incompetence of the managers. I didn't need the tree to tell me that this is the core problem. It was obvious to me right from the start."

"Jim, you are not fair." Brandon is uneasy with Jim's remark.

I'm more direct. "Jim, all of a sudden all managers are incompetent? Come on. To me, what you said sounds more like UDE number six—'Various functions are blaming each other for lack of performance.' Can you do the formal connection to our tree?"

"I'll try," he smiles back.

While they both are struggling with it, I examine the list in the attempt to find an UDE that can be an alternative explanation to Jim's suggestion of incompetence. UDE number five immediately presents itself: "Managers are trying to run their companies by striving to achieve local optima." I decide to wait for Jim and Brandon.

When they finish, I ask, "Why do you think most distribution systems don't improve fast and significantly enough?"

Half jokingly Jim answers, "Because they haven't developed the solution that you and your people implemented in I Cosmetics."

"That solution is nothing but common sense. What do you think prevented them from developing it themselves? Let me ask you an even tougher question. In any company that you know, do you think that it would be easy for a manager to convince the company to switch to such a system?"

That slows them down for a minute. Brandon is the first to answer. "No. It would be very difficult. As I already said, your system requires a change in the way plants are

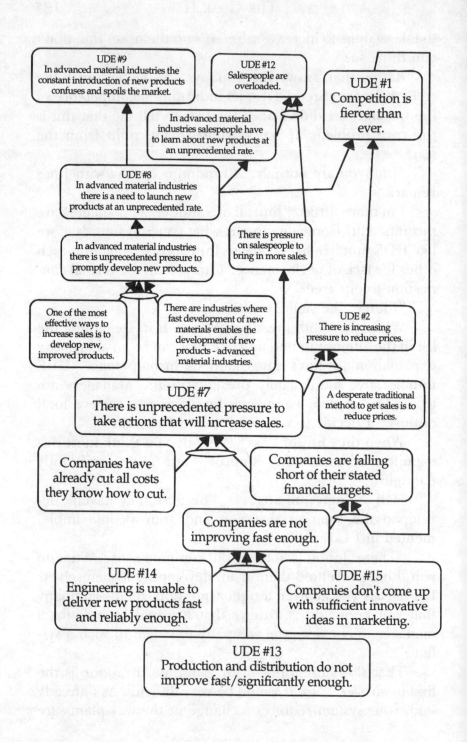

internally measured. It's not easy to get a consensus for such a change."

"And what about the cost accounting distortion that translates reduction of inventories into a huge artificial loss? Do you know that because of that distortion I contemplated reversing Bob's implementation?"

"I don't blame you," Brandon says. "This morning I was very close to suggesting it myself."

"If you agree with this, what do you think about the following? Let me start with a generic statement: 'For every mode of operation, managers develop suitable measurements.' " When they naturally agree, I continue, "If, 'Managers are trying to run their companies by striving to achieve local optima,' and 'For every mode of operation managers develop suitable measurements,' then 'There are important measurements that focus on local optima, e.g., cost accounting based measurements.' Do you agree?"

"At last!" Jim exclaims.

And Brandon explains, "We were warned that before the end of the trip you would fill our ears with fierce attacks on cost accounting. Some even say that you call cost accounting 'enemy number one of productivity.' "

"This is not a joke." I'm irritated. "All the improvements that I initiated in production and engineering were flying in the face of all cost accounting measurements. Efficiency; variance; product cost; you name it, I had to violate it. It was the only way to improve the companies. Let me tell you, more than once, I was sailing too close to the wind. If it was not for the speed with which our changes improved the bottom line, I wouldn't be sitting here now with you."

"Carry on," Brandon pats me on my shoulder. "We fully agree."

Still a little irritated, I decide to return to the tree. "Here is another facet of the same thing: 'Many actions that are needed for improving lead-time, reliability, quality, response time and service do not save cost, and/or increase

cost in the short run.' Before you ask, let me make it clear
that I mean 'cost' in the traditional sense. The way it is
measured by cost accountants in the plants."

"Unfortunately, we don't have any quarrel with you,"
Brandon assures me. "We examined very closely what you
have done in your previous division and we must agree.
You did violate every local measurement and at the same
time, everything you implemented made perfect sense.
Our only problem is the painfully slow pace with which
your improvements are picked up by others in UniCo. But
carry on, let's see where you intend to take it."

"Now it's just a matter of putting all of it together. If
'There are important measurements that focus on local optima, e.g., cost accounting based measurements,' and
'Many actions that are needed for improving lead-time,
reliability, quality, response time and service do not save
cost and/or increase cost in the short run,' then 'Production
and distribution do not improve fast/significantly enough,'
and also 'Engineering is unable to deliver new products
fast and reliably enough.' My dilemma is how to derive
from it the third member of the same group, 'Companies
don't come up with sufficient innovative ideas in marketing.' My hunch is that it's somehow connected."

"I think that you are right," Jim agrees. "And I think
that UDE number three is somehow involved in the connection."

I check the list to see what UDE number three is. It is
'In more and more cases the price the market is willing to
pay doesn't leave enough margin.' He has a point; what is
the difference between margin and product cost? One is
just price minus the other. If the concept of product cost is
misleading in operations, it might be that the concept of
margin is as harmful in marketing.

We play with it for a while but don't reach any firm
conclusions.

It's almost twelve and four UDEs are still not connected:

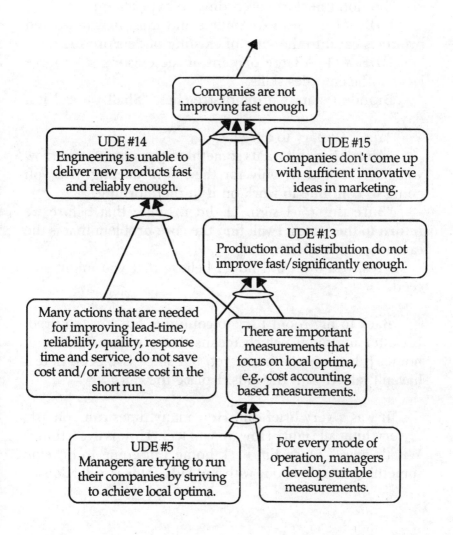

UDE #3: In more and more cases the price the market is willing to pay doesn't leave enough margin.

UDE #4: More than ever the market punishes suppliers who don't perform according to expectation.

UDE #10: Most new outlets and most new/improved products eat into the sales of existing outlets/products.

UDE #11: A large percent of the existing sales force lacks sufficient sales skills.

Brandon stands up and stretches. "Shall we call it a day?"

"Yes," I hurry to agree.

"Alex," Jim still wants something from me, "tomorrow you have to join us only for the noon meeting. Are you going to continue to work on it in the morning?"

"Sure thing," I sigh. "I did promise that before we return to the States, I will find the core problem that is the cause for all the UDEs."

"Yes, you did. And now I believe that you might succeed."

Back in my room I try to continue, but I'm too tired. It's after midnight, which means that it's after 7:00 PM at home. Julie won't be home yet, but since I've been here I haven't talked with the kids. I place the call.

It was a very brief call. How many times can you ask, "Everything all right? How do you feel? How is everything? What's new?" Once I'm back home I'm going to develop something to talk about with my kids. This is ridiculous.

16

Traffic is like a sales forecast, you can never predict it accurately. Knowing that London is even more congested than New York, we hurried through the last meeting; no one wants to risk missing his flight back home. So now we are stuck at Heathrow with more than three hours to spare.

The first class lounge in Terminal 4 is the best I've ever been in. A large variety of drinks, an impressive assortment of small, nicely cut sandwiches, delicious-looking cakes, and it's all free.

So why am I complaining? Do I prefer to be still stuck in traffic jams? People are strange. If reality doesn't mimic their expectations, if the precaution that they took turns out to be unnecessary, they feel disappointed. I even know people who complain about never collecting on their own life insurance.

I think that people deserve what they get. Just now, we got a real reason to complain—they announced that our flight is delayed because of a mechanical problem. They will tell us more in one hour. Yeah, sure, I've been here before, it's how the worst delays usually start.

Julie claims that you can always turn a problem into an opportunity. Well, not this one. Actually, I can. I'm unhappy with the gift that I bought her. It's a nice cashmere sweater but I couldn't find a color that will do justice to her complexion. I had planned to roam the shops this morning, but instead I worked on Jim's tree. Now I have some time, and they say that there are nice jewelry stores in this terminal. Maybe I can find something that will scream, "buy me."

Back in the lounge, with a unique platinum bracelet and a dent in my bank account, I'm relaxing over a bottle of cold beer. Over all, this trip went much better than I expected. I definitely scored big with Brandon and Jim. The negotiations for Bob's company are going better than I could have hoped; we are probably going to get a good price for it. The situation with Stacey's division is unclear, but the best thing happened with Pete's company. We didn't even discuss it, and we are not going to, until the dust clears.

What's going on there? This morning Pete was supposed to have a meeting with one of his buyers. I wonder if his optimism is justified. I wonder if he correctly read the initial response. I wonder if it wasn't just a polite way to tell him that his offer was not understood.

"Is Pete back in?" I ask his secretary.

"Yes, Mister Rogo, just a minute."

"Hello, Alex, how is it going on the other side of the pond?" Pete sounds cheerful . . . but that's how he sounds when he has to cover up for a big disappointment.

"Pete, how did your meeting go?"

"Better than expected."

I feel my muscles relax. Only now I consciously realize how much I've risked. If it had turned out that Pete's marketing idea was nothing but hot air I would have been in a terrible bind. Brandon and Jim would, no doubt, believe that I invented it to deliberately sabotage the sale. I shiver.

Calmly, I ask for more details.

"We went in. We went over the details. I gave a concession of another twenty-two thousand, and he signed the deal." Pete sounds as if he does such things at least three times a day.

It's okay. Everyone is entitled to show off a bit. Especially when it is well justified.

"Are you going to tell me how big the order is?"

"We signed the contract based on estimations of all his needs for the remainder of the year. It is six hundred thirty-four thousand, plus additions for every new design. But on those I had to promise a five-day turnaround. That was the last nail in the . . . marriage chariot."

"Are you going to have any problem meeting such fast response?"

"Not according to my prep room manager. He claims that he can meet four days without any hassle."

"Great." But I have to continue to ask, "What about the other buyer, the one you're supposed to meet tomorrow? Any news on that front?"

"Well, we are constantly on the phone," he answers. "Every few hours he calls to add some more stuff to the quote. He had probably involved his marketing department in it. He's driving us crazy, but I'm not complaining. Not at all."

Neither do I. "Pete, remember, we don't want to be in the hands of a few big clients."

"Yes, we are discussing that right now. It's important, it determines which prospects we should go after. As it stands now, with our 'Mafia offer,' we can get anyone we want."

He is flying. In his place I would be too. Next week I'd better pay him a visit. With such success he might overlook some snake in the grass. As long as the sale is hanging over our heads we can't afford any slip-ups.

Nice. It is really nice. I update Brandon and Jim. They are as pleased as I am. We raise a toast to Pete and his team.

"Are you ready to hear what happened to our tree?" I take out the big folded sheet and spread it over the table.

"More good news?" Brandon moves his chair closer to mine.

"I think so, but you be the judge." I am proud of what I constructed this morning. Really proud.

"Where do we start?" Jim is all business.

"From bottom, up," I answer. "That way it's easy to follow the logic."

Brandon volunteers to read. "If, 'Managers try to run their companies by striving to achieve local optima,' and 'For every mode of operation managers develop suitable measurements,' then 'There are important measurements that focus on local optima, e.g., cost accounting based measurements.' Yes, that's what we wrote yesterday. Oh, I see, here is the new stuff. If, 'Managers try to run their companies by striving to achieve local optima,' then, 'Most managers' perception of value of a product is heavily influenced by the local efforts required to design, produce, sell and deliver the product.' I don't know if I agree with this last conclusion."

"Yes, you do," Jim is decisive. "You yourself don't believe that's how we should regard the value of a product, but you must agree that this is the perception of most managers."

"You are right. Sorry, Alex."

"Keep going," I encourage him, "read the additional entity." I'm anxious to see their response.

Brandon doesn't need any encouragement, " 'The essence of cost accounting is to calculate the product cost.' Hmm . . . I'm not sure, but before I object, let's see what you are going to do with this statement."

He takes a deep breath and continues, "If, 'There are important measurements that focus on local optima, e.g., cost accounting based measurements,' and 'The essence of cost accounting is to calculate the product cost,' and 'Most managers perception of the value of a product is heavily influenced by the local efforts required to design, produce, sell and deliver the product,' then, 'Most managers believe that product cost is something real that quantifies the efforts absorbed by the product.' Whoa, that was long, let me read it again."

I wait for them while they digest this last mouthful.

At last Jim says, "No problem, I buy it."

Brandon agrees.

I can't control my impatience, "You see the unavoidable conclusion? It means that . . ." I'm looking for the precise verbalization written on my tree. "It means that 'Most managers believe that the product price should be equal to product cost plus reasonable margin.' "

They don't get it, rather, Jim is quick to conclude, "The key word is 'should', '. . . it should be equal . . .' I see, you're going to connect it to one of our UDEs. The one that states that, 'In more and more cases the price that the market is willing to pay doesn't leave enough margin.' "

No rush, in due time he will get it. Loudly, I say, "Correct. But, as it turns out, it takes some stages before we are able to connect to it. Bear with me, first we'll have to go through the mechanism by which prices are determined."

"You mean the struggle between supply and demand?" Brandon asks.

"Basically," I confirm. "But let's try to understand it a little bit better. The companies represent the supply side, and as we see, suppliers have a very precise perception of value of the product they supply—the value is supposed to be product cost plus reasonable margin. Naturally, they push for their perception of value to dictate the actual prices."

"Wait a minute," Jim says, "you are talking about suppliers as if they are one entity. That's not the case, suppliers fight amongst themselves."

"Exactly the other entity that we have to consider." I smile at Jim and point to the tree. "I haven't neglected it— on the contrary. I grabbed what we talked about yesterday, that 'Competition becomes more and more fierce,' which leads to the conclusion, 'Suppliers display a less and less uniform front.' "

"Thank you," says Jim, "and now you have probably got, somewhere here, the demand side?"

"Here it is," I point it out to him. " 'Market perception of value is in accordance with the benefits of having the product.' "

Before he has any chance to raise more questions I explain, "Rather than supply and demand, I prefer to show it as a clash between the companies' perception of value for the product they offer and the market perception of value for the same product."

"That's interesting," Brandon comments. "The two perceptions have nothing in common. The perception of value of the companies is based on the effort they had to put into the product, while the perception of value of the market is based on the benefits gained from using the product. No wonder the price is determined by arm wrestling; there is no agreed upon objective criteria."

"Exactly," I say. "And since we are now in a period when suppliers display a less and less uniform front, the unavoidable result is that," and I read from the appropriate place in the tree, " 'Prices and quantities sold are determined more and more by the markets' perception of value and less and less by the suppliers perception of value.' "

"Unavoidably," Brandon agrees. "And that leads to," he continues to read, " 'More than ever satisfying the market perception of value is key to success.' Which, not surprisingly, is a lesson that all of us have learned in the last decade. The hard way, I might add."

"First year course in economics," Jim says cynically.

"No, it is not," Brandon beats me by a hair's breadth, "and stop being such a smart aleck. Don't you realize what Alex wrote here? The pendulum is swinging to the market side, unrelated to the relation between supply and demand."

"What do you mean?" Jim is surprised by Brandon's fierce reaction.

"Let me explain," I try to cool them down. "What we said is when competition becomes very fierce, like the situation when it's also fueled by a technological race, when companies throw new products into the market every few months, in such cases prices will continue to go down, even when demand is higher than supply."

"But that can't be," Jim protests.

"If it cannot be, then you must point out to us where we went astray; where exactly the mistake is in our logic."

Jim bends over the table to reexamine our tree, but Brandon says to him, "Don't bother. Alex is right. Look, for example, at the electronic wafer industry. Demand is much greater than supply. All the wafer plants everywhere are huge bottlenecks. The backlog, right now, is well over a year. Nevertheless prices continue to dive."

"I guess you're right. I'll have to think it over. Brandon, if that's the case, then in many relatively high-tech companies we are invested in, we shouldn't expect that the recovery will lead to increases in their product prices. That is awful."

"Jim, didn't you suspect it? The recovery has been going on for almost a year now. Haven't you started to scale down the profit forecast of those companies?"

"Not enough," he admits.

"Can we continue?" I ask them. "We are about to connect to some more UDEs."

It doesn't help. Brandon continues to mutter, "First year economics . . ." Jim is probably trying to reevaluate the future of some of his investments. Who said that practical results don't come directly from the analysis stage?

Eventually I am able to continue to read. "If 'Supplier perception of value is product cost plus reasonable margin,' and 'Prices and quantities sold are determined more and more by the markets' perception of value and less and less by the suppliers' perception of value,' then, 'In more and more cases the price that the market is willing to pay doesn't leave enough margin,' which is our UDE number three."

"Simple, isn't it?" Brandon teases Jim.

I don't think that they'll continue to smile after the next few derivatives. "Let's view this branch," I suggest. "If, as we said before, 'Most managers believe that product cost is something real that quantifies the efforts absorbed by the product,' then, 'Most managers believe that selling below product cost leads (at least in the long run) to losses.'"

I examine them. They look at me. They look at each other thoughtfully. "Alex, don't you believe it?" Brandon asks.

"If I don't believe in product cost how can I believe it! I believe in the bottom line. But that's beside the point. Do you agree with this derivative?"

"We believe that most managers believe in it," Jim says. "As for us, for now, we would like to reserve our judgment."

So far, so good, I think to myself, and calmly continue to read, "If 'Most managers believe that selling below product cost leads (in the long run) to losses,' then 'Most companies are reluctant to accept orders with low margins and even go so far as dropping low-margin products.'"

"Alex," Brandon says slowly, "are you telling us it is a mistake when we tell the management of our companies to strategically prune low-margin products?"

"It depends," I keep a poker face. "When you 'prune' low-margin product you lose the money that you get from the clients who were buying that product. The question is do your resulting savings come to more than that amount."

"We cut the variable cost, but we don't always cut much of the fixed cost," he admits.

"Brandon, stop fooling yourself," Jim comes out strong. "Many times we don't cut even the entire variable cost."

"If the company doesn't have a bottleneck," Brandon slowly brings it together, "and we don't cut all the costs that were part of the calculated product cost, then. . . . Alex, you are telling us that we have actively participated in jeopardizing our own companies, aren't you?"

I maintain my poker face. It's not easy.

"I need a drink," Brandon says, and stands up.

"Make it a double," Jim follows him.

I guess that they are more interested in the last conclusion than in the way I have connected it to UDE number 4. That's fine with me. It won't hurt them to do some soul searching. Some people claim that the way to hell is paved with good intentions. From what I've observed and deduced since I've learned to construct common sense, these people are wrong. By now, the way to hell must be blocked by good intentions.

They return with coffee, bringing me one also.

"What happened to the drinks?" I ask.

Jim pats his stomach, "It's here."

"There is still one thing I would like to show you," I say.

"You have shown us enough," Brandon promises me.

"No," I object. "Remember, all of this stems from your demand that I show that one core problem is responsible for all the UDEs. We haven't done it yet."

"Yes, you have," Brandon sighs. "You have shown how everything is tied so tightly together. It's good enough."

"Besides," Jim raises his hand, "judging from your eagerness, I suspect another bomb is waiting for us. I think that we've had enough for one day."

"There is one link still missing," I insist. "You haven't seen how striving for local optima leads to the lack of innovative marketing ideas."

"Yes, that's important," Jim agrees.

"Okay, Alex," Brandon gives up. "We asked for it, we deserve to get it. Go ahead, show us."

He got the point. Next time they will not be so hasty to

suggest that I spend all morning constructing trees rather than leisurely buying gifts for my family.

I point to the area of the tree we haven't covered yet and start reading, slowly. "If 'Most managers believe that the product price should be equal to product cost plus reasonable margin,' then 'Most managers believe that there is essentially a single, fair price for a product.' At the same time, do you agree that, 'Different market sections might have different needs'?"

"Uh-oh. Here it comes," Jim trumpets. "Of course, what a dichotomy."

"No," Brandon corrects him, "what an opportunity. Keep on Alex, this is interesting."

I keep on, "If 'Different market sections might have different needs,' then 'Different market sections might have different perceptions of value for even the same product.' "

"Of course," says Jim. "Different perceptions, we can demand different prices."

"Not so quickly," I say. "Different perceptions don't automatically translate into different prices. My conclusion at this stage is only that 'To a large extent most managers ignore the market's different perception of value for the same product.' To answer your point, I have added another statement. 'Actions to guarantee effective segmentation can be taken.' But Jim, if a company neglects to find and institute these actions it must expect that two segments having different perceptions of value will both demand to pay the lower price."

"If one section knows about the other," he admits.

"Jim, at the end there are no secrets. At the end one will know about the other, and then what? You must take actions to guarantee that even if from the supplier point of view it is the same product, from the market's point of view it is not."

"Can you give us an example?"

"Sure. Look at the airplane we are about to board,

eventually. Go to the tourist section and check the prices people have paid. Do you really believe you are going to see only one price?"

"No," he smiles. "Not at all. It depends when they bought the ticket, where they bought it. It also depends if they bought their tickets as a group or as individuals."

"Yes," I agree. "It also depends on some strange things like the length of their stay. If you notice, none of it has any relation to the actual cost of flying a passenger across the Atlantic. They all will occupy the same space, in the same airplane, served by exactly the same crew. The airline took actions to segment the market, otherwise they wouldn't have survived. Even though, I must admit, that when you look deeper into it you get the impression that they probably over-segmented. If you know their system intimately you can find some crazy deals. Do you want another example?"

"No," says Brandon. "I think I can come up with many others. But tell me, what is your definition of segmentation?"

"Here it is," I show him. " 'Two sections of the market are called segmented from each other if and only if changes in prices in one section do not cause any changes in the other section."

Brandon reads it again. "So, you don't mean just niches?"

"No," I agree. "Niches are just part of my definition. I am talking about the fact that a company can take actions to effectively segment a market that right now looks uniform to them. Of course, provided that this market does contain sections with different needs."

"Keep on," Jim says.

"I must emphasize," I continue to explain, "that these actions to guarantee segmentation are very important. Look what happens when we don't do it, when we do have only a single price, no matter what it is. Do you agree with the following statement: 'Imposing a single price enables customers who have a high perception of value to pay a low price.'?"

They agree.

I continue, "At the same time 'Imposing a single price trims away customers for whom the price is too steep relative to their perception of value.' "

"What you are actually telling us," Brandon concludes, "is that most companies don't take advantage of the vast potential inherent in market segmentation."

"Precisely." They catch it much quicker than I was able to derive it. I suppose they have more experience than I do.

"Alex, what you are telling us is that due to lack of actions to segment we have UDE number ten?" Jim jumps to the next conclusion.

"Bravo!" I cannot hold back my admiration.

"What is UDE number ten?" Brandon asks.

I put my finger on the sheet and read, " 'Most new outlets and most new/improved products eat into the sales of existing outlets/products.' And I'm not saying it lightly. I spent quite some time this morning going over some cases where it did happen in my companies. In each case, if in parallel with launching the new outlet, I had taken some specific actions to segment the market, I could have minimized the damage."

"We'll take your word for it," Brandon says.

"Try to do better in the future," Jim pats me on the back.

"Now you see the next step," I continue, eager to finish. "From what we said, it is obvious that 'Marketing is not oriented to take advantage of the most promising and almost virgin direction—that of market segmentation.' "

"Almost virgin," Jim chuckles. "In a little while he will write, 'a little bit pregnant.' "

I throw him a nasty look.

"No offense, Alex. Just joking. I do appreciate where you are leading us. It is obvious now. Many companies are trying desperately to find new marketing ideas. We all know how difficult it is to come up with innovative ideas in a well-beaten direction. Everybody is trying to do it. While at the same time few are attempting to aggressively segment what seems to be a uniform market. We are simply blinded by the notion of a single price. You are absolutely right."

"Now that everything is tied together we can easily find the core problem," I declare.

"How?" Jim is still left with some curiosity.

"Trace the arrows. See which entity is the cause—directly or through other entities—of all the UDEs.

They bend over the tree, tracing the arrows down. They do it for a while. Then Jim raises his eyes, "Congratulations, you have made it. All our listed UDEs (and probably many more that we haven't listed) are derivatives of one statement. 'Managers are trying to run their companies by striving to achieve local optima.' And I'm not going to say that I suspected it right from the start."

"So what's next?" Brandon asks.

Before I can answer, Jim raises his hand, "No, Brandon. My head is spinning, and so is yours. If you want to know what is next, schedule another meeting with Alex, and count me in. But please, not next week. I've had enough for now."

17

"Thank you, Daddy." Sharon kisses me on the cheek, takes her barely opened gift and goes to her room.

"What's with her?" I ask.

"It's nothing." Dave is busy scattering around scarves. "Manchester United, Liverpool, Arsenal. Ha, this is a beauty, Austin Villa." He wraps it around his neck. "Did you know that last week they succeeded in. . . ."

Since the Mondial, Dave is fascinated with soccer, especially European soccer. What can possibly be interesting about soccer?

Happy that he is happy with my gift, I turn to Julie. "What's the matter with Sharon? I thought that having, what's his name, as a boyfriend put an end to her moods."

"It's Eric, and she's better but not perfect. Nothing to worry about," Julie assures me. "In a day or two she'll snap out of it."

"I think I'll go up and talk to her. It will be nice to cheer her up a little." I missed my girl too much.

"You can try." Julie doesn't give it much chance.

"May I come in?"

No answer, at least no answer that I can hear. I open

the door slightly. Sharon is lying on the bed reading a book.

"May I come in?" I repeat.

Sharon puts down the book.

I choose to interpret that as a yes, and sit myself on her bed. She moves a little to give me more room.

I entered. That's good, but what am I supposed to do now?

"What are you reading?"

"Some dumb book." She pushes it to the floor.

"How is Eric?" I try again.

"Okay."

"And school?"

"Fine."

I'm starting to bore even myself.

"You know Sharon," I try to be more direct, "I'd like to talk to you about something that really bothers me."

"What is it?"

"We don't have anything that we like to talk about. Not even a single subject that we like to discuss with each other."

"Oh Daddy, can we do it some other time? I'm too tired for it now."

Flop.

Okay, one last try. They say that teenage girls are sentimental. Maybe this will work: "Sharon, when I was in Europe the nights were very lonely. I missed all of you a lot. I didn't feel like doing anything. I didn't feel like reading, I didn't feel like going anywhere. For no real reason I was in this terrible mood where nothing seemed worth doing."

No response.

"Are you in the same situation? No real reason, just that everything looks plain dull?"

"Daddy!"

"Okay. I'll leave you alone. But tell me one thing. Do you have a real reason for your depressed mood?"

"Of course I do. What do you think?"

I gently smile at her. "I don't think that you do."

"What do you know?" She sits up. "Do you understand that I cannot see Eric until Monday? Do you know that I've been forced to betray Chris's trust in me? I don't have reasons? Do you know how irritating Debbie can be? Everything that I do with Eric is childish. This girl is simply jealous. I know that it sounds pitiful to you. Unimportant girls' stuff. Daddy, I'm not in the mood. Can I be left alone. Pleeeease."

I concede. "Yes, jealousy can be very irritating," I say, and stand up. "But sometimes we have to comply with it. That's life I guess."

"Debbie is my best friend. That's what makes it so hard."

"On the other hand," I'm opening the door, "if you want Debbie to continue being your friend and not a pain in the neck, you'd better do something."

"What?" She stands up as well. "What can I do?"

I go to her desk, pick up one of her pale pink pages and start to write. "Your objective, as I understand it, is to 'Maintain a good friendship with Debbie.' In order to achieve that you must 'Accommodate Debbie's behavior,' which under the current circumstances means that you must 'Tolerate Debbie's jealousy.' "

"But . . ."

"Yes, Sharon, you have a but, a big but."

"Thank you, Daddy!"

I ignore the pun. "You see, on the other hand, in order to 'Maintain a good friendship with Debbie' you must make sure that you'll 'Not allow friendship to deteriorate to ownership.' "

"Deteriorate to ownership . . . Correct! That's what I keep on telling her."

"Which means," I complete the cloud, "that you must 'Not tolerate Debbie's jealousy.' You are caught in a real conflict, my darling. And since I know how much Debbie means to you, no wonder you're bothered."

" 'Not allow friendship to deteriorate to ownership.' I'm going to tell that to her. She must understand that she doesn't own me. That I'm allowed to have a boyfriend. Especially someone so cool as Eric."

"What about the other reasons that you mentioned?" I politely inquire.

"Forget it. This is the real thing."

I think that it would be a mistake to stop here. If the other things were not important, Sharon would not go into a withdrawal. Debbie alone wouldn't have done it.

"Sharon, I think that we should continue on."

"Why?"

"Because you are too quiet. If it were just Debbie's jealousy, then probably you would have raved about her, you would have tried to find ways to put some sense into her skull, but it's unlikely that it would have caused you to crawl into your cocoon."

"Crawl into my cocoon? I didn't crawl into anything. Look, I didn't ask . . ."

"Sharon," I stop her before she goes too far. "The other things might not look really important. But I suspect that to you they are, and in a deeper sense than you yourself appreciate."

"I don't understand."

But at least she understands that I'm not trying to blame her or, even worse, to pat her on the head.

"I guess that I can help you find why the other things are troubling you to the extent they are. Do you want to try?"

"If you insist."

"Take a clean page," I say, and hand her the pen. "Now, let me show you how to start with a troubling event and finish . . ."

"Wait," she sighs. "What do you mean by troubling event?"

"You know, those irritating things that don't seem important but nevertheless haunt you for hours, sometime days."

"Yes," she smiles. "I have a few of them."

"You see, the mere fact that something troubles us more than it should indicates that this event has somehow caused more harm than is apparent on the surface."

She thinks about it.

"My speculation is," I carry on, "that the things that are bothering you cause you to compromise on something that is really important to you. Do you want me to show you how to start with one of these troubling undesirable events and reveal the real damage?"

"Do you think that I can do it?" She sounds skeptical.

"Let's see. What was the thing about Eric that you have to comply with? You said something about not seeing him for a while?"

"Yeah. He has some lousy exam on Monday. It's a long story."

"Okay. Write here, on the right, 'Not see Eric until Monday.' "

As she writes, she comments, "I will have to go alone to the party. Isn't it awful?"

"Now, below it write what you want."

"I want to see him every day."

"Fine. Write it down. Now, to the left of it, write why it is so important to you."

"What do you mean?"

"Why is it important to you to see Eric every day?"

"Because it is. He is my boyfriend. We have to be together. Isn't it obvious?"

"So write, 'Be close to Eric.' "

In my mind I quickly check the validity: In order to 'Be close to Eric' I must 'See Eric every day.' Why? I don't dare ask.

"Now comes the difficult question: In order to satisfy

what need do you comply with not seeing Eric? Why do you think you should not see him until Monday?"

"I told you, he has to pass the exam. He claims that it's important. At least to his mother it's important. Actually it is. If he fails again he will have to switch to a lower course and he wants so much to be an engineer."

"I'm happy to see that you don't allow your friendship to deteriorate to ownership."

"You mean den and to see him every day?"

"Yes. If you want a good friendship you must consider the other side's needs."

She thinks about it. "I guess you're right."

"So, in order to satisfy what need do you comply with not seeing Eric? Write the answer down."

"I still don't understand. What should I write? Because of Eric? That's what you want me to write?"

"In order to satisfy what need?" I repeat.

"The need to consider his needs." She's a little irritated at me being so picky.

"That's it," I say. "Write it down."

When she does I show her why it pays to be precise. "Try to read it now adding the words 'In order to,' and 'I must.' See if it makes sense.

"In order to 'Consider Eric's needs,' I must 'Not see Eric until Monday.' I still think that he could be more flexible. Now what?"

"What is your common objective? Why is it important to you to consider Eric's needs and at the same time be close to him?"

"Because, because . . . I know it, but . . ."

"Look at the previous cloud," I try to help. "The one we wrote about Debbie."

She glances at it and then smiles. "It's almost the same objective. 'Maintain a good friendship with Eric.' " She completes her cloud.

"In order to maintain a good friendship you must be with him, but at the same time you must consider his needs. You see, Sharon. Not seeing Eric until Monday puts you in conflict, which jeopardizes an important objective of yours."

She doesn't really listen. "Daddy? I think that my cloud about Eric is exactly Debbie's cloud about me." She looks again at Debbie's cloud.

It gives her a new perspective.

"Do you understand Debbie's behavior better?"

"You know what? I'm sure that Debbie and I can agree about what friendship is and what is becoming ownership. This will be a great discussion. Maybe Mom will allow me to sleep over at Debbie's house tonight."

And with that, my gazelle is gone.

Before I reach the door, she's back. "She agreed. Oh, thank you Daddy. Thank you so much."

It's a good feeling.

"Do you want to try to decipher your third complaint?" Not that it matters now, but I want to spend a little more time with my full-of-life girl.

"Why not," she agrees. "What was it?"

"Something about Chris."

"Oh yes." She is serious again, "It's bad."

"Rather than telling me what happened, why don't you write it down, as a cloud?"

"I'll try," and she sits down.

First she writes, "Give math homework to Kim." Below it, "Don't give math homework to anybody."

It's interesting. I wait patiently for further developments. After about a minute or two of twisting she writes to the left, "Keep my promise to Chris." And above it, "Save Kim."

"The objective is obvious, 'Maintain good friendships.' But does the whole thing make sense?" she asks.

"It does, if you've done the math work together with Chris," I say.

"That's exactly what happened. But Kim begged for it, I didn't have the heart to say no."

My poor baby. Three hits, from three different directions, all perfectly aimed at her most important thing—maintaining good friendships. And she didn't know how to handle even one, not to mention all three. No wonder she crawled into her cocoon.

Too frequently Sharon goes into her withdrawals. And we suspected that something was wrong with the kid. Maintaining good friendships is not an easy objective. It's very easy to get hurt. But it's certainly worthwhile.

Where were we? Why haven't we given her a hand? It's not so difficult to help. We certainly have more experience handling these types of problems. At least we have enough scars to prove how not to deal with them.

Will Sharon agree? Is she going to trust us with such a sensitive issue for her?

"Daddy?" Sharon sounds embarrassed. "You said something about not having anything that we like to talk about."

"Yes, Sharon."

"It's not true. I like to talk to you. You understand so much."

"Remember it next time you ask me for something and I say 'no.' "

That night, when Julie and I are sitting in comfortable, loving, silence, I return to Sharon's clouds.

When she started with her complaints I didn't see any connection between them. I don't think Sharon did either. Nevertheless, the objective of each cloud came out to be the same. Friendship is what's important to Sharon. That by itself is not a big surprise, we knew it long ago. But . . .

What would be the results of doing a similar analysis for myself? Suppose I pick three different, small but bothersome UDEs of my own? What will happen if for each I write the corresponding cloud? Will the objective come out the same for each? Even if I choose the UDEs from different aspects of my life?

Is personality much more focused than we give it credit?

"Julie?"

"Yes, dear."

"Let's check something. . . ."

18

"It's impossible to work with Hilton, I'm telling you." Bill Peach is deeply irritated.

"I must say that it took you quite a while to reach this startling conclusion," I tease him.

We are sitting in a restaurant having our monthly lunch. It's a tradition that started when Bill nominated me to be his replacement as a divisional manager. I enjoy these lunches. For a long time they had been my main channel for hearing all the juicy gossip from the high windows. Bill likes it because he's always known that I'm totally loyal to him. Today, I'm part of that close circle, which makes our lunch meetings even more fun.

"Come on, tell me, what happened this time?" I'm all ears.

"That bloody rattlesnake. That no good double-crosser. You won't believe what he's done." Bill still has to release more steam.

"As long as we are discussing Hilton, I'm afraid that I won't have any difficulty believing anything."

"You know that Granby has to submit an investment plan to the board?"

"Yes, I know." I'm not smiling any longer. I also know

where the money for those investments is coming from. It's my companies' blood that they are fighting over.

Bill is too busy being angry at Hilton to notice me. "So, naturally, Granby turned to Hilton and me to prepare a plan. We decided to be gentlemen about it. Hilton a gentleman, what a joke. I should have known that it would never work. Anyhow, rather than fighting about the money, we decided that each of us would submit a plan for exactly half the sum."

"And then you find out," I've been with both of them long enough to guess, "that you have submitted a plan for half and Hilton submitted for all of it."

"Who told you about it? No. It's so obvious, huh? But you should have been there, when he persuaded me that this time it would be okay. How he proved that it is the only way that makes sense for both of us. And I, the fool, fell for it."

"You deserve it," I say.

"Right. Every one who believes in anything Hilton promises deserves it."

Vultures deserve whatever is coming to them, I think to myself. We are going to sell my companies and they are already fighting over the blood. Damn Hilton, that's for sure, but also damn you, Bill.

We eat our club sandwiches in silence.

I'm not fair. What the hell do I want from Bill? That he will not fight for investment for his group? If he was the one that initiated the sale of my companies then it would be another story. But he wasn't. He was not involved at all.

"You know, Bill, Bob and Stacey are taking it very hard. They don't like the idea of being sold, one bit. And neither do I."

"It's understandable. No one wants to be in your shoes. But that's life. The periphery is always sacrificed to protect the core."

"I guess so. By the way, when the time comes, I'm relying on you to find a proper place for Don. Will you?"

"Any time."

"I'd like him to have a line position. He is ready."

"I can always use a person like Don. But why do we have to talk about hypothetical situations? Listen, do you know what that creep Hilton suggested? That we invest twenty-two million to buy that worthless company in Idaho."

"Why?" I'm surprised. "We already checked it out. Their patents are dubious, the real brains left them years ago. Besides, why so much?"

"Hilton had to inflate his plan to show that he needed all the one hundred and thirty million. You see, he didn't want to use any of the suggestions that Trumann said were no good, so he threw in everything else he could think of. The only criteria was that it look good. And you must admit, on paper that company looks quite good."

"It's all a big show," I sigh. "Granby wants to look better and be able to blame Trumann and Doughty for selling too low, so he pretends that my companies can be sold for much more money than is realistic. Hilton wants to be more powerful, so he pretends that he needs all the money for his group even though he needs it like a hole in his head. It would be funny if it weren't my people and I who have to pay for it all."

Bill doesn't agree. "You are right about Hilton but not about Granby. The old man is as straight as an arrow."

"That's what I thought until now," I admit. "But how else can you explain using such a gross overestimation for my companies?"

"What are you talking about?" Bill is honestly surprised. "One hundred and thirty million is a very conservative estimate."

"Bill, I don't have much experience buying and selling companies, but I was not born yesterday, and I do know how to read financial statements. For each of my companies we'll be lucky to get thirty million. To say that we'll get one hundred and thirty for the lot is simply ridiculous."

Bill looks at me. "Want coffee?" he asks.

"Forget the coffee. Tell me what is going on."

Bill is busy trying to catch our waiter's eye. I'm starting to get irritated. Then, without looking at me, he asks, "What do you think Pressure-Steam is worth?"

"Maximum thirty million, not even that. Look Bill, their market is stable and in stalemate. Stacey succeeded in bringing her company to a quarter of a million profit. Maybe, with a lot of effort, it is possible to bring this company up to making two or three million profit a year, but that is the maximum."

"Alex, what is the value to any one of the competitors if they can close the division and take its clients?"

I feel like someone clobbered me on the head. Hard.

So that is the plan. Of course. How naive could I be? A competitor that does it will gain our market share. They all have excess capacity. Material is only thirty-five percent of the selling price. A competitor that takes over and dismantles my company can increase his profit by maybe even forty million a year. Not to mention that it would break the stalemate, they would become the largest and most dominant in this market. How stupid could I be?

Now I understand the conversation with that disgusting wheeler-dealer. Now it all makes perfect sense, including the price. No wonder I smelled something bad. I smelled the body of my company being torn to pieces.

And Trumann and Doughty, those butchers. They were careful not to tell me a thing. They look on both sides of the equation, oh yes. And I know what they'll tell me when confronted, "We must sacrifice a part to save the whole." My foot.

"Are you all right?" Bill actually sounds concerned.

"No, I'm not," I almost shout at him.

"Yes, you are," he smiles at me. "I can almost hear the sounds of the trumpets. Dragons, run for your life. Saint GeoRogo is going to war."

"You bet your ass I am."

I get into my car and start the engine. Where to? It doesn't matter. Just to drive, I need to think.

For miles, I'm fuming. At Trumann, at Doughty, at Granby, at Hilton, at Wall Street, at the world. Even, a little, at myself.

After a long time I call myself to order. Being mad is not enough. What am I going to do? Fight for a nice pricey severance for the employees? What a lousy solution. Besides, how much can I persuade UniCo to pay? One month's salary per year of employment? Two? Maybe three? No way will they agree to even two months per year. And that's nothing. Yes nothing, to a person who cannot use his expertise anywhere else.

And Stacey? What chance will she have? With a track record of heading a company that was sold to the cleaners? That black mark will devastate her for life.

And me? I'm also going to carry the same mark of Cain on my forehead.

No way. No way am I going to allow any of it to happen. But how can I stop it?

The cloud is clear. I've known it for a long time. It is also clear how to break it, we must find a way to increase sales. Significantly and rapidly. The problem is that until now I didn't believe that it was really possible. Now I don't have any choice. I must assume that it is possible. I must take it for granted. That's the only way I can gather the stamina to go and look for it.

A knight who doesn't believe in the Holy Grail will never find it. And one who does? Try and stop him.

There must be a way. There must be a way to increase sales. Actually I have proof, Pete's company. There we succeeded. With no advantage in technology. With no budget to invest in equipment or advertising. With nothing. And in less than one month, look where we are. Now we have what Pete is calling a Mafia offer—an offer so good, no one can refuse it.

But where am I going to get more of these brilliant ideas?

How brilliant must it be to guarantee that Stacey's company will not be thrown to the shredder? Very. Even if we grow the profit to five million a year, it will not be enough. Not even ten. The price they can get by selling it to the wolves is simply too high. They do have a realistic chance to get close to one hundred million dollars. It's not a fantasy.

It will not be enough to find a marketing break-through that will increase sales. We have to find something that is powerful enough that we eat the competitors for breakfast. That's the only way.

No, I probably don't know the real cloud, and increasing sales will not be sufficient. But I do know how to find the solution. It's in my head, hidden, fragmented, maybe even grossly distorted, but if it exists, it's there. I must use Jonah's Thinking Processes to bring it out into the open. To surface and polish it.

I've already done the most difficult part. Due to Brandon and Jim I've already built the Current Reality Tree of the current competitive market. I have to continue on.

And I have to do it myself, I cannot push it on Stacey and Bob. It's my responsibility, and besides they are likely to look at the situation too narrowly. I must find the generic way. Later, each of them should use it to construct the specific solution for his and her own needs.

Stop procrastinating, I urge myself. The Current Reality Tree points out the core problem; managers are using local optima. The next step is to state it much more precisely. I have to figure out what prevents management from doing much better. Jim is wrong. According to Jonah, we shouldn't assume ignorance or incompetence on the part of managers. We should assume that they are captured in a conflict that is preventing them from doing the right thing. So, if I want to do it by the book, I should state what the right thing is for them to do and what the conflict is that is preventing them from doing it.

What should I select as "the right thing"? How would I like my managers to run their company?

Isn't it obvious? I ask myself. They should strive to achieve global optima.

Hmm. I have a problem with that.

Not that I'm against global optima, but . . .

If optimum was the best we could do, how come a breakthrough solution gives results that were inconceivable before?

After a while it starts to register. Optimum is doing the best within the box, while what I'm looking for is . . .

Exactly. We desperately need breakthrough solutions. Anything less will not be sufficient. We must find solutions outside the box.

So what am I suggesting? That managers run their companies by always striving to find breakthrough solutions?

No. There is no need to exaggerate.

I think that I'll be happy with "Managers arrive at good decisions." This way I leave the door open for breakthrough solutions when needed, without unnecessarily demanding them as the norm.

I think about it. It's simple, but it does make sense. I decide to take it as the desired objective.

Now I have to clearly verbalize the conflict preventing managers from achieving this objective. According to Jonah's guidelines, this conflict should be quite apparent in the Current Reality Tree. I have a problem. I think that I know this tree inside and out. If there is an apparent conflict, I'm sure I would have noticed it.

From my experience I've learned that the best way to save time is to follow the guidelines. I've got to look at it again, but how?

I take the first exit and stop at a gas station. "Fill it up. Super, please."

I reach into the back seat, grab my briefcase and pull out the tree. Immediately the conflict stares at me. I guess that when you know what you are looking for, it's easy to find. I write the conflict. "Consider the clients' perception of value," versus, "Consider the supplier's perception of value."

Now I have to prove that this conflict is what is preventing the objective from existing in reality. It doesn't take long to complete the cloud. I check it by reading aloud, "In order for 'Managers to arrive at good decisions,' they must 'Consider the need to get enough sales.' " This is correct at the top level.

No, it's correct for all levels. I think it's correct even when decisions are made at lower levels; in distribution, production or engineering.

"You are all set, sir. Eighteen dollars and thirty cents."

I hand him my credit card, and continue to read aloud.

"In order to 'Consider the need to get enough sales,' managers must 'Make decisions and act upon the client's perception of value.' This is good."

I turn to the bottom side of the cloud, "In order for 'Managers to arrive at good decisions,' they must 'Consider the need to get reasonable product margins.' " Under the prevailing corporate culture, it's a must. Actually, in most companies, even those people who understand that they shouldn't do it, still have to. Unless, of course, someone wants to become a martyr.

I read the last connection, "In order to 'Consider the need to get reasonable margins,' managers must 'Make decisions and act upon the suppliers' perception of value.' "

I sign the slip, start the engine and find my way back to the highway.

I glance at the cloud. Once it's written, it's so obvious. Throughout UniCo, I see managers constantly vibrating on the conflict arrow.

"I don't think we should accept the order." "I think

that we should." "Don't accept the order." "Accept it."
"DON'T." "Why did you accept it?" "We had to." "No we
didn't." "We did!"

Alex, I say to myself, you illustrated the point very
clearly. Come on, continue.

Which arrow in this cloud makes me feel the most
uncomfortable?

It's very easy to answer that question. In order for
"Managers to arrive at good decisions," they must "Consider the need to get reasonable product margins." In the
last years I've proven, over and over, that when the market
is segmented we can increase profits now as well as in the
future—even if we sell for negative product margins. Especially when all the work is done by non-bottlenecks.

In my group, I hope that no one considers product
margin as a criteria to accept an order. Orders are accepted
only according to their impact on the overall throughput
and overall operating expense.

We have broken the cloud.

So why are we still in trouble?

Then it hits me. We ignore product margin and it
works. We have turned around all three companies from
bottomless pits into break-even. It worked—but not
enough. Every time we find a segmented market, we are
happy to sell our excess capacity for prices lower than our
average. It improves our bottom line but it's a waste. A
waste that we can't afford anymore.

The real problem is we've run out of niches. We don't
dare sell below our prices in our core markets, and we
don't dare start a price war. It might ruin us. So now, in
every one of our companies, there is a lot of excess capacity.

Besides, the constant decline in prices is eroding the
gains that we do get from our improvements. We must do
something much more powerful. For us it's not a matter of
gradually increasing profits. To save our companies we

must sell all our capacity at higher than average prices, not lower.

How?

That's exactly what I'm trying to figure out. I have to find a much more effective way to break the cloud. I'd better look at the assumptions behind the other arrows in the cloud. If there is a better answer it must be different than what I'm already doing today.

The road is clear. I read the next arrow. "In order to 'Consider the need to get reasonable product margins,' managers must 'Make decisions and act upon the suppliers' perception of value.'"

Here the assumption is that product margin must be based on product cost. Which as I know, leads to the impression that a product should have one fair price.

Based on the tree, the obvious injection is to be able to command a multitude of prices. Which means, to take actions that will segment an existing, seemingly uniform, market.

Yes. This direction is clear from the Current Reality Tree. But if the cloud is useful, it should provide me with more alternatives. I don't think that figuring out the generic way of how to segment a seemingly uniform market will be a short or easy task. Besides, this type of work requires a pencil and paper.

Before I turn toward home to do it, I should examine other arrows in the cloud. Maybe they will provide me with easier alternatives.

I glance over at the next arrow. It's the conflict arrow. According to Jonah, if you can break it, it usually provides the most powerful solutions. If there ever was a time I needed a powerful solution, it's now.

"Make decisions and act upon the clients' perception of value" is mutually exclusive to "Make decisions and act upon the suppliers' perception of value." This is plain common sense. What's the assumption? That the two perceptions are different? It's too obvious.

"It's obvious after constructing the Current Reality Tree," I dryly say to myself.

So what can I do with it? After a while I realize that the assumption is more restrictive. Suppose the client's perception is very high, much higher than the supplier's perception. In that case managers would not face any dilemma.

If they're not greedy, that is.

The assumption is something like, "The client's perception of value of the product is significantly less than that of the supplier." Only then are the managers facing the dilemma.

With one eye on the road I scribble it down.

What can we do to change this assumption? Do I have an injection, any idea how to change it, I ask myself?

Yes, I do, but it's too simple. "It's not something concrete," I mumble.

So I'll have to go through the process of converting it into something concrete and practical. What's the big deal? I know this process, I have time, what I need is a direction. And this one looks very simple. So simple that it cannot be wrong. Too simple.

For a few miles there are signs announcing the next rest area. Where is it?

I roll into it and stop.

"Take actions that sufficiently increase the perception of value the market has for the company's products," I write down.

This is what I call simple with a capital S. But it is a direction. And if Jonah's methods do work, it should lead to a solution.

According to the guidelines, I now have to choose the strategic objectives. It's not a big deal, they're just the opposite of the undesirable effects. This shouldn't be too difficult. I have the list here. . . . Somewhere.

It doesn't help. This list was composed by Trumann and Doughty and it encompasses UDEs from all their companies. We don't necessarily have to upgrade our sales force's skills or improve engineering. As a matter of fact, we cannot afford the time it requires. For us, I laugh dryly, it will be enough if we can somehow gain a dominant competitive edge.

No, wait a minute. Even that won't be enough. We must achieve something that most companies don't have to. We must be able to quickly demonstrate impressive, bottom-line results.

Slowly I write the first objective: "Sell all the capacity without reducing prices."

Considering the amount of excess capacity that we have it will result in an impressive bottom line. The problem is that we'll have to convince everyone that we can sustain such results for the long run. This is just as important.

I add another objective, "Have an apparent, dominant, competitive edge."

Yes. That will do it. What I have to do now is figure out how, by starting from my suggested direction, we can reach these two objectives. I'll have to build a Future Reality Tree.

If there is one thing that is more tedious than constructing a Current Reality Tree, it is constructing a Future Reality Tree where the starting point is something that looks no more real than flying pigs.

But it's possible. I know it is.

I start the car and decide to head back. I look for signs. It's not a bad idea to figure out where I am. Wilmington? Where the hell is Wilmington?

So what am I waiting for? I pick up the phone and call Don.

"Where are you?" He is apparently worried. "The budget committee meeting is supposed to start in ten minutes, I don't think I can fill in for you."

"Yes, you can. Just ask Bill to allow it. He will. Oh yuck, at one-thirty I was supposed to have a meeting with the CFO."

"You're telling me?" He sounds a little irritated.

"Don't worry, I went instead. It was okay. But where are you? Are you coming back today?"

"I don't know. Listen Don, remember the Current Reality Tree that I gave you last week? Take it home and study it. By tomorrow morning I want you to know it inside and out."

Oh, God. It's Milford. I'm more than one hundred miles away from home!

"Okay, Alex. Can I ask why?"

"You can easily guess."

"Does this mean we are going to try to figure out how to increase sales?"

"Yes."

"Hurrah!" I instinctively move the phone away from my ear. This man has well-developed lungs. "We were waiting for it. All of us."

"See you tomorrow at eight."

"Should I order a conference room? In your office we are bound to be constantly interrupted."

"Good idea. And prepare yourself."

"For what?"

"For a lot of work. We are going to kick some ass."

19

When the coffee is served, I gather enough courage to raise the real issue. "I want to convince you that we shouldn't sell my companies. It will be a huge mistake."

"Alex, we went over it again and again," Brandon Trumann sounds a little irritated. "This subject is closed."

Jim Doughty signals his agreement with Brandon.

"Is the subject closed even if the situation has changed? Come on, you're more open-minded than that."

"What can possibly change to that extent?" And in a patronizing voice he adds, "Alex, let it go. It's a lost battle."

"Just give me some time," I say, "and I'll turn my companies into geese that lay golden eggs."

"And what makes you think you can do it? Two weeks ago you were not optimistic at all."

"I'm optimistic because of you two. You had . . ."

"Don't count on us. We're the bad guys," Jim laughs.

"Alex, I thought I explained it to you," Brandon tries to knock some sense into my thick skull. "We don't have a choice. The financial situation of UniCo is too fragile. We like you, we appreciate what you're doing, but don't ask for the impossible."

I let him finish and then calmly continue, "You had me do the analysis of companies in the current competitive market. You started it all. Don't you want to know what came out of it?"

"Oh yes, we do," Jim says. "But Alex, if you think that some theoretical analysis will cause us to reverse our decision, you are more optimistic than I thought."

"It's not entirely theoretical, I had a very real starting point. I have the printing company turnaround to extrapolate from."

"We appreciate what you have done with that company," Brandon tries to pacify me. "What you've done there verges on miraculous. But do you believe that you can repeat the same thing over in I Cosmetics and in Pressure-Steam? They are very different from the printing industry."

"And from each other," Jim adds.

"I know, but I'm not starting from scratch. I've used what Pete did as a guide, and continuing our analysis I built a generic blueprint of how to do it anywhere. Having this blueprint, it should be relatively easy to build the specific solutions for the specific companies."

"Do you really think you can outline the generic procedure for taking a market?" Jim Doughty asks.

"Yes," I say, confidently. "That's what I want to show you."

"Any market? Even if we don't give you any money to invest and we impose a tight time limit?" Brandon is astonished.

"Depends what you call a tight time limit—but six months should be sufficient." I have learned what you can accomplish in a company in three months. Most people regard it as nothing, I see it as an eternity.

"I'm not promising anything, definitely not six months," Trumann says. "But if you're so sure of yourself, I'll buy a round of drinks and then you can show us," and he starts looking around expectantly.

"Bring the beer."

The lunch crowd has cleared out, and the place is relatively quiet. Our waiter is gone. Trumann goes off and returns shortly, frosty mugs in hand.

"Excellent. Thanks, Brandon." I take a big swallow, wipe off my mouth and start. "In order to significantly increase sales we have to increase the perception of value of the market for our products."

"Yes, if you can do it," Brandon agrees. "It's much better than reducing prices."

"Usually we think that in order to increase the perception of value of the market we have to come up with new, improved products."

"That appears explicitly in our tree," Jim concurs. "And you know how much I dislike this approach. Considering the huge investments and the low chance of success, it simply doesn't make any business sense. I always say, let the competitors pave the way, we'll follow."

"There is another way," I say. "A way that does not involve investments or high risks."

"Now you've piqued my curiosity," Jim admits. "I'm all ears."

"We can see the alternative way when we examine what Pete has done. He didn't touch the physical product, he upgraded something else."

"What do you mean?" Brandon asks.

I try to explain. "From the supplier's point of view, the product is the actual physical product. This view gives limited options for improvement. Look at it from the market's point of view. From the market's point of view the product is much broader. It includes the service that goes with it, the financial terms, the guarantee. . . . The product is the entire offering."

"Makes sense." Brandon is slowly nodding his head.

"All suppliers know that," Jim is more critical. "Look how much importance is given to customer service these days, to due date performance, to short lead times."

"Nevertheless," I argue, "when we, the suppliers, talk about upgrading the product, instinctively it translates into investments in engineering, equipment, and massive amounts of time. What Pete noticed is that in order to drastically change the perception in the eyes of the market, he doesn't have to upgrade the physical product. He can change the periphery, the section of the offer that is not the product itself. And this, my friends, can be done with almost no investment, and very quickly."

Jim doesn't seem enthused. Far from it.

Brandon is more polite. "I'm all for it," he says. "However, Alex, is this practical or just a theory? I mean, it sounds great, but there's a problem. How are you going to find out which changes in the offering will have a big impact on the clients? Changes that your competitors have not implemented yet?"

"Oh, that's easy," I smile. "But let me start by giving some background. Remember what is really determining the perception of value of a product in the eyes of the market? It's not the effort to produce it, it's the benefits derived from having the product."

They nod their heads; we've discussed this before.

"We know that there are two types of benefits. Adding something positive or eliminating something negative. Look at any advertisement. Look at how a car is advertised. It's comfortable, reliable, or comes with a great factory rebate. If you noticed, only the first one, comfort, is an advantage. The other two are the elimination of negatives.

"What is the meaning of reliable? You won't have to take the car to a garage as often. Reliability is not a plus on its own, it reduces a negative that is inherent in having the product.

"A price reduction, or factory rebate, is the same thing. Paying is an inherent negative that comes with the product. But, if you buy ours, it will cost you less."

"This distinction between plus and less negatives—this minus minus—is quite interesting," Jim chuckles. "But why do you mention it?"

"Because you are putting me under time pressure. I

believe that the more powerful way to increase the perception of value of the market is through bringing additional positives. But we can get the easiest and quickest improvements by concentrating on eliminating the negatives. They are intimately well known to the customer, you don't have to persuade him that they exist, and you don't have to persuade him that he wants to get rid of them. It's the path of least resistance.

"Think about it, this is exactly what Pete did. First he chose to define his market as the buyer's, since they are the ones who directly interact with him. They are the ones who, when Pete succeeds in improving their perception, can react almost immediately. Then he solved the major problems of the buyer. No wonder the buyer's perception of value for Pete's offering took a quantum leap."

"Wait a minute," Jim is on guard. "What you're saying is that you have to know the client, you have to make sure that you address his needs."

"Precisely."

"I'm sorry, Alex," he looks disappointed, "but this is lesson number one in business. Everybody is trying hard to find the real needs of their clients and address them better than the competition. I don't see anything new in what you tell us."

"No, Jim. Every company claims that that's what they're doing. But almost nobody is."

"I'm not sure I understand," Jim is more careful now.

"Okay. Tell me, how do you think companies find the real needs of their clients?"

"I don't know the details, but they do it. I know that they invest a lot in market surveys, for example."

"Excellent example," I agree. "Only four months ago we got such a survey on Pressure-Steam's market. Our market research department gave us a two-hundred-page document, with lots and lots of data. I bet that every UDE the clients have, especially with us or our products, was listed in tables, diagrams and histograms. A lot of benchmarking, every cross-section that you can think of was there. But do you know what we've done with it?"

"Probably nothing," he admits.

"Almost. We were impressed. We even launched some activities to try and address some of the UDEs, but it really didn't tell us anything that we didn't already know, or at least suspect."

"So, what's your point?"

"My point is that you're right. Everyone is trying to address the UDEs of the client. But compare it to what Pete did. See the difference?"

I drink some beer and wait for them to catch up.

"There is a difference," Jim admits. "And not a small one. But I can't quite articulate it. . . ."

"That's just because you aren't so used to our terminology. The difference is that everyone is trying to address the client's UDEs. Pete is addressing the client's core problem."

"Yes, of course," Brandon says. "I have always claimed that dealing with symptoms is ineffective. We should aim at the root causes."

"Not enough." I have to make sure they see how it really fits together. "Root causes are not enough for me. We should try to correct a core problem, one that is responsible not just for one or two UDEs, but for a whole gamut."

"I see," says Jim. "And you seem to have the perfect tool to do it. The Current Reality Tree. You demonstrated to us that you can start with a list of seemingly unconnected UDEs and end up with a core problem. What a demonstration. I'll never forget it."

Boy, Jim sure is sharp.

I try to summarize, "Remember your concern about finding out which changes in our offering would have a big impact on the clients? Now you see why I'm so sure we will be able to do it, Brandon?"

He still fudges, but his expression is more relaxed and confident.

"So let me see if I understand your suggestion," Jim pushes on. "First, you're going to survey the market to get the UDEs."

"Jim, I don't have to survey the market, I think surveys are a waste of time and money. My people know the market well enough to come up with a good representative list of UDEs, and even if they didn't, just meeting with two or three clients surfaces enough UDEs. You don't need to have every single UDE to write a good Current Reality Tree, a representative sample is usually enough to identify the core problem."

"Right. So, you are going to take the UDEs of your markets, build a Current Reality Tree, and through it identify a deep enough problem." Jim stops and gives me a questioning look.

I nod approval, and he continues, "Then you are going to see what changes you have to make, not to the physical product, but to the offering as a whole, so that you are better addressing a deep problem of the market. This is intriguing."

"Intriguing? It's ingenious," Brandon slaps the table with approval.

I lean back, and finish my beer. They do the same. After a while, Jim asks, "How do you know that you haven't forgotten something? That you haven't neglected an angle that might come and bite you?"

"Good question," I say. "Let me enhance it. You know that when many of a person's problems are eliminated, that person might change his behavior. Here we are talking about addressing a deep problem, which will eliminate a lot of UDEs. We must expect that the market behavior will change as a result. What guarantees that this change will be to our benefit? Who says it won't boomerang on us, and after a while leave us worse off than we were before we started?"

"Good questions," Brandon says. "But I think that with any change we have to take some risks."

"Some level of risk is unavoidable," I respond. "But I am too paranoid not to try and reduce the risk as much as possible. And we have the perfect mechanism for that.

"You see, once we have built the Current Reality Tree of the market, we are well aware of the underlying causalities. Then what we do is start by assuming that we are launching our new offer, and logically predict what must be the unavoidable impact on the client. In other words, we build the Future Reality Tree of the market."

They seem to understand.

"Now we are going to use the most abused, but powerful resource that we have. At our company, like at any company, we have no lack of people whose instinctive reaction to any suggestion is 'Yes, but . . .' Small yes, big but. So we take this Future Reality Tree that we have built and send it to as many functions within our company as possible, asking for reservations."

"No doubt you will get them. Piles of them." Jim laughs.

"It is very important not to ignore these nasty reservations. Each one of them is a pearl, because if we do take them seriously, if we write each reservation as a logical Negative Branch, we can identify everything that can go wrong."

"And a lot that cannot," Brandon adds wryly.

"Now, the Negative Branches that lead to real hazards have to be trimmed, which means we have to complete our offerings with additional actions that will almost guarantee that the identified negatives will not occur."

"Yes, very smart. This way, if it works, you'll end up with an excellent offer, one that will significantly increase your competitive edge. Alex, how long should this process take?"

"I don't know. But my guess is less than a month. I

have to leave time for implementing it and getting the orders."

"To the orders!" Jim raises his mug. We look. All our mugs are empty. Jim grabs his water glass. Brandon and I do the same, and we all join in the toast.

"Alex, what about market segmentation?" Jim asks. "This beautiful idea that came out of our Current Reality Tree? You're not going to use it?"

Again I marvel at how much they learned from that tree. "Maybe not in the beginning, but I am definitely going to use it."

"The point was to cause the segmentation in what is now a uniform market, not to just go after niches. Do you know how to do this, how to cause this differentiation?" Jim is relentless.

"I think so."

"Well?" Once again, they're getting pushy with me.

"Well, it's quite simple." Maybe it is, but again I wonder how to explain it so that it's clear. "Actually, it's a derivative of what we've been talking about. You see, Jim, we've left an open question: what is the market of a company? We can define it as the person who the company interacts with. We can define it as the companies to which it sells its products. We can define it as the companies that buy from the companies whom we sell to. Or we can go as far as describing the market as the end consumer.

"I suspect that we can do the analysis for each stage, and as we are coming closer and closer to the consumer we will get more powerful solutions. Of course, the implementation will become more involved, we will have to convince the intermediate links to collaborate."

Have I lost them? I'd better try to answer Jim's question quickly.

"The real interesting question is, how many Current Reality Trees should we write if we are serving two different markets? What do you think?"

"Two, I guess." Brandon decides to participate.

"And if these two markets have overlap, in other words, it is not so clear cut where one market ends and the other starts?"

"Still two I think."

"And if in one market we could look at it as two groups of clients, where the only difference between them is that one group has, on top of all the UDEs of the other group, some additional UDEs of their own? What then?"

"It's interesting how you're distinguishing between markets, according to their UDEs. But to answer your question, I still say two."

Jim nods in agreement.

"I think it's a mistake. Look at it this way. If we build only one tree, still distinguishing which group has which UDEs, we can adopt our offering to be comprised of two components. One that solves all the common UDEs and an additional component that solves the additional UDEs.

"From our point of view, since the changes are in the periphery and not in the physical product, we will tend to look at it as one product. But look from the eyes of the market. For the group with the additional UDEs the expanded offer is much more valuable. And they will be willing to pay a higher price."

"Very smart, Alex. That's how you generate the segmentation." Jim seems pleased with my answer. Finally.

Brandon is still nodding his head, "Fascinating."

I decide that the time has come to go for the throat, "So can I assume that my companies are off the hook?"

"You mean, that we should stop all activities to sell your companies?" Jim smiles at me.

"Yes. For the time being at least."

"Alex, be realistic," Brandon uses his patronizing tone again. "Your plan of action is very innovative, and we are all for it. But don't tell me that you haven't noticed the weakness.

"First, what guarantees that when you finish the analysis of the market we'll not find that you and your competitors are already addressing the market's core problem? Second, even when it turns out that you aren't, what guarantees that you will be able to address the market's core problem? Maybe it has nothing to do with your offering. Third, even if the core problem of the market relates to your offering, who said you will be able to implement changes that will affect it? Maybe the required changes are outside your control or require major changes in the product itself?"

Now I see why Brandon is in the powerful position that he is. I don't think that I could grasp it so quickly. There's definitely no way I'd be able to pinpoint, on the spot, all the weaknesses. That's impressive.

"That's not to say," he continues, "that we think that you don't stand a chance. You might succeed. The printing company is proof that sometimes it might work."

"Are you willing to take the risk? If I have a chance to succeed and you don't give me the time, you might be selling a gold mine for pennies."

"We're not taking any chances," Jim explains to me. "Anyhow, in the next few weeks no major activities are scheduled. By then you'll know if your scheme has a chance of working. Keep us updated. If it turns out that you can effectively address the core problem of a company's market, we'll know what to do. Remember, we didn't have any problem adjusting to the success in the printing company. And we won't have any problem handling any other such successes either."

"No, we won't," Brandon assures me. "Just remember to keep us in the picture. Good work, Alex. Excellent work."

No, it wasn't a waste of time. Not the meeting and not the meticulous work that we did to develop the ideas I presented. Now it all depends on us. If we continue to use the Thinking Processes and implement the common sense conclusions that emerge, we're bound to win.

I'm not afraid of the points that Brandon raised. They

are not new to us, they were all spotted in the analysis. I think we have good ways to handle them all.

Doing the analysis wasn't easy. Constructing logical trees is not fun, not glamorous, and the high points of discovery are buried in the gray background of "if-thens." Don and I slaved for two whole days, using Jonah's Thinking Processes to arrive at the, now obvious, conclusions. I remember, in great detail, how it went.

20

When I arrived, Don wasn't there yet.

So I decide not to waste any time. I drag the flip-chart from the corner and flip until I find a clean sheet. From my pocket I take out a thick pad of post-its. On one I write, "The company sells all its capacity without reducing prices." On another, "The company has an apparent, dominant, competitive edge." I stick them at the top of the page.

"Nice objectives, good morning," Don greets me as he enters.

"Good morning," I answer, and start to write another post-it.

"Coffee?" he asks.

"Yes, please," and I stick the post-it at the bottom of the page. I read it out loud, " 'The company takes actions that sufficiently increase the perception of value the market has for the company's products.' "

"What is it?" Don asks. "The theme of today's analysis?"

"In a way," I agree, and take the cup he hands me. "It's also the injection that I got from the cloud." When I see his expression, I add, "I know that it's not much, but this is our starting point."

"This is what you call a starting point?" Don is surprised. "To me it looks more like an ending."

"Let's say that, at this stage, it's more like wishful thinking," I admit.

"What are we supposed to do with it?" He is not happy. "I thought that you'd come up with something more concrete. A real starting point. How are we going to construct a Future Reality Tree with this?"

Don does not have a lot of experience in constructing Future Reality Trees, especially when the starting point is wishful thinking.

"The same way that we always do," I try to cool him down. "We'll start with this injection and, using if . . . then . . . arrows, we'll try to reach these two objectives. We'll use additional statements that are correct even now, and, if necessary we'll add more injections, until we reach the objectives."

"More statements, more injections? Come on Alex, with such a starting point I can reach the objectives no sweat. But what's the point? The result will not be a Future Reality Tree, it will be a Future Fantasy Tree! How are we going to reach what you call the starting point? That's the real problem."

"I know. And you know that I know. So stop fussing around and let's do the formal connection to the objectives."

"But, Alex," he continues to argue, "if we don't have even a clue how to achieve the injection, if it's only a pie-in-the-sky, does it make any sense to continue?"

"Yes, it does," I firmly say. "Before we rack our brains finding out how to achieve it, first we should know if we want to, if it will do the job. I'm not as sure as you are that this injection, by itself, is sufficient to reach our objectives."

"But. . . ."

"If it's as simple as you say, why are we arguing? Let's just do it."

"I guess that it makes sense to see the total picture

before slaving on the details." Don is not overly enthusiastic.

"If, 'The company takes actions that sufficiently increase the perception of value the market has for the company's products,'" I say, starting to build the Future Reality Tree, "then, 'The perception of value the market has for the company's products is higher than the current prices.'"

"Why do you claim it?" Don is aggressive.

"Because of the word, 'sufficiently.' How would you interpret the words 'sufficiently increase the perception of value' if it isn't increased above the current price?"

"I see what you are doing," Don's frowning face starts to clear. "Through constructing the Future Reality Tree you hope to gain more understanding about your injection."

"Exactly," I say. "And if Jonah is right, it should give us a detailed understanding. So detailed that we'll know how to accomplish it."

"Good idea," Don smiles. "Can I continue?"

"Be my guest," I hand him a post-it pad.

He writes another note and reads, "If, 'The perception of value the market has for the company's products is higher than the current prices,' then 'The market doesn't have any quarrel with the company's requested prices.'"

"Good," I say, "but not good enough. This still doesn't guarantee a competitive edge."

"Right," Don agrees. "The market might not have any quarrel with our prices but at the same time it might have even less of a quarrel with our competitors' prices. You're right, we'll have to add another injection. Something like, 'The perception of value the market has for the company's products is higher than the perception it has for the competitors' products.' This will give us a competitive edge."

"Considering that we have to reach a 'dominant competitive edge' I suggest you change 'higher' to 'much higher.' That will take care of it."

"The paper suffers all dreams," Don mutters as he corrects the injection. "Now it looks like we can connect to one of our objectives: 'The company has an apparent, dominant, competitive edge.' I told you that it would be too easy."

"Don," I patiently say, "you addressed 'competitive edge' but you haven't substantiated that this competitive edge is apparent. To do that you have to prove that our market share grows."

"You are right, I need both injections." He is not impressed. "If, 'The perception of value the market has for the company's products is much higher than the perception it has for the competitors' products,' and 'The market doesn't have any quarrel with the company's current prices,' then 'The company increases its market share.' Now we've reached the point where the market prefers us over the competitors and as a result we increased market share. Is it okay with you to connect to the appropriate objective?" And he draws the corresponding arrows.

"Don, I think that you are being too hasty. I don't think that you have established a dominant competitive edge."

"What else is missing?"

"What guarantees that the competitors will not immediately copy our actions and wipe out our advantage?"

"I see." He thinks for a minute. "I guess we'll have to add another injection. Something like, 'The actions the company takes are hard for the competitors to follow.' "

"That will do," I agree.

When he finishes adding it to the tree, he says, "Based on the same logic I can connect to the other objective as well. 'The company sells all its capacity without reducing prices.' Okay?"

"No, it's not okay, I think we have to add another injection," and I hand him a post-it. "We have to make sure that we increase the perception of value in a big enough market or markets. Much bigger than our available capacity."

He reads the post-it: " 'The market that the company targets is much bigger than our available capacity.' No problem," he sticks it on the big, white sheet and completes the tree.

"It's very easy to formally achieve your objectives when you are allowed to use dreams," he comments.

"Yes," I laugh. "It looks like our injections will be real about the time that pigs fly. But, you must admit that so far we haven't wasted our time. Now we know what's needed. It's not enough to increase the market perception of value to be above our requested prices, we also need to increase it to be much above the market perception of value for the competitors' products. We need to do it in a big enough market, big enough to exhaust all our capacity. And we need to do all of it in a way that will be difficult for our competitors to copy."

"That's all? No sweat." He tries to be sarcastic. "So now instead of one flying pig, we have four. This is what I call progress."

"It's not really four. The injections that we added are elaborating on the original one, they make it more explicit."

"Not explicit enough, at least not for me," he sighs.

"We haven't finished yet," I try to encourage him. "What we have to do now is use the real power of the Future Reality Tree, Negative Branch Reservations."

"What good will that do?"

"It might help us trim the wings of these pigs."

"If you say so," he mutters, without much hope.

I copy the original injection, flip the page and post it at the bottom. I read it again, " 'The company takes actions that sufficiently increase the perception of value the market has for the company's products.' Don, what increases perception of value?"

"A better product."

I know that we cannot afford it. This is the real reason why our injection seems to be a flying pig. But, according to Jonah, following this route is supposed to lead us to a practical solution. I hope he is right. Since I don't have any other alternative, I take the time to write it properly.

Don reads what I write: "If 'The company takes actions that sufficiently increase the perception of value the market has for the company's products,' and 'The market appreciates better products,' then 'It is apparent that the company has successfully launched better products.' The negative branch is obvious, it takes investments of time and money to launch a new product. Things that we don't have."

"Correct, but we should write it down. If, 'It is apparent that the company has successfully launched better products,' and 'It takes investments of time and money to launch a new product,' then 'It is apparent that the company has invested money and time.' As you said, 'We don't have money and time,' and thus the conclusion is, 'We are replaced as the management of the company.' Negative Branch, no doubt."

I stand up and take our cups for a refill. "Don, in our negative branch, where do we switch from positive to negative? The injection is positive. Successfully launching a new product is positive. The next step, investing time and money, is negative. Here is where we have to concentrate. What is the assumption under the connecting arrow?"

"Alex," Don clears his throat, "we are assuming that the new product is actually new."

"What do you mean?"

"Maybe the new product is just the old one with small modifications? Then the company doesn't have to invest a lot of money and time. No, this is not a flying pig, it's realistic. Take Pete's solution as an example. He made minimal changes in his offering, and it didn't require any investment or time to implement."

"Yeah, good idea. Let's put it back into our Future Reality Tree."

"How?"

"Here, take your cup," I hand him his coffee and flip back the page. "We have a new injection, 'The company introduces small changes that sufficiently increase the perception of value the market has for the company's products.'" And I post it at the bottom of the page. "Now our original flying pig is not an injection but a derivative.

"See, if 'The company introduces small changes that sufficiently increase the perception of value the market has for the company's products,' then 'The company takes actions that sufficiently increase the perception of value the market has for the company's products.'"

"I must admit that our new injection is more down to earth. But we still don't have a clue where to look for the small changes that will make a difference. Our new injection still has wings," he says flatly.

"Which we'll have to trim." I'm not losing my optimism.

"How?" Don is discouraged. "I don't see even a negative branch that we can write."

"When all else fails, read the Current Reality Tree again," I'm quoting Jonah. "If there is a clue that can pave the way, it is there."

Don is beyond arguing.

We read the tree, again. To my surprise I do find a clue. Right at the bottom.

"Listen to this, Don. 'Market perception of value is in accordance with the benefits of having the product.'" I write it on a post-it and stick it near the bottom injection.

"I don't see the relevancy."

I ignore him. Now, at last we're getting somewhere. "If, 'The company introduces small changes that sufficiently increase the perception of value the market has for the company's products,' and 'Market perception of value is in accordance with the benefits of having the product,' then, 'It's apparent that the small changes the company introduces bring high benefits to its market.' Come on Don, what are the things that bring benefits? What additional benefits did Pete's solution bring?"

"You said it. Pete's solution brought a solution."

For a second I don't get it. Then I realize how perceptive Don's remark is. "You are absolutely right. Pete's solution was not just a solution for his company, it was a solution for the dilemma of his clients. How can we generalize it?"

"No sweat," he says, and starts to write, erase, move post-its around, and write again, until finally he posts the following statement: "A product that relieves prospects' problems brings benefits—the more and bigger the problems that it relieves, the greater the benefits."

"Very nice," I fully agree.

"If we accept it and we accepted that 'It's apparent that the small changes the company introduces bring high benefits to its market' then the unavoidable conclusion is that 'The small changes the company introduces are those that relieve many of its market (prospects') problems—the more problems relieved the better.' Alex, it's close, but I still don't know what we can do with it."

"What are you talking about? We have made it. We grounded our pig!" I jump out of my chair. "Don't you see?"

He doesn't. Not yet.

"Don, what is more effective, to address a symptom or its cause?"

"What is this? Trivial Pursuit? Of course addressing the cause is more effective than addressing the symptom."

"What is more effective," I continue to ask, "to address the cause of one problem, or the cause of many problems?"

Don starts to smile. "The cause of many problems. And how can we find the cause of many problems of the market? We know. Oh yes, we know. What a simple solution. How come we didn't see it before? It's so obvious. If we want a marketing solution for our company we shouldn't analyze our company, we should analyze the company's market. The solution to marketing is in the market. So simple. So obvious."

"Yes," I join in. "Everybody knows their UDEs, but very few know their core problem. If we want to bring a lot of benefits to the market we'd better address its core problem, not the symptoms, as everybody else is doing. And we are in a unique position to do it. We have the perfect tool for it, the Current Reality Tree."

Don stands up, and we shake hands.

"Alex, I must tell you that I didn't believe that anything would come out of your starting point. In my eyes it wasn't a flying pig, it was a flying whale. But now, now it's a different ball game."

"Come on Don. Let's rewrite the Future Reality Tree. This time starting with a tangible injection. Let's see where it will lead."

Don posts the new injection, "A Current Reality Tree on the company's market is constructed." "I bet this injection will trim the wings of all our original injections. They will no longer be dreams. I'm sure that they will turn into derivatives."

"Let's see." I encourage him to continue. He is right. Maybe we'll need some more injections, but we are over the hump. No more flying pigs.

"Okay. Now let me add that 'A Current Reality Tree is a very effective way to connect problems, UDEs, to their origin.' The derivative is that 'The company can determine which are the deep causes in the Current Reality Tree that can be removed by the company's type of offering.' Alex, wait a minute. How do we know that there will be a deep cause that the company's offering has anything to do with?"

"We know, Don. It's okay. In any realistic case the market has more than one UDE that relates to the vendor.

Not just due to its product but also due to its service, financial terms, et cetera."

"I see," he agrees. "And since there is more than one
UDE that stems from us, we're bound to reveal a deep
cause that we can handle. That's beautiful. It means that we
will not have any problem identifying what are the small
changes we have to implement in order to bring high benefits to our clients. Let me add it to the tree. It will turn our
original injection into a mere derivative."

I agree that we're bound to reveal a deep cause that we
can handle. I pray that we can handle them with only small
changes. Probably that's the case, since there are so many
UDE's that stem from our service.

As he does it, I'm concentrating on the next injection.
How can we guarantee that the market perception of value
for our products will be higher than for our competitors?

To my surprise I realize that no additional injection is
needed. The market has several existing UDE's that relate
to our type of product (including the way it is currently
offered). This means that currently no one is successfully
addressing the core problem responsible for these UDEs. If
we do it, the market is bound to have a higher perception
for our products. No sweat.

I know that for the markets of each of my companies
these UDE's are not small. Relieving all of these UDEs will
be highly beneficial. We are going to get a dominant competitive edge.

When Don finishes, I go to the flip-chart and post in
the appropriate statements and arrows. When I finish, the
injection, "The perception of value the market has for the
company's products is higher than the perception it has for
the competitors' products," is no longer an injection. It's a
derivative, a result.

"I see why you insisted on writing the Future Reality
Tree even though it was a pie-in-the-sky," Don is beaming.
"Now it provides us with a clear map. We know exactly
what we have to address."

"So let's address it. What is the next injection we have to connect to?"

" 'The actions the company takes are difficult to follow by its competitors,' " he reads from the board. "How can we guarantee that the competitors will have trouble copying our offering?"

We continueed the process, hammering out every detail and building a rigorous map for Bob and Stacey to follow.

21

I half sit, half lie in front of the TV, barely watching the news. It was an exhausting day, especially with the bomb Pete laid on me just before the day ended. It's a big problem. And if it's not solved immediately, everything might collapse.

Stacey's company will be sold to the shredders, Pete and Bob's companies will be sold for peanuts, and before long they too will be destroyed. And me? I'll be thrown out, disgracefully, into the street. Trumann and Doughty will guarantee it. Everything depends on a quick solution to this unexpected problem. Well, not exactly unexpected. I suspected it right from the start, but who could have anticipated it would be so severe?

Why is it that exactly when everything seems to be under control, reality proves that it isn't? If there is one thing I can't complain about, it is living a dull life. Some excitement is fine, but this roller coaster I'm on is a little too much.

The worst thing about it is that I personally cannot do a thing. My hands are tied. The only thing I can do is sit tight and wait for Pete and Don to straighten out the mess. One thing more nerve-wracking than being a warrior is being the one waiting behind the lines for the warriors to win.

Do I have a real reason for my concerns? It all started at four this afternoon, when Fran passed me a call from Pete.

"Alex, I think I'm running into a little problem."

Knowing Pete's British heritage, I suspect a big problem. "What is it?" I calmly ask.

"My people are unable to sell our new offer," he says without emotion.

"How come?" I am sincerely surprised. "According to your reports, you have closed three more deals in the past two weeks."

"Yes, Alex. That's the problem. I have closed them, not my people. My people have succeeded in closing nothing so far. Not that they haven't tried. They have. By now they are so desperate that they refuse to try anymore. I am afraid we'll have to revise the forecast back down."

"Wait, Pete, not so quickly. Tell me more."

"There is nothing more to tell," Pete sounds down. "I just finished a sales meeting. Each one of our salespeople has tried to sell it and has failed. They claim that our offer is too complicated, and that the buyers don't understand it. My VP of sales is leading the rebellion. He has tried it four times, with four hot prospects. Now he's convinced that it is unsellable."

"How many times have you tried it?" I ask.

"Five."

"And?"

"And we have five nice contracts. But that's not the point. I can't be the only salesperson in my company. And I can't push them anymore."

"Wait," I say. "Let me think."

After a minute of silence, I ask, "Pete, did you find the idea hard to sell?"

"No, not at all. That's what baffles me."

"Did you tell your people exactly how you do it?"

"Of course I did. I even wrote the whole procedure down. They swear that they have followed my instructions to the dot. I don't know what's going on."

It's a long time since I've heard Pete sound so desperate. They must have hit him badly in the sales meeting.

"So your people are claiming that you devised an offer that only you can sell?"

"Correct."

"That you are a super salesman, but a company's offer should be good enough to be sold by mere mortals?"

"That's what they claim, word for word. Alex, almost half of their compensation is based on commissions. I must do something, and fast."

"Pete, stay cool," I try to calm him down. "Since we both know that you are not a super salesman, it must be that the offer is good, and salable."

He laughs nervously, "That's what I was trying to tell them. But they won't listen. Not anymore that is."

"If there is one thing I have learned in my life," I tell him, "it's that in reality there are no contradictions. There is always a simple explanation, and the only simple explanation I can see is that in spite of what your people are telling you, they aren't presenting it the same way you are. They must be deviating in some way, and their deviations are fatal."

"Makes sense," Pete replies, "but probably I'm too close to the situation. Last time I went with my VP of sales to a meeting, I swore to myself that I would not open my mouth, I would just observe. After three minutes, I took over. We got a sale, but my VP of sales became even more disenchanted. That is probably when I lost him. Listen, Alex, what I really want from you is that you'll send Don to help me."

"What do you mean?" I am not entirely surprised.

"I want him to accompany my salespeople on some sales calls. He is not as emotional as I am about the offer; he won't have any problem watching them butcher the sale without interfering. At the same time, he knows the logic of our offer inside and out. Maybe he can put his finger on what they are doing wrong."

I think about it. Pete is right, but I need Don to work with me. No, there is nothing more important than guaranteeing that Pete's solution does work. My whole plan is dependent on Pete demonstrating that such a marketing solution can quickly turn around a company. It is essential for the entire group's survival.

"When do you need him?" I ask.

"The sooner the better. Starting tomorrow would be ideal."

"Let me see what I can do. I'll call you back."

I went directly to Don's office.

"Dad?" Dave interrupts my gloomy thoughts. "Can I ask your advice?"

I can't believe my ears. When is the last time Dave came to me for advice? I can't even remember.

"Of course." I turn the TV off and look at him. He seems normal. "Have a seat," I say.

"I prefer to stand."

I wait, but he doesn't say a word. He just shifts his weight from one foot to the other.

"Carry on," I encourage him. "What's your problem?"

"It's not really a problem." He looks uncomfortable. "It's more . . . like, a situation."

"A situation that you don't know exactly how to handle?"

"Yeah, sort of."

"You've come to the right person," I assure him. "I'm the expert of sticking myself into unpleasant situations."

"You?" Dave is surprised.

I just smile. Let my kids hold on to their illusions about their father. "Tell me about it." I decide to take a businesslike approach.

That makes him more comfortable. "You know Herbie," he starts.

I nod my head. Of course I know Herbie. How could I not know him when he spends half his time at our house, constantly raiding the fridge.

"Well, he came up with an interesting idea."

"Yes?"

"It has many pluses . . ." He starts to fudge. "You know . . ."

I know my boy. The next sentence will be, "Sorry, forget it" and he'll disappear.

"Dave, what is Herbie's idea?"

"You know that Herbie is as crazy about old cars as his father is."

"And as you are," I cannot resist the temptation to add.

He smiles. "Nothing compared to them. You know the collection that they have. Six antique cars. One cooler than the other."

"Yes, I know," I assure him before he tells me again about Herbie's father's hobby. It's nice to have such a hobby. The problem is that first you have to be a millionaire.

"So," Dave returns to the issue, "Herbie wants us to buy an old wreck and rebuild it. He found a fifty-six Olds ninety-eight convertible. It's falling apart. The engine is one solid block of rust but the chassis is okay. And the body can be nicely restored. It could be a real beauty."

I keep quiet as he rambles on.

"Herbie knows where we can buy the parts that we'll need. He even located an old transmission. It's a fifty-nine model but we think it'll fit. Herbie and I are pretty good mechanics. I think that we can turn it into almost a collector's item. It has a lot of potential."

"So what's your problem, Dave? Do you want me to lend you money for it? That's the advice you want?"

"No, not at all." He seems somewhat offended, as if he

never before asked for money. And for much worse purposes.

"Sure?"

"Quite sure. I think that we can manage with less than
fifteen hundred dollars. And I have enough for my share. I
still have most of the money I made last summer. Besides,
grandma promised me five hundred for my eighteenth
birthday. Maximum I'll need is a short-term loan."

From past experience I'm starting to suspect that
short-term loan, in my kids' vocabulary, means to be repaid
from their inheritance. And my mother intended the gift to
be for Dave's pocket money this fall when he goes to college. But what the heck, rebuilding a car from almost
scratch will be good for him. I think that he can do it.

"I'm not sure about a loan," I say. "But if that's not the
problem, what is?"

"I don't know," he says. "I have an uneasy feeling
about it."

"Any real reason?"

"I don't know. I'm afraid that Herbie won't be able to
come up with his share, and I'll end up financing the whole
thing myself."

"How are you going to manage that?"

"Don't worry, Dad. It will never happen. I'd rather
drop the project in the middle. I don't think it's likely,
Herbie claims that he can get the money. I don't know.
There are more problems than that."

"Like?"

"Like, who will take the car, when? Right now we go
out together, but . . . ." He starts to fudge again.

I let him ramble for a while. "I think I understand," I
finally say.

"So, Dad, what should I do?"

I don't know what to answer. Herbie's idea sounds
okay, it seems they know what they're getting into. But
there are pitfalls, many things that might go wrong. Should
I advise him to go ahead? Or to drop it?

Whatever I recommend, one thing is sure, before long I'll be blamed for my recommendation. I almost cop out by saying, let me think about it, when I realize what I should do.

"Dave," I start slowly, "whatever advice I give you, will you follow it without question? I hope not. So ask yourself, what good will it do?"

"It will help. I respect your opinion Dad."

"Frankly, I don't know what advice to give you. It's not a simple matter, there are pluses and minuses on both sides."

"Yes," he sighs, looking disappointed.

"But there is a way I can help you," I say. "I can teach you how you can make the decision. Without compromises, and without guesses."

"Oh, come on. Can you? Even when it looks like there is no decisive answer?"

"Let's go to my study," I say, standing up.

"I hope it's not too complicated," he mutters, following me.

We sit down at my desk, and I give him a dime. "Heads is go ahead. Tails is tell Herbie to drop it."

"That's your method?" he asks.

"No, that's just the way to pick a starting point. It really doesn't matter."

"Whatever you say." He flips the dime. It comes up heads.

"Okay. So let's assume it's a go. Start by listing all the positive things you see in the idea."

After writing two lines, he hesitates.

"What's the matter, Dave?" I ask. "Are there some positives you don't want to tell me?"

"Sort of," he grins.

Even better, I think to myself. "Let me describe a situation very similar to yours when I used this technique. I think I even have the work I did."

As I look for it, I start to tell the story. "It happened

about four years ago, when we were still living near your uncle Jimmy. One day he came to me and suggested we buy a boat together."

"What a neat idea," Dave says.

"Yes," I agree. "It had a lot of pluses, but similar to your case, I felt uneasy about it. Let me show you what I did. Where is it? It must be somewhere here in this drawer."

I flip through the papers. I forgot how many interesting things are stored here. Dave almost gives up.

"Ah, yes, here it is. Of course, at the bottom. The first page is a list of all the positive aspects of buying the boat."

"You flipped a coin before you started this list?"

"Probably. I don't remember. In any event here are the reasons to buy a boat with Jimmy: I will have a boat in my possession; I will share the financial burden of purchasing and maintaining a boat—the only realistic way to make it possible."

"Those two are identical to my situation," Dave interrupts.

"No wonder, the situations are very similar. Probably the other positives are applicable to you as well. Like: I don't have to do all the maintenance myself; or due to Jimmy's superior mechanical ability, the boat will be well taken care of."

"No, that last one is definitely not applicable," Dave laughs.

"Here, read it yourself." I hand him the page.

He glances at it. "Yes, most of these points are good for me, except for the last one." And, grinning, he reads, " 'I will have an ally to help persuade Julie to allow me to spend money on my dream, a boat.' Quite a persuasive list, so what happened?"

"Look at the next page, the negative list is not less persuasive."

" 'We might disagree about the selection of the boat,' " he starts reading. "I don't have this problem, we already know what we want to buy. Next. 'We might disagree about who will use the boat when.' Yes, that's a problem, but not as big as in your case. We are double-dating."

"Even in our case," I say, "it wasn't a big problem. You know your mother likes to spend time with her brother, and I like him too."

"Yeah, but what about Aunt Jane?"

I ignore his question. "Read on."

He continues down the list, making funny remarks. I don't know who enjoys it more, him or me.

"Nice," he says when he finishes. "A nice summary. But how did it help you decide? Now it looks even more difficult than before you started."

"This is not the end," I tell him. "It's just the beginning. Now, starting from, 'We agreed to buy a boat together' I have used if-then logic to reach each of the negative arguments. The same way I did when you asked to use my car. Remember?"

"Yes, Dad. And thank you. There was no problem, was there? I did take care of the car. And I don't bug you for it now."

"No, not more than before," I admit. "So when I finished connecting to each one of the undesirable effects, I started to check whether or not I could take actions to trim them."

"What do you mean by trimming them?"

"Figuring out if I can take an action to guarantee that the negative will not happen. For most of the negatives it was possible. But for one, every idea I came up with needed Jim's collaboration."

"Which one?"

"The one that says it would be a problem if one of us had to sell his share."

"You were thinking long term," Dave is impressed.

"Is there any other way?" I ask.

"Probably not," he admits. "Anyway, what did you do?"

"I slaved on it some more, polishing the words so that when I showed it to Jimmy, he wouldn't be offended. Here, look at it." I hand him the negative branch.

"See, first I stated my starting points: we agree to buy a boat together; you might want to get rid of your share; I don't have enough money to buy a boat alone. Not that type of boat anyway. You see the conclusion?"

"Yes, it is quite obvious. You can't afford to pay for Jimmy's share."

"Couple it with the fact that I am very picky about who my partner is, and you see the result. Jimmy might get rid of his share to a person I don't approve of.

"Now you see? Whatever choice I made, we were bound to end up badly. I might not compromise, which meant that I would have to sell my share as well. Not a good option; at that point in time we could safely assume that I would be in love with the boat."

"I see," Dave concludes, "you wouldn't like Jimmy too much for forcing you to sell."

"That's for sure," I say.

"And the other possibility is not so good either. You might compromise and then you'd be stuck with a partner you didn't like. Then you'd have an even bigger grudge against Jimmy.

"And as you know," I summarize, "if there is one thing I don't want, it's to stand between your mother and her brother. So I took this page and read it to Jimmy, asking him to come up with a resolution."

"And what happened?" he asks with interest.

"You know what happened. We don't have a boat and we have a great relationship with Uncle Jimmy."

"So what are you suggesting? That I don't rebuild the car with Herbie?"

"Nothing of the sort. What I'm suggesting is that you write all the negatives, and connect to them with if-then logic. Don't leave them just hanging there substantiated only by gut feel."

"Why is it so important to do it?"

"For two reasons," I say. "One is that once you detail the logic, you are much more able to really examine which actions you can take in order to trim the negatives."

"And the other?"

"The other is even more important. If you don't see how to trim a negative by actions depending entirely on yourself, if you need Herbie's collaboration, don't suggest any actions to Herbie. That might lead to unpleasant arguments. Instead, show him your logical derivations, exactly as I've done with you. Read it to him step by step. If there is a good solution, he will come up with it and you can both polish it. In that case, since there are no more negatives left to worry about, there is no reason you shouldn't rebuild the car together."

"And if he can't?" Dave asks. "What happens when I show him why a negative effect is expected, and he can't come up with a way to avoid it?"

"Then you will both have to make a choice. But it is no longer you against him due to the problem; it is you and he against the problem. In any event, your friendship is protected."

"Good idea. Maybe I'll try it. Dad, can I borrow these papers?"

"Only if you promise to put them back where they belong."

"Sure," he smiles at me. "At the very bottom of the drawer. I know."

22

I'm preparing my presentation for Granby when Don enters my office.

"Congratulations," I greet him. "Pete just called, praising you to the sky. What have you done to him? Put him under some type of spell, or just used your natural charm?"

He laughs, clearly pleased. "Did he tell you that this morning I got him a nice order?"

"Yes. He mentioned that as well."

"It was a piece of cake." Don drops into a chair. "It went by the book. No surprises, not even one."

"What was it?" I ask. "Why did you play salesman? I thought that you went there to find out why Pete's sales force is ineffective."

"Oh, we did. Each of his four salespeople already has a sale under his belt. They love it. They think it's the greatest thing since sliced bread. But, you see, after slaving on it for two weeks, I had to see if I could do it myself, not just teach it. So they arranged a meeting for me with a small prospect. Almost a cold call. And it worked like a charm. I really liked it."

"Maybe you should switch to a career in sales," I tease

him. "Tell me, what was the problem? I'd like to hear it from you. In detail."

"As you suspected," he starts, "they simply didn't know how to present it properly. I think that the biggest mistake was that they started a meeting with a buyer by talking about how great this new offer is. How much it would save the buyer, how low the inventories could be. You know, all the good stuff."

I don't get it. "What's wrong with that? Isn't it what they are supposed to do?"

"If they want to ruin their chances of getting the sale, yes. Otherwise, no."

"Don, will you please stop with your riddles and start to explain."

"I am. Look, Alex. Put yourself in the shoes of a buyer. Here is a salesperson praising his offer. What is your natural reaction?"

"If I'm a typical buyer, I'll try to play it down," I say.

"Exactly," Don concurs. "You will start to object. You'll object to his claims about how unique his offer is, to his claims about how badly you need it. And if some of his claims seem to be exaggerated, as is the case with our unconventional offer, you will probably express your skepticism."

"Yes, that's probably what I'd do," I agree.

"And the more objections the buyer raises, the less likely the salesperson is to make a sale. This correlation is established by broad-scale studies."

"You don't need studies to prove it, every salesperson knows it from experience. So, what are you telling me? That a salesperson should not start by presenting his product? Especially when his offer is non-conventional?"

Instead of answering, he goes to my white board and starts to write a cloud. As he writes, I read it out loud. "The objective is, 'Bring the buyer to see your product as the best value for his money.' I hope that you didn't have any problem convincing Pete's salespeople that that should be their objective."

"No, not at all. They're professionals."

"Fine," I say, and continue to read. "In order to 'Bring the buyer to see your product as the best value for his money,' you must 'Show value to the buyer.' That's obvious. At the same time you must be careful to 'Not cause the buyer to object.' I agree to that also. Now, let's see the conflict.

"In order to 'Show value to the buyer,' you must 'Present your product.' Of course. But in order to 'Not cause the buyer to object,' you must 'Not present your product.' "

"Remember," Don hurries to explain, "what we just discussed. You start by presenting your product and instinctively the buyer starts to object."

"Yes, lovely conflict," I agree. "No wonder salespeople are dancing between the drops, trying somehow to build rapport with the client, before they go to the real business. So, how did you break this conflict? What are they supposed to do?"

"Pete and I built a detailed Transition Tree for it. Want to see?"

"Sure."

Don goes to his office to get it. I look at the cloud again. It is generic. Nothing in this cloud is unique to Pete's case. Maybe Don's solution is also generic? I hope it is, because this cloud shows to what extent we will face difficulties selling our breakthrough solutions. Since they are, by definition, going to be unconventional, they are bound to cause the prospects to raise many objections.

Where is Don? What is taking him so long?

"I thought it would be better if you had your own copy," he says as he returns.

I look at the two pages he hands me. A typical Transition Tree: the "how to" tree; the detailed logic of how to transfer from the present into the desired future. At the bottom there are statements that describe the present state of mind of a buyer—that is the starting point. At the top of the second page is the objective, "Congratulations, or in depth analysis of the failure." How typical of Don to write it like that.

Along the right side of both pages there are several square boxes; these are the recommended actions. Some of them don't make any sense to me.

"Shall we read it together?" I suggest to Don.

"With pleasure. We started by describing a typical buyer. 'Many buyers see their job as pretending that they don't necessarily want to buy.' "

I smile. "Yes, there are too many buyers like that. I can't stand them."

Don continues to read, " 'Buyers don't usually have full trust in the salesperson regarding his praises about his products.' "

"Nice understatement."

He grins at me. "Look at the next one, 'Usually buyers don't exactly have a delightful history with printing companies.' "

"This is not just an understatement, this is a British understatement," I tease him. "Did Pete write this one?"

"Of course. Now, do you agree that each one of these starting conditions leads to the same conclusion, 'It is likely that a buyer will greet a conventional presentation of our win-win offer, not with enthusiasm, but with deep skepticism'?"

"Unavoidably," I agree.

"Now, look at it from the point of view of Pete's salespeople. They knew that our offer would definitely be a great deal for the buyer. He pays the lowest prices, he is holding surprisingly low inventories and he doesn't suffer any obsolescence. At the same time, they were far from sure that this offer was good for them. They were not sure at all that they were going to get more sales. Under this frame of mind, how do you think they reacted to the buyer's skepticism?"

"They are giving him what he really wants and he plays hard to get." I can envision the situation. It's funny. "I hope they were professional enough not to give their opinion in too many words."

"No. Like I said, they are professionals, but there is something called body language. You can imagine that from there the meeting went downhill."

"Yes, I can. So what did you do differently?"

"The first thing was to guarantee that they would have enough time to present it properly. We made sure that the meetings would be minimum half-an-hour."

"I see, that's what you mean by, 'The salesperson and the buyer meet without time pressure.' "

"Correct. Now our salesperson starts by presenting the buyer's Current Reality Tree."

"Wait a minute," I say. "What Current Reality Tree are you talking about? I don't remember that Pete did any Current Reality Tree. He started directly with the buyers' cloud."

"Correct, but as it turned out, we couldn't escape doing it." Noticing that I'm still confused, he elaborates. "When Pete developed the solution his intuition was strong enough to allow him to jump some steps. But when we tried to figure out how his salespeople could explain it to the buyers, the only way was to go back and construct all the trees according to our generic map. You'll see in a minute."

"So one way or another the entire work must be done. Interesting," I say, not fully understanding why. "Let me see the Current Reality Tree of Pete's buyers."

He hands me an additional page. "No surprises," he clarifies. "Basically what we discussed when Pete presented his solution to us. At the bottom are the printing company policies, and you see how we rigorously derived all the buyer's UDEs. The idea is that our salesperson reads it, from the bottom up, to the buyer. Since it begins by pointing the finger at us, the buyer is not displeased with such a start to a meeting. This is important, otherwise he will tell the salesman to cut the crap and give the offer. He will give it, and the spiral down starts."

"Doesn't the buyer have problems understanding the tree?"

"Not at all. Why should he? Everyone understands if-then. It is part of our language."

He is right. I tend to confuse the difficulty of constructing a tree with the difficulty of understanding one. When the tree is written on a subject a person is intimately involved in, nobody has difficulty understanding trees, not even kids. Not even someone who has never seen such a tree before. "Carry on."

"Then the salesperson supplements it with a numerical example, just to clarify the concept of price-per-usable-unit." He hands me another page.

"Did the buyers have any problem with that?"

"No, not at all. As a matter of fact, they all regarded it as a very useful concept. They immediately started to use the term. I suspect they knew it all along, what was missing was just the verbalization."

"I see. So, 'The buyer follows with interest.' That's what you're telling me?"

"Oh, yes, they commented, they remarked, but not one of them objected to anything in the Current Reality Tree. They simply have too much intuition about their own job.

"Now we reached something really important. You see, the Current Reality Tree vividly shows how the printing company policies make the buyer's life miserable. Do you know what was the result? The buyers realized that at last there was a salesperson who really understands them."

"This is a real achievement," I concur. "I can see how you broke the cloud. Rather than starting by presenting your product, you start by presenting to the buyer his own problems. And you do it in a way that he really appreciates. That's the way to build rapport. Not based on riffraff but on real substance. You know, Don, to reach this level of rapport usually takes months, even years."

"I guess so," he says. "Anyhow, at this stage we found out that the salesperson should, once again, show the direct link between our policies and the buyer's UDEs. It helps to summarize the page. The result is what you would expect," and he reads from the Transition Tree, " 'The buyer responds with a sigh, a nasty remark, or something similar, but he does not attack the salesperson.' "

"Of course, at this stage the buyer knows that the salesperson is on his side," I agree.

"Right. And now the salesperson explains that we have realized that as long as our policies create problems for the buyer, that by itself is a problem for us. We are simply blocking our own sales."

"I'm sure that every buyer loved this confession."

"Yes. Most responded by asking what we were planning to do about it, which opened the door, nice and wide, for the salesperson's next step. He hands the buyer his Future Reality Tree, saying 'here are our new policies.' "

"May I have a copy?"

"Certainly."

At the bottom are the injections: Ordering in batches of two months and receiving it in shipments of two weeks; the right to cancel after the first shipment without any penalty or explanation. Don is right. These injections do represent changes to our existing policy.

Don continues to explain, "The salesperson reads to the buyer his Future Reality Tree. This gives the buyer a vivid understanding why these injections will unavoidably lead to the positive outcomes."

"Interesting," I say to Don. "You were careful to use only the if-then logic that the buyer already agreed to when you read his Current Reality Tree. That's smart. It almost guarantees that he cannot object to it."

"None of them did, but don't think that we got the sale at that stage. If you switch back to our Transition Tree, you'll see the next obstacle: 'A buyer facing what he perceives to be seller's generosity becomes suspicious.'"

"Naturally. So how did you convince him that there aren't any snakes in the grass?"

"We decided that the easiest way was to show him a snake. We told him that this was not the entire offer. You see what the next recommended action is? We give the buyer the negative branch."

"Which negative branch? What are you talking about?"

"Oh, sorry." He gives me another page.

I take the time to read it. It is the negative branch that I highlighted to Pete; the possibility of the buyer abusing the offer, by declaring a one-shot small order as a big order, getting a lower price-per-unit, and then canceling after the first shipment.

"What was their response to this?" I ask.

"All over the map. But in each case they found a way to trim it. A way that was acceptable to us."

"I see," I say. "That way you made the buyer part of constructing the offer. He must have known that at this stage he had actually bought in."

"Yes," he laughs. "At this stage it was apparent to me as an observer that the buyer was preparing himself to defend against our salesperson's closing attack. To overcome it, we tried something unique. We instructed the salespeople to say to the buyer that he probably needs time to think about it, and to suggest scheduling another meeting. This is guaranteed to increase the buyer's trust in the salesperson, and the offer. But, only in one case was a meeting scheduled."

"And in the others?"

"In all the others, the buyers insisted we continue right then and there."

"Even better."

"Here is a nice twist," Don continues to surprise me. "Knowing that closing a deal is a sensitive step, we decided not to take any risks. Pete composed a list of obstacles that usually stand in the way of the buyer before he can sign the order. We simply present this list to the buyer."

"Wait a minute," I can't believe my ears. "You are giving the buyer excuses why he shouldn't buy? Are you trying to convince the buyer that he cannot sign the deal?"

"So it seems," he laughs. "But Alex, don't forget. At this stage the buyer knows that our offer is his dream. There is no fear that he will walk away."

"I see," I get it. "A role reversal. If you take the position of raising the obstacles, he must now take the position that they can be overcome. That's gutsy."

"Not really. What happened in reality is that the buyers played down some obstacles and discussed with our salespeople how to overcome the others. And you know the results. Whenever it was a small deal it was signed on the spot. In other cases, when we discussed business with buyers of large accounts, they asked us to prepare a quote for more business than we expected. It's looking good. Pete's problem now is how to slow down. The shop needs time to digest this tidal wave."

"Super job, Don. Really super job. You have done much more than I expected. We will need this blueprint for Bob and Stacey, once they figure out their own breakthrough marketing solutions."

Don leans back in his chair, rightfully proud of what he has accomplished.

"Don, as a reward, go home now and pack."

He stands up and stretches. "Unpack, you mean."

"No, pack. We are flying to Bob's."

"Alex, I was away for two weeks. I have plans for tonight."

"No problem. You can stay here, and take tomorrow off. I'm going to Bob's to examine the solution they've come up with. I just thought you would want to be part of it."

"Wouldn't miss it for the world." He heads for the door muttering, "With this schedule, no wonder I'm a bachelor."

23

I had asked Bob to hold the number of participants to a minimum, to invite only the people who actively participated in building the marketing solution. I expected about a dozen. He brought Susan Lomark, his VP of sales, and Jeff Dillman, his VP of operations. I know Jeff quite well, he was instrumental in building our approach to distribution. A very capable person. Susan, I know much less. I never worked closely with her, but Bob thinks the world of her, so she must be good.

"What about the others?" I ask Bob as we help ourselves to coffee and donuts.

"There are no others." Responding to my raised eyebrow, he adds, "Alex, since it got out that we are up for sale, this place is swarming with rumors. And rumors don't make it easy to operate. Before we know that we have a solid marketing plan, approved by you, I'm not going to leak it out. I don't need any more disturbances."

"I understand. Shall we start?"

Bob signals Susan to present. "We followed your tree," she says, and goes to the flip-chart.

"Did you believe that it would work?" I ask out of curiosity.

"I can't say that we believed in it. It made sense, but

frankly, who would believe that it's possible to systematically develop a marketing breakthrough?"

"But it worked?"

"We think so," Bob answers for her. "Otherwise we
wouldn't have called you here."

"We'll know that it works when sales start to roll in,"
Susan says. "Until then it's only a neat idea."

"I like this approach. Carry on."

She flips the first page. "Here we listed some of the
market UDEs that we used as a starting point."

"We elected to choose the shops as our market, not the
end consumers," Bob interjects.

"Why?" I ask.

"We followed your guidelines," he answers. "You want
fast results, so we concentrated on the link that we have
direct contact with."

"Besides," Susan adds, "to bring whatever new message to the consumers would necessitate increasing our advertising budget."

"Which we assumed you would have a hard time ap-
proving," Bob completes her argument.

"Good choice," I concur.

I read the UDEs of the shops. No surprises. Even I,
who never worked in the cosmetics field, know all of them.
Things like: "Shops have to give considerable discounts on
relatively obsolete products"; "Many times shops are out of
an item a customer wants"; or "Many shops have difficulty
meeting payments to the vendors."

"Then we built the Current Reality Tree of the shops,"
Susan flips one more page.

"Was it difficult to construct this tree?"

They look at each other and grin, "Embarrassingly
easy," Bob admits.

I let Susan continue.

"According to your guidelines we should rewrite the
tree so that the core problem is expressed as a policy of the
vendor. In our case we didn't have to do any rewrite. It

came out naturally like this," and she starts to read the tree from bottom up. " 'Cosmetic companies give discounts in proportion to the size of the shop's order,' and 'Discounts for large orders are substantial.' Take this policy of ours and consider the fact that 'Shops are usually in fierce competition with each other' and you see the unavoidable result, 'Shops are forced to order in large quantities.' "

"Yes, I see, but let me digress for a second. An equivalent conclusion is that shops cannot afford to order in small quantities. Bob, didn't you tell us that shops are not taking advantage of your new distribution system, of your offer to replenish to them on a daily basis? This might be the answer."

"Yes," he laughs. "And I accused them of resisting change, of being locked into purchasing habits. Nothing of the sort. At the same time that my distribution managers were begging them to order on a daily basis, our sales policies were discouraging them from doing it. Smart, isn't it!"

I prefer not to comment and signal Susan to continue.

"Let me first go into the financial branch. A direct result of buying in large quantities is that 'Shops have to carry a lot of inventory.' As you know, 'Most shops don't have much cash.' Remember we are not selling to the big chains, most of our outlets are small shops, like drugstores. So the need to carry a lot of inventory means that 'Most shops must borrow heavily.' "

"And you see the result, 'Shops' financial expenses are heavy,' which translates into 'Shops' profitability suffers.' "

"The situation is quite bad," Bob elaborates. "I constantly hear complaints from small shop owners that they are really working for the bank. To that extent the burden of the loans is heavy."

I nod my head. I've heard about it. And not just in cosmetics.

Susan continues. "If, 'Most shops must borrow heavily,' and 'Shops' credit is limited,' then 'Some shops have difficulty meeting payments.' 'We, the vendors, want to be paid . . .' "

"How nasty of us," Bob must interject.

"And as a result 'Some shops have trouble getting merchandise,' which, of course, has a major impact on their profitability."

"How bad is it?" Don asks.

"Quite bad," she answers. "Every year many shops declare bankruptcy. We, and our competitors, are well aware of the cash pressure, so we all give quite good payment terms. The standard in the industry is ninety days."

"And reality is," Bob adds, "that our receivables are running at about one hundred and twenty days. It's a real problem."

"Shall I continue?" Susan asks.

"There is more," Bob promises, "a lot more." He smiles at Susan.

"Here is another entry: 'Shop forecast of future sales is quite inaccurate.' Couple it with 'Shops are forced to order in large quantities,' and you get the next nasty result: 'There is considerable mismatch between the shop inventory and actual customers' demand.' This leads directly to 'In spite of the large inventories, shops suffer from shortages.' "

"What do you mean by shortages?" I ask, just to make sure.

"Shortage means a customer entered the shop, asked for a particular item, this item is not in the shop and the customer refused to buy an alternative item."

"So according to this definition, a shortage translates directly into a lost sale?"

"Yes. That is the derivative," she points to the tree. "And you see what makes it even worse. Here is your conclusion, 'Shops cannot afford to buy in small quantities,' which makes shortages a chronic condition. The shop will live with the shortage until it can afford another big purchase."

"And this," I follow the arrows, "leads to a substantial reduction in shops' profitability."

"Very substantial," Susan agrees.

"Alex, you've got to see the last branch," Bob is clearly proud of their tree. "You won't believe how crazy this industry is. Susan show him."

Susan is not overflowing with enthusiasm. In a dry tone she continues, "As you know 'Brands are constantly releasing and advertising new product lines.' "

"Now more than ever," I say.

"Yes, definitely," she confirms. "Combine it with 'There is considerable mismatch between the shop inventory and actual customers' demand,' and the result is obvious: 'Shops are holding a goodly amount of relatively obsolete products.' They know that they cannot hold these 'old' products for long, and therefore, 'Shops offer considerable discounts on relatively obsolete products.' This doesn't help their profitability."

"You see, Alex," Bob explains the obvious, "exactly when we invest a fortune to persuade the consumers to buy the new line, the shops are going out of their way to persuade them to buy the old line. Talk about a mismatch."

"Let me understand," I say. "From your tree the core problem is clear. It's our policy that drives the shops to buy in large quantities. How large is large? I mean, in terms of the shop's weeks of sales?"

Susan volunteers an answer. "It depends on the size of the shop, but in any event I think that it's more appropriate to talk in terms of months than weeks. If I judge by the frequency shops are ordering from us, I would say that a big shop orders from us in batches of one to two months. For a small shop . . . about six. The average is somewhere around four months, I guess."

"I see. That's good."

"Why do you say that?" Don is surprised.

"We are a major part of the problem," I answer. "This

means that we can be a major part of the solution. Okay Bob, let's see your proposed solution."

Bob turns to Jeff, who until now hasn't said one word. "Your turn," he gestures to the flip-chart. Susan can barely hide her sigh of relief. Why are they afraid of me?

Jeff clears his voice. "The solution is quite obvious." He flips a page. "Basically the Future Reality Tree is a mirror image of the Current Reality Tree. We started with two injections, 'Discounts are not based on the size of the order, but on the dollar amount the shop orders per year,' and, 'The shop is replenished on a daily basis.' From these two injections, and following the logic outlined in the Current Reality Tree, everything fell in place." And he sits down.

I scan the Future Reality Tree. No surprises. These two injections lead nicely to the opposites of all the UDEs. Jeff is right, there's no need to read this tree aloud.

"If you notice," Bob says, "one of the injections is based on our new distribution system. This will guarantee that our competitors will not be able to offer the same. At least not for a while. Knowing them and the way they operate, it will take them at least two years to copy us."

"Great work," Don is beaming. "Our road map does work. You have done a great job."

"Your road map was excellent," Bob agrees. "It was a no-brainer."

There is a problem, I think to myself. There must be a big problem, otherwise why hasn't Bob revealed this solution to his people? He must suspect that I will not approve it. Why? It looks perfect. I can ask him, but it will be better if I find it myself. Think.

I stand up to refill my cup. This is my standard way to gain time. It doesn't help. I still don't have a clue. Before I give up and ask Bob for the pitfall, I turn to Susan, "How much, do you think, will this offer increase our sales?"

"In the long run, a lot. Maybe even thirty percent. Maybe more."

"And in the short run?"

"It's hard to tell," she fudges.

"What's your guess?" I press.

"Probably sales will drop. But not by much."

"Sales will drop? Why?" Don is astonished.

Now it's clear. It is a big problem.

"Because this offer gives the shops an incentive to drop inventories," I explain. "Susan, how much inventory are the shops holding now, and how much do they need to hold for proper visual display plus reasonable stock? Don't exaggerate in the amount of backup stock, remember, according to your suggestion we are going to replenish them on a daily basis."

"This does not mean that they will immediately realize that we can do it, but a fair estimate is that they'll be able to reduce their inventory by half. Maybe a little more."

"Which means," I quickly translate it, "that launching this offer will translate to about two month's lost sales for us?"

"It will be compensated somewhat by their orders to cover for shortages, and hopefully by shops that we can attract to us, shops that right now we aren't doing business with. I think that the drop will be closer to one month rather than two. That's roughly the size of the bullet we'll have to bite."

"Can we afford it?" Bob asks innocently. As if he hasn't been worrying about this problem himself.

"I don't know," I hesitate. "We already took one shot this year, the finished goods inventory reduction. It was a big one. Almost ten million dollars. What we are talking about here is even bigger. Almost two months of lost sales will increase this year's losses to unbelievable numbers. I don't know how I can pass it by the board."

"But this will guarantee that next year and the year after, this company will register record profits," Don tries to argue. "Trumann and Doughty will understand it. They are shrewd businessmen."

"Yes, they are," I say. They are shrewd enough to realize that if we go ahead, there is no way we can sell Bob's company this year. Can I persuade them? Maybe.

"I have a suggestion," I say. "You all go have lunch. I'm going for a walk. You gave me a lot to think about."

24

Bob's headquarters are located in the middle of a nice park. The weather is pleasant, the big trees provide almost a pastoral atmosphere. I don't notice any of it. I'm pacing the narrow paved trails, fuming.

Once again, this devastating, short-term pressure. "Time is money," I can almost hear Brandon. "Can you guarantee that we will make more than inflation? The credit rating of UniCo is too low. We cannot afford to continue taking such an exposure." Yes, I know it all. But it's absurd to give up on such an apparent opportunity.

Maybe I can persuade Brandon and Jim to postpone the sale? I can guarantee making more than inflation. What will be the return on investment if we implement this solution? The investment is giving up on two months' sales.

Actually it's not giving up on anything. If we understand that as long as the shops haven't sold, we haven't sold, then all this frantic push on the shops takes an entirely different posture. By forcing the shops to hold more inventory, we have simply removed ourselves further from the market. How much inventory do they carry now? Four months? In an industry that constantly releases new product lines, to be four months removed from the market is devastating.

Forget it. For now I have to consider the impact on our books—and on our books, sales means sales to the shops. We'll lose two months' sales. How much are we going to gain? According to Susan, we're probably going to increase sales by thirty percent. Maybe more. I think I can take her estimate as realistic. She is conservative. She is the one who will have to deliver, and she's been in this business all her life. She knows it inside-out.

Let me use as a conservative number an increase in sales of only twenty-five percent. That's beautiful. It means that in the long run each year we'll get an equivalent of three months' on the two months lost sales. That's one hundred and fifty percent annual return. Who is talking about inflation? That's better than a gold mine.

Wait. How long do we have to wait until we reach the long term? I don't like pies-in-the-sky. When will net sales increase? When shops finish reducing their surplus stocks. That's not too remote. It should happen in about four to six months. In some cases, less. With this argument I stand a chance of persuading the board. I'll have to do it meticulously.

What exactly do I want to persuade the board to do? To postpone the sale of I Cosmetics. Until when? Until at least next year, then they'll be looking good.

No, it won't do. Oh, my God, I'm in a deeper hole than I thought. If I succeed in convincing them to postpone this sale, I'm dead.

They must take care of the lousy credit rating of UniCo, that I can't change, which means they must get enough money from selling my companies. They are talking about needing over one hundred million dollars. If I persuade them not to sell I Cosmetics, by that act, I've signed the death sentence for Pressure-Steam. Then they will have to sell it to the shredders.

No. I must protect Stacey's company. Bob is okay. With this beautiful marketing solution I think I can persuade any buyer to allow Bob to continue to run his company without interference. I think that I can even present it in such a way that proper prospects will be willing to pay a higher price. Yes, this I may be able to do.

Shall I leave it at that?

I don't feel comfortable with it. It means that Bob and his people will have to postpone the implementation until the sale of their company is complete. That is stupid. And I don't care what our crazy financial statements are saying. There must be a better way.

But there is another thing troubling me also. It's obvious that the negative branch of this marketing idea was bothering them. Bob, Susan and Jeff knew it all along. How come they didn't succeed in trimming it?

Their intuition about it is huge. Their desire to protect their company is even bigger. And they know that the only way that they can do it is to come up with a good marketing solution. This is an excellent one—except for this negative branch. According to Jonah, people who have the intuition and drive to the extent that they succeed in writing a Future Reality Tree leading to the desired effect will always succeed in trimming every negative branch. Why haven't they?

Did he say something about it? I can't remember. Maybe he did.

I go back to the main building and take possession of an empty office. Everybody is still at lunch. Julie should be at home.

I explain my puzzle to her. She listens attentively. When I finish, I ask, "Did Jonah ever say anything about this?"

"Yes, he did," she assures me. "He said that often people dismiss an injection that can trim a negative branch."

"Why should they? We want to trim this negative branch. We want it desperately."

"He said that it happens when the injection leads to new negative effects," she explains. "Then people tend to regard the injection as impractical, and they will simply ignore it."

"I see."

"From my experience, this is a common mistake. Often, if you stick with such an injection, you find that the negative branches it causes can be trimmed, usually pretty easily."

"You think that's what might have happened here?" I wonder. "You think maybe they have an injection that they dismissed?"

"Maybe. Alex, what do you have to lose? Check it out," she says.

She's right. I must cut this negative branch. Too much is at stake.

"Yes, I will. Thank you, darling."

"And Alex," she gives me some last minute advice, "even if you see that their injection leads to many new negatives, continue the process. At the end it does work. You'll see."

"I'll tell you tonight. Thanks again. Bye."

I go back to the conference room and write the negative branch on the flip-chart. Starting with the statement in their Future Reality Tree, "Shops drop unneeded inventory," and ending with the fact that we lose the equivalent of about two months' sales. Shortly after I finish, they all enter.

"What's the verdict?" Bob asks.

They are all waiting to hear my answer.

"What verdict?" I ask. "We haven't finished the analysis yet." And before anyone has the chance to object, I continue, "We were discussing this negative branch," and I point to the flip-chart.

"How can we possibly trim it? I want to hear your ideas, even if you already discussed them and decided that they are impractical."

"Yes, we did discuss some possibilities," Bob admits.

"But none of them made any sense. We're stuck. So what will happen if we can't trim it? Are we going to move ahead or drop it?"

"I haven't decided yet, it's too early. Now I would like to hear some of these impractical injections. Please."

They don't want to continue. They want the verdict now. I can't blame them. They live under immense pressure. It's not at all easy to work in a company with such an uncertain future. Right now, for them, any answer is better than this uncertainty. But I can't afford to give it to them. Not until I'm convinced that there is no other way. And I'm not yet convinced.

"At least give me the opportunity to realize that there is no way to trim this branch," I try to persuade them to continue. "Do you want me to decide on such an important matter before I'm convinced that I have all the facts? Bob, will you please give me the injection that looked the most promising. Even though at the end you decided that it's impractical."

"What we were playing with," Jeff speaks up, "is the underlying assumption that we can't increase sales in the near future. We were toying with ideas of how we could."

"Good thinking," I say. "Right into the heart of the problem. And . . ."

"And we came up with something, but the medicine is worse than the disease. And besides, there is no chance you'd approve it."

"Try me."

"Well, we could give our merchandise to the shops on consignment terms. No obligation when we ship to the shop, but it has to pay upon selling. Susan claims that this would increase sales to new shops more than what we'll lose from the existing shops reducing their surplus inventory. Yes, we know that it's impossible. You'll never authorize the cash injection," Bob says.

"Besides," Susan adds, "it has many other negatives. If

we give our goods on consignment the shops will have much more cash."

"What's bad about that?" I ask, still trying to figure out if I can get them some cash to do it. Maybe short term. I'll have to check.

"What's bad about it?" she echoes my question. "The shops are going to use this money to buy more from our competitors."

"Live and let live," I say.

"No. It's going to hurt us. The shops have limited display space. We are going to end up with less display space than we have now. And you know, whatever is not displayed is not likely to be sold."

"Susan," I ask, "can we condition our offer on agreed upon display space?"

"You mean, that the shop commits to dedicate certain predetermined space to our products, like brand names in the big chains? I don't think that would be a problem, especially when they can fill up the display without any hassle. And that's the case if we give it on consignment, it doesn't require any cash investment from them. And with our delivery ability they won't have any blanks. I think that we can actually ask them to guarantee us more space than they currently give us."

"This will increase our sales?"

"Oh, yes. No doubt. It will also give us some more immediate sales. In order to fill this space many shops will have to expand what they carry from our product line. You see, most of them are not carrying all our product lines, and they don't want to display a lot of repetitions. Yes, this will help. Considerably."

"But," she turns gloomy again, "how can we control them. We are working with thousands of shops. It's impossible."

"What do you mean by control?"

"Look," she tries to explain, "if we give our goods on consignment, the shops don't have to pay when we ship."

"They don't pay for it now, as I understand. They pay only after ninety days."

"Yes," she tries to control her impatience, "but the sale is done when we ship it to them. If we switch to consignment, then they'll have to pay only when they sell it. Most of them are so pressed for cash that I'm afraid they will simply not report sales. We can't control it. We can't build a police force that goes and counts what they actually sold. It's impractical."

"Susan, that's not a problem," Jeff says in a quiet voice. "We are not going to ship them merchandise the way we are doing it today. We are going to replenish to them. This means that in order to get merchandise, they will have to report what they have sold to us on a daily, or at least a very regular basis. I think that we can easily build an amicable system."

"Hmmm. . . . Maybe. Let me give it some thought."

"It's all very nice," Bob says. "But are you going to give us the cash. Consignment means that the shops are holding our inventory. Do you think that we can get back the cash that we released to UniCo when we dropped our finished goods inventory?"

By now I know the answer. Susan provided it. I decide to teach Bob a lesson. "Yes, I'll get it for you. As much as is needed. But before I leave here, I want to know exactly how much you need."

"No problem," he says. "I asked Morris, my new controller, to calculate it. I'm sure he has the numbers."

"How much is it?" I ask.

"Frankly, I don't know. You see, a day after I asked him, we decided that it was impractical. So I never asked for his answer. But I can call him in."

"Please."

Until Bob's controller arrives, they debate what to do with the shops' obsolete product. They come up with some neat solutions. The more they examine it, the better it looks. They are on a high. My promise to provide them with the cash they need has lifted a ton off their shoulders. It's fun to watch.

Eventually Morris arrives. "I took the time to double-check the numbers, just to make sure."

"How much is it?" Bob asks him.

"About thirty-four million, three hundred thousand dollars." He hurries to add, "Based on the number Susan gave me, that the average time from our shipping until the shops sell is forty-five days."

"Wahoo!" Bob is impressed. "Alex, are you sure that you can get us so much money?"

"Check your assumption," I say. When he doesn't get it, I turn to Morris. "Assuming that this reduction in receivables does not affect sales, will you please tell Bob who is giving this money to whom?"

"Isn't it obvious?" he innocently asks. "Right now, we have fifty-seven million, ninety thousand dollars in receivables. This is roughly one hundred and sixteen days. According to Susan, it will drop to only forty-five days. As I said, if she's right, we'll be able to give back to UniCo about thirty-four million, three-hundred thousand dollars."

I burst out laughing. One by one, they join in.

25

At dinner I'm telling my family about the marketing solution for I Cosmetics. Julie and Sharon are naturally interested. What is surprising is to what extent Dave is involved.

"Why don't you buy more companies that sell other merchandise to the same drugstores?" Dave asks. "If it's so good for I Cosmetics, it will be good for them as well."

He has a point. With this type of offer—asking for shelf space rather than hard cash and promising daily replenishment—it's bound to be good business.

"You can use the same distribution network," he echoes my thoughts. "You said that the regional warehouses are almost empty today."

"Dave," I say, "it's a good idea, but I'm afraid that UniCo doesn't have the cash to invest in it."

"That shouldn't be a problem," he continues to develop his idea. "You said that Bob's offer will reduce the receivables from over one hundred days to about forty-five. This is a cash machine. Borrow money, buy the companies, convert their receivables into cash and pay back the loan. What's the problem?"

"It's not so simple. But Dave, carry on this way and

you'll become a very successful businessman." I'm very pleased with my son. He's sharp.

"Dave is already a successful businessman. He has an antique Cadillac," Sharon brags. "A real collector's item."

"Yeah, sure," I laugh. And to Dave I say, "So, you decided to restore the old car? Good luck."

"Didn't I tell you? I guess not," he is a little embarrassed. "Thanks, Dad, I used what you taught me and that's the result. Herbie and I are going to restore a car. But Sharon's right. It's not going to be the fifty-six Olds. It is a nineteen-forty-six Caddie. We've already started to work on it. Can you imagine me in a big, shiny Cadillac?"

"How cool," Sharon squeals. "Remember, you promised to give Debbie and me a ride. All the girls will die. Yahoo!"

"Cool down, Sharon." What a lively imagination. "They first have to fix it. Right now I doubt if it even has an engine."

"Yes, it has," Dave assures me. "The original, and it's just been rebuilt. It runs like a dream. But of course, there's lots of work to do before we can put it on the road. Lots and lots."

"How did a fifty-six Olds become a nineteen-forty-six Cadillac?" I wonder what's going on. "Where did you get the money? A forty-six Caddie with a good engine is not something that you can get for fifteen hundred dollars. Not even fifteen thousand."

"It's all thanks to you, Dad."

"To me?"

"In a way. I took your work, you know, Jimmy and the boat, and . . ."

"What boat?" Sharon is all ears.

"Keep quiet, shrimp. I'll tell you later," Dave promises her. "Anyhow, I wrote my negative branches. Actually they boiled down to only two . . ."

"Dave, don't try to sidetrack me by talking about the

Thinking Processes. Where did you get the fortune to buy the car?"

"I'm telling you," Dave sounds irritated.

"Let him tell the story," Julie says. "It's fascinating."

"So I wrote two negative branches." Dave is still a little put out. "One dealing with all the problems of sharing and maintaining the car between Herbie and me. You know, like what you had with Jimmy. The other was about Herbie's problem getting the money."

I barely listen. The kids had a hard time scraping up fifteen hundred dollars. Where the hell did they get the money for such an expensive car? How much was it? Thirty grand? Forty? Maybe even fifty?

"I started with the easy one," Dave continues. "The one about the problems of sharing. I went over the logic with Herbie. I forced him to read every word. If I spent so much time writing it, he could spend the time to read it. He trimmed it in five seconds."

"Tell your father how." Julie makes sure that I get to hear all the details.

"Oh, it was simple. We both have to leave for college in September, so we decided that at the end of August we'll sell it. That's not much time, until then we'll manage."

"When will you finish the car?" I ask.

"Early July, we hope. I'm telling you, there really won't be time to fight about it."

"So the first negative branch was trimmed. Great. What about the second one?"

"The second branch was more sensitive. As I told you, I was concerned about where he was going to get the money. Well, it turned out he was planning to sell some grass."

"What! You didn't tell me this part."

"Mom, cool down. You know that I would never agree to such a thing. Herbie knew it too. That's why he didn't tell me about it before."

"So that was the end of that idea," Julie states.

"Yes, but it wasn't the end of our idea to restore a car. Herbie used our first injection to develop the second one. He said that since we were going to sell the car anyway, why not borrow from the future buyer. We knew approximately how much the car and the parts would cost us; about fifteen hundred dollars. Remember, at that stage we were still thinking about the Olds, we didn't know about the Cadillac. On top of the cost to us, we estimated that we were each going to put about three months' work into it. So we thought that offering it for twenty-five hundred would be a good bargain."

"Whom are you going to sell it to?" I ask.

"To you," he smiles at me.

"You are still talking about the Olds? Why do you think I would be interested in an Oldsmobile?" Really!

"That's exactly what gave us the real idea," Dave beams at me. "You see, I remembered what you told me about the difference between the perception of value of a supplier, and the perception of value of the market."

"What does that have to do with it?" I ask, baffled.

"The way we figured the value of the car—you know, what it cost us and the labor—is the way a supplier would derive the value," Dave explains. "But when we started thinking about persuading you, we decided to look from your eyes, and the only good argument we could come up with was that I would promise that if you bought the Olds, I would never touch your BMW."

"I see." My sneaky son.

"But then we decided that if that's the type of argument we were going to use, we would be much better off approaching Herbie's father. You know that sometimes Herbie succeeds in convincing his father to let him borrow his cherished antiques, and you also know that sometimes it takes a small fortune to repair the damages."

"So you concluded that Herbie's father's need for such a promise is much greater than mine," I say, relieved. "Did you ask him? What happened?"

"Herbie's father had a much better idea. He'd already purchased this Cadillac, and the major parts. So he offered us the job of restoring it. Of course, he first forced Herbie to sign that he will never ask to borrow one of his other cars again."

"And what are you going to get out of it?" I ask.

"Oh, until I go to college I can use it on an equal basis with Herbie. And if we get it running and it goes twenty-five hundred miles with no problems, Herbie's father promised me a thousand dollars. This way I don't have to spend my money, I can save grandma's gift, and I will have even more money to spend at college. How do you like it?"

"I like it." I like it a lot.

"So you see, Dad, you helped me twice." Dave summarizes. "Once with the negative branches, steering Herbie smoothly into a real solution rather than a real fiasco. And the second was explaining to me the differences between perceptions of value."

"Good job, Dave. You really put it to use nicely. You even pushed the concepts further. When I was talking about the suppliers' and markets' perception of value I was talking about companies producing products on an ongoing basis. You applied it to one-shot deals. And you're right. It works there as well. Come to think about it, it should work for any sale."

"Including the sales of your companies?" Julie jumps in. "They are each a one-shot deal."

"No," I reply. "Here the rules are rigid."

"What rules?" Dave is interested. "How do they determine the value of a company?"

"It's quite involved, but basically, you look at the net profit of the company and multiply it by the profit/earnings ratio for that type of industry and you have a good starting point. It also depends on the assets the company has. That might modify the picture."

"But that's purely based on the perception of value of the supplier," Dave insists. "You are only looking at the company. It's like looking at the product, rather than the needs of the buyer, Dad."

"You have a point. But that's how it is done."

"Not necessarily," Julie interjects. "Not according to what you've told me about Stacey's company."

I think about it. She's right. If you look at Pressure-Steam in isolation, the value is very low. But when you look at a particular buyer—a very particular buyer, Stacey's competitor—in regard to his needs you get a totally different number. Four times higher.

I raise my eyes and look at her. "Julie, you are right. Maybe we are going about it in the wrong way. Maybe we can get much more for Pete and Bob's companies if we look at the needs of the potential buyers. But what do I know about their needs? Nothing."

"Well, who are the potential buyers?"

"For Pete it is large companies in the printing industry. For I Cosmetics, we are approaching a much wider spectrum. The real experts on it are Brandon and Jim. I'll have to talk to them."

"Alex," Julie continues, "you must know something about the printing industry. Last year you spent a considerable amount of time at Pete's company."

"Yes, I did, but . . ."

She waits a minute, watching me. "Well?" she pushes.

"When I got Pete's company it was a good representative of the industry," I admit.

"Which means what?"

"Everything was run in order to save costs. Not real operating expense, but cost-accounting costs. You can imagine the results, I've told you about it a thousand times. It's hard to believe, but that's how most of this industry operates. That's the reason I'm afraid to sell it to someone who will interfere with the way Pete is running it."

I love to talk about Pete's company. When I start, it's hard to stop me. "This company is now a beauty, in every aspect. In quality, in delivery, in quick response to whatever the clients want. And most importantly, with their innovative approach to the market, it's bound to become very profitable, even this year.

"Profitable. The word does not describe it. It's going to be much above anything that anybody in the printing industry has ever seen. Let me tell you Julie, from every imaginable aspect, it's a model. A model of how this business should be run. I'm really proud of it."

"You deserve to be." Julie smiles at me.

"Doesn't somebody need such a model?" Dave asks.

"You mean," I slowly say, "selling it not based on the financials but rather on the fact that it can be used as a model for its industry? Interesting thought."

"Alex," Julie chips in, "I think that Dave might be right. You said that companies spend a lot of money on benchmarking. What is better for them than to have the best performer in their own backyard."

"Yes." My mind is racing; I develop it further, "And they spend a fortune on consultants. In their business, Pete and his people are better than any consultant out there. They not only understand what to do, they have done it."

"So they will be the teachers," Sharon concludes.

They all look at me. "Let me understand what we are talking about," I try to recoup my thoughts. "For a big printing company, and I'm talking about really big, Pete's company can be the source of a paradigm shift in performance. It's a perfect model of how to schedule and control a printing operation, not based on the paradigm of artificial cost but on what really makes sense, short and long-term bottom-line impact.

"They are an outstanding example of how to handle the prep room. A job that might take another company weeks, Pete is turning around in four days, no sweat. But most importantly they know how to develop unique marketing approaches. They can be the benchmark, the school and the consultants at the same time."

"But Pete and his people don't want their company to be sold," Julie reminds me.

"Are you kidding? They would love to be in the position of being the catalyst of change for a large printing company. It's the ideal job and a great opportunity for them. On the contrary, here at UniCo they are in a strait jacket. They are not part of the core business, they are stuck out in the periphery."

I'm excited. This idea has a lot of merit. The jump in the financial performance of the company guarantees that we can sell it for a nice bundle. But if we can sell it as a lever for change to a large printing company, then the sky is the limit.

And everybody will benefit. The buyer. UniCo. Granby will come out smelling like roses. Trumann and Doughty will be very pleased. But most importantly, Pete and his people will be in the best position they could ever hope for.

And what about me?

I'll manage.

"So what do you say?" Dave cuts into my thoughts.

"What I say is that you are right. For a big printing company it's a unique opportunity. I wonder if I can present it so that they'll understand how unique and valuable it is?"

"We're sure that you can," they all tell me.

26

When we are alone, Julie raises the issue, as I knew she would.

"Alex, what about your job? It looks like your companies are going to be sold, and I think that you're doing the right thing making sure that they will end up in good hands. But what about you?"

"I don't know," I sigh. "I really don't know."

"Until now," she says in a soft voice, "I was careful not to push you, but things are starting to fall into place. You are taking care of your people. What about a little taking care of yourself?"

"And my family," I finish her thought. "Julie, what do you want me to do? Start pulling some strings? Put my resume in the appropriate hands? I can't do that. Not in my position, not now. Besides, the war is still going on. I won some battles, but the major ones are still on the horizon. I cannot afford to be distracted. Don't you see?"

She thinks about it. At last she says, "I would feel much better if I knew that you had a plan. Not just for your companies, but for yourself. Is it too much to ask?"

Contrary to the common opinion, I hate to plan. Especially when Julie is involved. I know my wife. When she is talking about a plan, she doesn't mean some vague list of actions. She will maneuver me into performing a meticulous analysis. In this regard, she is more Jonah than Jonah.

However, nothing is bad about it. It's good to have a plan.

"I must agree with you," I say. "The time has come to put together a rigorous plan."

"Do you have enough intuition about the subject?" Now Julie is all business.

"I think so." It's not as if I haven't thought about it the last few months.

"Good." A pad appears in her hand. "As long as we're talking about you—not UniCo, not your companies, not your people—but you, do you have any quarrel with the following objective: 'Get an equal or better job'?"

When Julie moves, she moves.

"No quarrel." I try to be as practical as she is.

"If that's the case, I think that we agree on the Thinking Process we should use," she says categorically.

"Yes. The Prerequisite Tree." I'm also a good student of Jonah's.

"Okay, start to raise obstacles."

Now, I know that this might sound strange. If we want to reach an ambitious objective, why start by raising obstacles? Isn't it counter-productive?

But this is Jonah's way. As he puts it, "Always start with a step that people are expert at performing." And everyone of us is an expert at bitching and moaning. In other words, coming up with all the reasons why it can't be achieved, raising obstacles.

"We still don't have a marketing solution for Stacey's company. This is a big problem." I start to bitch.

"Agreed." Julie writes it down. "More."

"The profits of Pete's and, even more, Bob's companies are still far from being satisfactory. I know that we took the proper actions but it's not yet in the bag. If we have to sell them now we are not going to get much."

"I'm writing it as two obstacles," Julie informs me.

"One is 'Profits of Pete's and Bob's companies are abysmal.' And the second, 'Values of Pete's and Bob's companies are low.' Okay?"

"Fine," I agree. "Now take what we discussed at dinner. This issue is not yet complete. In spite of what I said I don't yet have a clear understanding of the buyers' needs. At least not to the extent that I can put together a persuasive enough presentation."

"Why is it so important?" she asks.

"What are you talking about?" I'm surprised. "How else can I leverage the price of Pete's and Bob's companies?"

She writes it down and then says, "Alex, will you please start to address the real obstacles. If you want to get an executive vice-president position in a substantial company, you must have excellent recommendations from respectable and powerful people. It's essential."

"Yup, it is. Add it to the list."

"Well?" she says.

"Well, what?"

"What about some more obstacles of that sort. You know much more about it than I do."

"You are doing very well," I encourage her. "Please carry on."

"As I understand it, there aren't many jobs like that waiting to be filled." She doesn't like that she has to bring it up.

"What an understatement. But remember, to get one of the few that are there, recommendations are not enough. I must have an outstanding record. Otherwise I don't stand a chance; the internal people are the first to be considered. And Julie, so far, as an EVP, I don't have an outstanding record."

"Turning around your companies from bottomless pits into what they are today is not enough?"

"No. Not if they are sold for less money than what they were bought for. Besides darling, you're ignoring Stacey's company. As it stands now, it's going to be sold for demolition. Any executive carrying a black mark like that can kiss good-bye any chance of getting an equivalent job in another company."

Julie is not getting excited. She's heard all of it before, one way or another. "Do you have more obstacles to add to our list, Alex?" she asks in a matter-of-fact tone.

"Just the fact that Trumann and Doughty are not kids. They are the shrewdest, most clear-minded business people I have ever met. I guess that when you're talking about recommendations, you are talking about them?"

"Yes. As I understand it, they think highly of you. As they should."

"Darling, this is a tough world. Trumann and Doughty would never make a recommendation that they didn't feel totally comfortable about. They must protect their reputations. If they recommend somebody, he or she better be good."

"I still don't understand the problem." My loyal wife.

I try to explain. "If Trumann and Doughty do not get enough money from the sale of my companies, and it doesn't matter what the reason is, they will not be impressed with me. In my position I must deliver results, not excuses. Just results, nothing else counts."

Julie is not impressed with my emotional speech. "Anything else?"

"Let me see the list," I say. I read it carefully. "No. I think we have all the major obstacles. Can we move to the next step?"

Starting with the list of obstacles is not as devastating as you might expect.

What's the next step? The obvious. We all know that when the objective is ambitious it stands to reason that the plan to achieve it will contain several intermediate objectives. Where are the intermediate objectives coming from? The only reason for an intermediate objective is to overcome an obstacle that stands in the way of reaching the desired end objective. There is no other reason.

Therefore for each obstacle on our list we have to figure out the corresponding intermediate objective; the thing that if we achieve it the obstacle will be overcome.

"The first obstacle that you mentioned," she starts, "is 'There is still no marketing solution for Stacey's company.' What intermediate objective do you have in mind? How can you overcome it?"

I'm trying to be as professional as she is. It's not easy. In her job she has developed a remarkable ability to remain analytical, no matter how emotional the issues are. She must.

"Nothing fancy. I just need enough time to implement the necessary actions. You see, the guidelines that Don and I developed are so powerful that I'm really not too concerned. Stacey needs time, nothing more."

She writes it down and continues, "The next obstacle is, 'Profits of Pete's and Bob's companies are abysmal.' I guess that the intermediate objective is the same. Once again, 'Have enough time to implement the necessary actions.'"

"Yes, and there is no problem in getting the time. I've already scheduled a meeting with Brandon and Jim. They will grasp Bob's solution in no time and they'll be happy to wait. You see, implementing this solution will bring more cash in the next few months than what they hoped to get from selling the company. And then we'll end up with a company that can be sold for at least three times the current reasonable price. Nope, there's no problem buying time for Bob. As for Pete, there was no problem to start with."

"Excellent. The next one is 'Values of Pete's and Bob's companies are low.' I guess that the intermediate objective is to reach 'Values of Pete's and Bob's companies are high,' and you already took the actions that will guarantee it."

"Nothing in business is guaranteed. But yes, conceptually you are right. What's the next obstacle?"

"I wrote it as, 'Not enough knowledge to construct persuasive presentation for potential buyers.' What do you have to do to overcome it?"

"Many tiny details. I'll spend time with Brandon and Jim to construct it. I think that between us we know enough. Besides, it will be a good idea to make them part of this process. In the end they're the ones who will have to do the actual sale. Basically it boils down, once again, to having the time to do what's needed. No big deal." I'm quite confident about it.

"And this will pave the way to taking care of the next obstacle," she says. " 'Value of Pete's and Bob's companies is not leveraged,' is answered with something like 'The appropriate buyers are persuaded to regard Pete's and Bob's companies as models.' "

When I nod in approval, she continues. "So far so good. Now let's address the biggies. 'Recommendations from powerful people are essential.' I understand that Trumann and Doughty are your best shot?"

"Yes. And also Granby. A good recommendation from your ex-boss maybe doesn't carry a lot of weight. But a cold recommendation is devastating."

"I'm writing, 'Trumann, Doughty and Granby are willing to give high recommendations.' I think that if you achieve the previous intermediate objectives, this will come as a result."

"Probably."

"The next one is, 'There are not many open positions at the required level.' Alex, the obvious intermediate objective is 'The right open positions are identified.' What are you planning to do about it?"

"According to Jonah's guideline you are supposed to ask questions like that only after we sequence all the intermediate objectives," I tease her. "But darling, as long as I don't take care of the other obstacles there is no point applying for any position. After I take care of them, I'll have more than ample time to look for a job. You see, accomplishing all the other intermediate objectives will guarantee that I'll get a lucrative golden parachute from UniCo. I'll have enough time to look around."

She is not too happy with my answer, but after a slight hesitation she continues. "The next obstacle is . . ."

It's no hassle coming up with the other intermediate objectives. Then we start turning the resulting list into a plan.

We have to figure out which intermediate objectives we can achieve in parallel, which only sequentially.

Here the fact that for each intermediate objective we already have verbalized its corresponding obstacle helps a lot. Actually it makes sequencing the intermediate objectives into a relatively easy task.

How? Well, ask yourself what can possibly be the reason that we must achieve intermediate objective X first, and only then can we achieve intermediate objective Y? It must be that there is an obstacle that prevents the achievement of Y, and this obstacle is overcome by achieving X. That's why X has to be accomplished before Y. Make sense?

To sequence we just have to find which obstacle blocks which intermediate objective. It's that easy.

When we've finished, we examine the resulting Prerequisite Tree. It looks good. It's solid.

Julie remarks, "According to the tree, 'Identifying the right open position,' is not conditioned on any other intermediate objective. You can start now."

"But . . ."

"But you are right. There is no point in addressing it now. It is only one of the three necessary conditions that are essential for the final objective. And relative to the other two, having an impressive track record and the high recommendations, it is relatively trivial. Yes, there is no need to address it yet."

After a while she adds, "I like your plan, my smart

hero. Now I see that every action that you took, right from the start, was on the right issues. Thank you, dear." She puts the pad aside and comes to cuddle in my arms.

She's relaxed. I wish I felt the same. Stacey is not moving at all. The news about what is planned for Pressure-Steam has paralyzed them. I have to go there. But can I move them? I doubt it. And if the situation there is not resolved, nothing else counts.

Besides, there is a lot of work on all the other fronts, and frankly, I spend too much time on worthless corporate issues. The paperwork takes more than half of my time. Am I spreading my efforts too thin?

According to this Prerequisite Tree, I am. What it tells me is that: I must make sure that Stacey develops a solid marketing approach that will guarantee her division a decisive competitive edge; I must work with Brandon and Jim to make them embrace the concept of selling Pete's company (and later Bob's) as a "model for excellence"; I must ensure that Bob's solution is implemented as smoothly as possible.

But most importantly, nothing should be allowed to distract me from doing it.

27

This was an excellent day. A week ago, the morning after Bob, Susan and Jeff presented their solution to me, I suggested to Brandon Trumann and Jim Doughty that I come to New York to update them. We met in Brandon's offices, on one of the top floors of the twin towers.

What a sight. All the world is at your feet. On the other hand, it's a long fall from here.

One of my objectives for this meeting was to gain time for Stacey. I had to convince them that we do have a realistic chance to develop a marketing breakthrough solution for Pressure-Steam. To accomplish this, I decided to start by bringing them up-to-date on Bob's solution. My assumption was that it would be enough to show that this solution was not the result of an ingenious intuitive flash, but rather the result of meticulously following the generic process that Don and I had constructed. The Future Reality Tree of how one should go about developing a competitive edge. They were already familiar with that tree.

I gave them a copy of the client's UDE list that Bob, Jeff and Susan put together. Brandon and Jim examined the list, no surprises there. Then we read the Current Reality Tree that was built from this list. Brandon commented that to construct this Current Reality Tree is child's play compared to the one we built together. Jim agreed.

Once we finished reading the Current Reality Tree, they didn't have any difficulty translating the core problem into the natural solution. The cloud was almost redundant. And then we went over the Future Reality Tree. That was important. It convinced them that the solution will be very attractive to the shops.

Of course they raised negative branches, lots of them. That was the fun part. They couldn't come up with any negative branch that Bob's group hadn't already analyzed in depth. So, in response to each reservation they raised, I simply handed them the appropriate page, showing which injection Bob came up with, and how it not only trims the negative, but leads to more positives. It was great.

When they had exhausted all their reservations, they started to raise a long list of implementation concerns. I was well prepared. Bob's team had given me all the ammunition I needed. Trumann and Doughty were impressed. No, not just impressed, they totally bought in. Frankly, only when I had finished explaining it all to them did I realize to what extent Bob's solution is really powerful.

And my plan worked. Brandon said that he is now a believer in the Thinking Processes. Jim even asked if I can take the time to teach them how to become masters in using Jonah's techniques.

Then I played my trump card. I suggested that we do the calculation of how much cash Bob's company will generate in the next four months. They couldn't believe their eyes; they checked the numbers over and over again. But there it was. Under the most severe assumptions, shortening the collection time on the receivables will bring in more cash than what we hoped to get from the sale of the company. You can imagine that I didn't have any problem convincing them that it would not be a wise move to sell the company before we get the cash.

I was ready to move to my next step. I knew that I

couldn't simply ask for a delay for Stacey. They need to start having results, and results for Trumann and Doughty means more cash for UniCo. A lot of cash.

I suggested estimating the future annual profits of I Cosmetics. I wanted them to see the magnitude of the numbers. When we finished the calculation it came out that implementing Bob's solution will bring I Cosmetics to a profit of eighteen percent on net sales. Not on the current sales, but on the increased sales. This means approximately thirty-seven million dollars net profit a year. Not bad for a company that just a week ago we were willing to sell for less than thirty million.

The return on net assets, when you take the crazy way we use to determine net assets on our balance sheet, comes out to be almost sixty percent a year. Sixty percent RONA for a company that doesn't have any patents or proprietary technology.

You can imagine that Brandon and Jim hurried to calculate the selling price. Yes, they still intend to sell the company. They need the money to improve UniCo's credit rating.

To estimate how much we can sell I Cosmetics for, we used a profit/earnings ratio of seven. The value of the company came out to be about two hundred and fifty million dollars! No wonder, a remarkable jump in profits causes a remarkable jump in value.

Brandon was quick to point out that there is no way we will get this amount. Not when profits are based on forecast rather than hard numbers from past history. But he thought we could shoot for one hundred and fifty million. What a change. They were praying to get this sum of money for all the diversified group. Now they want it from just Bob's company alone.

At that stage I was ready to move on the issue of Stacey's company. The negotiations with Pressure-Steam's competitors are moving at a snail's pace. A snail's pace compared to what Trumann and Doughty want to see; an express train relative to what I want. At the current rate they have a good chance of signing the deal before the end of the year.

So I just speculated what would happen if Stacey develops an equivalent competitive edge in her field and starts to eat into the competitor's market share. They were quick to realize that it would be like sticking dynamite in the competitors' behind. It would also enable us to ask for a higher price. It was easy to squeeze a promise that they'll freeze negotiations for the next six weeks. Right now they have more confidence than I do in our ability to rapidly develop a competitive edge for Pressure-Steam.

Once I knew that I'd won this battle, I moved on to my next objective. I reminded them of their estimate of the amount that we can get for Bob's company, and declared that we can get much more, that we're going about it in the wrong way. They were not surprised. I don't think that I can surprise them anymore, whatever I claim. Anyhow, I laid on them the realization that I learned from Dave. You know, why are we putting ourselves in the trap of evaluating the company through its financial performance. We should evaluate it in relation to the benefits a buyer can get by acquiring it. And these benefits are not restricted to only the direct profits that can be made by the purchased company.

We discussed the concept of selling our companies as models of excellence, as catalysts to raise the performance of a much larger company. Initially it was hard for them to accept, but when I switched focus to Pete's company, to the printing business, it was much easier for them.

The last three hours we spent attempting to construct a presentation for big prospects in the printing industry. Even though it was very helpful in bringing Jim and Brandon to buy into the idea, I didn't like the results. It is not a good presentation, not at all. I will have to teach them how to construct a Transition Tree. This is the only way we can smoothly deliver such a complicated message. We scheduled a weekend two weeks from now at a resort area. We are going to try to bring our families, too.

Should I tell them then that in this meeting I was following a Transition Tree? That would be a bad idea, they might feel manipulated.

I'm going over what I achieved with them. I gained enough time for Stacey's company. Bob's company will not be sold for the next four months. In the meantime, we are going to prepare a dazzling presentation for the printing industry. Then we'll be ready to concentrate on cementing the deal on Pete's company.

By the way, we intend to sell Pete's company for more than one hundred million. That's their number. I think that if our presentation is really good, we can get close to two. We'll see.

Not bad. Not bad at all considering where I was less than three months ago, when the board's resolution hit me like a ton of bricks.

Now I am on my way to visit Stacey. Don will meet me at the airport, and tomorrow morning we are going to spend time with all Pressure-Steam's top management. I must find a way to move them forward, to infuse them with the stamina to construct a solution. They must do it. They have the intuition, they have the know-how, and they are the ones who will have to implement it.

I don't think that I will have any real problems, not when they hear that I have secured a sufficient window of time for them, when they hear that Trumann and Doughty are willing to wait.

At the gate I'm greeted not just by Don; Stacey comes too. As we go to the parking lot I break the good news to her. She doesn't seem enthused.

"Did you complete the Current Reality Tree of the market?" I ask.

"Are you kidding?" she bitterly answers. "We couldn't agree even on the market's UDEs."

"When will you?" I try to disguise my irritation.

"Alex, you are asking for the impossible. I haven't even managed to get my people to move seriously on the distribution system."

"How come? I thought you'd finished hammering out the details over a month ago?"

"Yeah. So what."

"Stacey, what's the problem?" I ask. "Do you think that I didn't buy you enough time? That six weeks won't be enough to construct your marketing approach? It took Bob's people only two weeks to polish it."

She doesn't answer.

I'm starting to get fed up. "Of course six weeks won't be enough," I say in a hard voice, "if it takes you more than three weeks to write an UDE list. Listen, I bust my behind to buy you time. I can't understand why you allow your people to waste it."

"Alex, with all due respect, I think it's you who doesn't understand. You're asking for the impossible. Do you know what is going on in my company?" I've never seen Stacey so depressed. "Have you seen my last report? Sales are down. Shipping is down."

"I can imagine that morale is low, it's understandable." I try to be responsive.

"It's not low," she corrects me. "It's hit rock bottom."

This is too much. "Stacey, are you telling me that your people are declaring defeat?"

"What I'm telling you is that they are realistic. They have families to take care off. Many don't have savings, but they do have mortgages. How can I blame them when all they can think about is finding another job.

"Listen Alex. Since UniCo bought this company four years ago, what have these people seen UniCo do for them? How much did UniCo invest in modernizing this company? Zilch. Not even a penny.

"And now UniCo is going to sell them out. UniCo is going to make a bloody fortune and they are going to be thrown into the streets. Will you please stop pushing for the impossible? Nobody here is willing to collaborate."

This is a totally defeatist attitude. If Stacey doesn't wake up, there is only one line of action open to me. To fire her and immediately take her place. I have to talk some sense into her. I hope that she listens.

We reach the hotel. I turn to Stacey and wait until she looks at me. "No, Stacey, you are wrong. Bloody wrong. You are taking from these people the last chance that they still have. And yes there is a chance, a real one. We can turn it around. We can secure these people a good job in a prosperous company, in Pressure-Steam. But not with the attitude you are taking. Not by declaring defeat before the battle has even begun.

"You are the president of this company. It's your responsibility to make sure that it will continue to survive and prosper. And what are you doing? Deciding a priori that there is no chance? How can you do it?

"So what if upstairs they want to sell you to the cleaners? Does it mean there's no way to reverse that decision? Of course, based on the current performance there is no way. But in whose hands is it to change this abysmal performance? And who said that we don't have enough time? If we plan our actions carefully, if we deliver the correct intermediate results, we have all the time in the world.

"You can blame the board, you can blame me, you can blame the market conditions and even your people. But at the end Stacey, it's all up to you. You can decide that you can, or you can decide that you cannot. In either case, you are right.

"See you tomorrow morning. Come on, Don, let's go."

28

At the entrance, Don and I are directed to their main conference room. They are all waiting for us. Stacey has packed the room. Not only with the entire sales staff, even the production supervisors and union stewards are here. They had to arrange for extra chairs along the walls.

As I go to take my place at the head of the long table, I shake hands with the people I know. They are very formal, but there is no open hostility. Don takes a seat at the back, near the door. Smart move.

"Good morning," Stacey starts.

"Good morning," she tries again. It takes a little while until the room quiets down.

"Here is Alex Rogo, our executive vice president," Stacey introduces me. "He is here because he believes in the future of Pressure-Steam. He believes that it's within our power to prevent it from being dismantled. Yesterday, Alex sat with the two senior board members to buy us time. He persuaded them that there is still a chance and succeeded in stopping all negotiations to sell our company, for the time being."

Some sporadic claps.

Will Stacey back me up? Will she grab the baton? If she doesn't, we are going to have another severe setback. A setback that we cannot afford. Early this morning I decided that I have to gamble on her. She can do it, no doubt. The question is, will she?

"Let's hear what Alex has to say to us." Stacey sits down. It's my turn to stand up.

I look at them. They are confused and defeated. I'll have to start by giving them the overall picture. But I must be careful to present things as they are, a pep-talk would be devastating. I also know that I must wake them up to take actions. But how?

"I am from headquarters," I begin. "For me, numbers talk, especially the green numbers. All the companies in the diversified group have improved substantially in the past year, but none are doing well. They improved from heavy losses to roughly break-even, but what we are looking for is profits.

"UniCo needs money. UniCo needs money badly. None of our three companies is bringing in any money to speak of. It's no wonder the board decided to sell the diversified group. It's business. It's hard, plain business.

"About three months ago, the board decided that all three companies were to be put on the block. All were under threat of being, in one way or another, destroyed. There is no way we can reverse the board's decision. There is only one path open, to improve performance fast. To improve performance to the extent that no new owner will mess around with the way the company is being run.

"For that we need to increase profits. Not by ten percent. Not by a hundred. Not by five hundred. Each company needs to increase its abysmal net profit to staggering numbers.

"It is impossible to do it by cutting costs. It is impossible to do it by working harder. You probably think it is impossible to do it, period."

At last I get some response. Unfortunately they are agreeing with my last statement.

"The only way to do it is to find new, smart approaches to increase sales."

I don't need to be a super expert to read their body language. If there was any hope left in them, it's dissipating.

"Listen," I demand. "One of your sister companies has already succeeded. Two months ago they were forecasting nine hundred thousand dollars net profit for this year. Now it's clear that they are going to make well over ten million. No, UniCo didn't give them a penny for investment. No, their market didn't improve. They have done it themselves. They constructed a new, unconventional approach to the market."

I stop to let them digest, and then continue.

"I Cosmetics was in a worse starting position than you are. Last year they lost almost a million dollars. This year their forecast was to break even. Now they, too, have found a breakthrough in marketing. Everyone is sure they will deliver over thirty million dollars net profit. You can imagine that in the rest of the diversified group, no one is now afraid of losing their job. They are secure.

"Now it is your turn. You must find a marketing breakthrough in your industry. You must think unconventionally."

They look at me with poker faces. I can feel the cold front.

No wonder. They are beaten. Speeches and references will not make a difference. They are beyond this stage.

They need to see a clear and tangible way out. They need to see their marketing solution, and they must believe that it's within their power to implement. Otherwise they won't even lift a finger.

"What is preventing you from getting more sales?" I ask. Nobody volunteers an answer. I try again.

"What are the major complaints of your customers?" This is starting to be embarrassing.

"What demands do your prospects make?" I don't

give up. "What do they demand in order to place an order with you?"

"Cheaper prices," comes the answer from several places. They are starting to enjoy my discomfort. They enjoy putting the big boss from corporate, who doesn't understand anything about their real world, in his place.

I cannot even get their market UDEs. I'll have to try another tactic. They take some distorted pleasure in showing me that there is no way out. Maybe if I can construct their cloud it will help? Maybe, if I'm able to bring them to agree on their cloud, I can use it to break out a solution? Fat chance, but what do I have to lose?

"Cheaper prices, I see. And what will happen if you do reduce prices?" I start to work on their cloud.

"Nothing," Joe, the VP of sales, bluntly answers.

"Why?" I ask him.

"Because the competitors will match our prices on the spot."

"So something will happen. Our profits will go down." They don't even bother to smile.

I switch on the overhead projector, saying, "The objective is to 'Increase sales.' In order to 'Increase sales,' you must 'Respond to the prospect's needs.' Which means you must 'Reduce prices.'

"On the other hand, in order to 'Increase sales,' you must 'Take actions that your competitors cannot immediately imitate,' which definitely means, 'Do not reduce prices.' "

I look at the image projected on the screen for a moment, giving them a chance to let it sink in, before I turn to them. "Is this the case?" I ask.

"Yes," Joe answers quietly.

"I am asking all the sales people here, is this your conflict?"

"Yes," they all answer.

"Tough problem," I admit. "A very tough problem. Joe, will you come help me?"

He stands up reluctantly. "Help you do what?"

"Help find out if there is any way out of this box."

He twists his lips in disbelief, but comes to the front.

"Joe, which part of this cloud do you dislike the most?" I ask.

He takes his time examining the cloud before he answers, "I don't have any quarrel with the bottom part. . . . And I like to please our customers. What I definitely don't like is reducing our prices."

"Does everybody agree with Joe?" I want to make sure that they are all in on it.

Some say yes. Others nod.

"Fine," I acknowledge them. "Let's expose the hidden assumptions. In order to 'Respond to the prospect's needs,' we must 'Reduce prices,' because . . . Come on Joe, because . . . ?"

"Because that's what they ask for," Joe completes the sentence.

What an answer. "Joe, don't avoid the issue. Try to relate to the prospects' needs."

He doesn't like my remark. Salespeople are always supposed to relate to their prospects' needs. A legend.

"Reduced prices is what they need," he says in a formal voice.

"Why?" I play the ivory tower executive.

"Because almost all our clients are under financial pressure from corporate. They are industrial companies. They are like us. Always under pressure from corporate to improve on their financials."

He still has enough spirit to fight me. That's good.

"Now we are getting somewhere," I pretend not to notice his cynicism and turn his words into a clearly verbalized assumption. "In order to 'Respond to the prospect's needs,' we must 'Reduce prices,' because 'The only way to respond to the prospect's financial pressure is to reduce price.' That's what you said?"

"What our clients want is that we'll reduce prices," he

repeats to himself. "That's for sure. But if we listen to them they will try to put all their financial burden on us. You know that some of our clients want us to give them spare parts on consignment. Can you imagine such guts?" It's apparent that Joe is irritated with the whole subject.

He's not cooperating, but I see a way to use what he's said. Maybe it's not fair, but we have to make progress. I look at Joe, at the cloud and then turn to face the group. "So Joe doesn't think that our assumption is valid. Reducing prices is not the only way that we can respond to the customers' financial pressure. For example, as Joe said, we can respond to their financial pressure by giving them spare parts on consignment."

Joe is too flabbergasted to speak.

Phil, the sales manager for the East Coast, can't take it any longer. "But sir, what's the difference? Isn't consignment just another way to reduce prices?" If it weren't for my position, he would have been more blunt. That's for sure.

"Phil," I patiently say, "there is a vast difference between reducing price and giving spare parts on consignment."

"I don't see it," Joe returns to the battlefield.

"Let me demonstrate it by an example. Suppose that a client holds one hundred thousand dollars worth of spare parts, and he uses, on average, about ten thousand a month." I write it on a transparency. "A typical medium-sized client. What will be the financial impact on the client, if we reduce the price of spare parts by ten percent?"

"That will be a disaster," Phil cannot restrain himself. "We'll lose income, and I don't think that we'll increase our spare parts, sales by even one unit. Are we really going to do that?"

"We are only going to do things that make business sense," I assure him. "At this stage we are just trying to answer your question, what is the difference between reducing price and consignment? You claimed that there is no difference. I claim that there is. Shall we find out?"

Nobody is happy. I hear murmurs of "Academic discussion." "We shouldn't waste our time on that." "Let him continue."

I ignore it, point to the numerical example and repeat my question to Joe. "What will be the impact on the client's finances?"

"If we reduce our spare parts' prices by ten percent, then we'll get one thousand dollars less per month. That's all. It doesn't look to me like a sensible business decision." Joe insists on not looking at it from the client's point of view.

As long as I do not bring them to see their offering from the market's perspective, we don't stand a chance of developing anything meaningful.

"In other words," I rephrase his answer, "the client will have a direct positive impact of one thousand dollars a month on his profit and the same for his cash. Now suppose that instead we offer—from now on—to give him spare parts on consignment. What is the financial impact? On the client, not on us."

Joe doesn't answer.

Phil says, "For the impact on the client's finances we have to ask his comptroller."

I ignore him and continue to talk to Joe. "Joe, if we switch to consignment, what must happen? The first month the client takes from his inventory the equivalent of ten thousand dollars. We replenish it, but on consignment terms. The result is that the client improved his cash by ten thousand dollars and reduced the inventory he holds on the books by the same amount. This means that our offer is very attractive to him, much more than giving a ten percent price reduction.

"Now the month after that, the client . . ."

Joe can't take it any more. "Yes, our offer is very attractive to him. No wonder, his cash improves by ten thousand dollars, our cash suffers by the same amount. His inventory is reduced by ten thousand, ours went up by the same amount."

"Not correct. Steve?"

Steve, Pressure-Steam's controller, answers as I expected. "Our inventory will go up only by two thousand five hundred dollars. That's the value that we carry on our books. We don't carry inventory at sales value."

"So what." Joe is very upset. "Excuse me, but if you are going in this way, why don't we give the client the original equipment on consignment as well?"

"Interesting idea," I calmly say. "That would solve his problem of an investment budget."

"But . . ." Joe is out of words.

"It will also enable the client to improve his return-on-investment. His corporate would love it. And if your prospect belongs to a company like ours, you'll have a really attractive offer, since it doesn't put any immediate demand on his cash."

"Are you joking!"

"No, I'm not joking," I answer dryly. "I'm just examining what is attractive to our prospects."

This pushes Joe over the edge. "Attractive! I can tell you many things that are attractive to our customers. The problem is that none of them make any sense for us."

"Give me an example."

"If you want something really attractive," Joe doesn't hesitate for a second, "give the customer everything. The best would be if we own and run the customer's needs for pressure steam for him. This is ridiculous."

I stare at him. For a long time. Here is the answer. So simple. Can it be?

He starts to fold under my gaze.

Suddenly Stacey speaks up. "Joe, repeat what you just said. Exactly, word for word."

"If you want to be attractive to the customer, let's run

his pressure steam needs for him," he says in angry desperation.

"Why not?" Stacey stands up. "What if we own the equipment, the spare parts, the maintenance people—all of it? We take care of whatever the client needs for pressure steam. We could sell him pressure steam. Not equipment, not spare parts, but pressure steam.

"Oh, don't worry, we are not going to give it for free. We'll charge for it."

"How are we going to charge for it?" Joe spits.

"I don't know," she says. "Maybe according to kilocalorie, or BTUs."

"That will not do," he says. "We must take the distance from the furnace into account. Pipes, valves, everything that goes with it are a major part of the system."

Well, well. He's walking into the trap.

"Maybe we should charge according to BTU per yard?" someone thinks aloud.

"I'm sure we can sort it out," Stacey says. "That won't be the problem." Turning to all of them she asks, "What do you think? Let's not sell the physical iron but sell the real thing that the client wants. Pressure steam. Where he wants it, when he wants it, in the amounts that he needs. What do you think about the concept?"

Nobody hurries to answer. Some nod their heads skeptically. Some stare at the ceiling or at each other. But there is no negative reaction. They simply are thinking about it. I sit down.

Phil is the first to talk. He says only one word. "Xerox."

"Yes, Xerox," Stacey repeats. "Our large copying machines. We didn't buy them. We don't own them. We don't maintain them. The largest ones we don't even operate. It's all done by Xerox. And we pay them. We pay them a flat fee per month plus a small sum for each copy. They didn't sell us copying machines, they are selling us copies of whatever we want copies of. Joe, what do you think about it?"

"It won't work. Most of our income and all of our profit comes from spare parts. If we are going to give them on consignment, we'll starve."

"Who said anything about consignment?" Stacey is surprised. "What I'm talking about is giving this new offer to new clients. Companies that are building new plants or expanding existing ones."

"Ah, that's another story." Joe is more relaxed.

"Well, what do you think?"

"I don't know." Joe is much less aggressive now. "It might work. There isn't much to lose. In any event, in order to penetrate we already sell the original installation for only the raw material cost."

Stacey continues to consult with him. "Do you think that if we offer it for a flat monthly fee plus charging according to usage we can get the deals?"

"Depends on the prices. But for the right price we'll get it. The real question is what price gives us a break-even point?"

"Our break-even depends on how much it costs us," Stacey says. "A major burden is the spare parts. If we implement the new distribution system we can bring every part that is needed within a few hours. This will mean that we'll need to hold much fewer spare parts at the client's sites. It will substantially cut our costs."

"To some extent," Joe grudgingly agrees.

"I also believe," Stacey continues, "that we can maintain their system for a fraction of the maintenance cost that they spend."

"That's for sure," Phil speaks up. "They don't know how to maintain our equipment. Sometimes what they call maintenance, I call sabotage."

"Which means that we can maintain their system for a fraction of what it costs them. Joe, we can give them a good price. A very good price."

"We'll have to do the calculation." Joe is still skeptical.

"We don't have to do any calculation to know the answer. Look, Joe, we have a tremendous amount of spare capacity," Stacey reminds him of the obvious. "If you think that with this offer we can take the new market, any reasonable price will guarantee us a lot of profit. Don't you see?"

"If it's good, the competitors will immediately copy us. What's the use?" He digs in his heels.

"We can make sure that will not happen," Phil says. "If we can have all spare parts within a few hours, we will be able to guarantee extremely high reliability. Let's offer to pay penalties for every breakdown that lasts longer than . . . say twenty-four hours."

"Penalties? Why penalties?" Joe is immediately on guard.

"Because that way we'll ensure that our competitors will not immediately follow," Stacey says.

"And if they try, they'll break their heads," Phil completes the picture.

Joe doesn't answer. Many are grinning. Only now I start to realize to what extent they don't like him. Frankly, neither do I.

Stacey turns to the group and suggests, "Shall we examine, seriously, to what extent this offer will be attractive to the prospects?"

They start to argue about it. More and more people are drawn into the debate.

Before long Stacey takes a blank transparency and writes at the bottom, "We offer pressure steam where, when and as much as needed." Slowly, the Future Reality Tree starts to emerge. Every time that they succeed in overcoming another reservation, a few more entities are added to the tree.

After two stormy hours, three pages are already finalized. They are over the hump. No one is now against the solution, they are polishing it. Making sure that it's okay.

Their Future Reality Tree clearly shows how big and diverse the benefits are going to be. The benefits to them and to the clients. It's impressive.

The details in their case are very involved, but the concept can be explained in a simple way. The offer that they are examining now, relative to the way they always did business, is like the difference between buying a car and leasing a car. You know that tax reasons make leasing quite popular. But that is just a tiny part of the story in their case.

To realize the real magnitude of it, imagine that currently you don't have to just buy the car but also a fully manned garage to maintain it, an inventory of spare parts, and a gas station.

What they offer is to give you the car that you want, and to charge according to the miles you drive, as you drive them. The price is very fair. In total, considering the expense of maintenance people and carrying costs, it's cheap.

Now imagine that you must have a car but you are measured on return-on-investment. The difference between the two offers is night and day.

Knowing how corporate thinks about these things, I'm quite convinced that if Pressure-Steam presents it well, they're bound to win almost every new installation. Considering the fact that they have a lot of spare capacity, they're bound to make a hefty profit. How much? I'll have to wait for a week or two until I get their detailed plan.

They are about to break for lunch when Phil says, "Why offer it only to new installations? Why don't we offer it to our competitors existing clients? With this offer we can eat them for lunch, and they can't do a thing about it."

This remark starts the madhouse. Everybody is talking. There are many negative branches they'll have to hammer out. Many.

I decide to leave. My presence isn't contributing a thing—maybe even the opposite. Stacey is firmly in control and action-oriented. Nobody thinks anymore that there is no way to increase sales, on the contrary, they are bloodthirsty. Their competitors' blood.

Don wants to stay on. Stacey doesn't have any problem with it, on the contrary, she is glad to have him.

29

Six months later we are sitting in my office.

"How long does it take them?" Bob asks for the tenth time.

"More coffee?"

He ignores me. "These bloody lawyers. What are they doing in there? Sharpening pencils? How much time does it take to insert a few minute changes?"

We are waiting for the lawyers to put in the last-minute changes that were agreed on. Then Granby and Nelson will sign and I Cosmetics will no longer be part of UniCo.

Bob stands up and starts to pace. "And I still say we sold it short."

"Bob, let it go. Two hundred and seventy million is a fair price. Besides, what is it to you? In an hour or so, you are them. You change camps. Any last-minute regrets?"

"Not really." He sits down again. "You know I didn't have any real problems with it. Especially after talking to Pete."

"Yes," I laugh, "he is as happy as a cat in a dairy."

"Why shouldn't he be? He is expanding like there is no tomorrow."

"I think that what really counts for him is that he can now teach people how to do things the right way. You know how much Pete likes teaching. As I heard it, they plan to rotate all their managers through his company. Even the corporate comptroller has to spend two weeks there. Can you imagine what Pete will probably do to him?"

Bob's laughter fills my office.

"By the way, Alex, you never told me how you managed to pull off that miracle. To get one hundred and sixty-eight million dollars for that small pimple."

"I don't think you want Pete to hear you calling his treasured company a pimple."

"If he does, I'm dead. But Alex, with all due respect, it's a small company. How much were they doing? Must be less than seventy million a year. You got more than twice their total annual sales!"

"They were also cranking out fourteen million profit a year. But the real answer is—we got it the same way we are going to get a fair price for your company. We didn't sell just a company. We sold a valuable concept. The company and its management are the essential instruments to implement that concept."

"I see." He quiets down. "I could still learn a lot from you. Maybe I'm making a mistake leaving UniCo?"

"Are you crazy? Do you think that you'd get such an opportunity here?"

"No, Alex, just teasing. Who could ask for a better opportunity? Not only am I keeping I Cosmetics under my direct control, but on top of it I'm going to run the entire drugstore supply group. Your kid's idea worked beautifully! What a job! Five companies. Nine plants. Over two hundred sales reps. A hefty budget. I can't wait. What's with these bloody lawyers?"

He starts again.

I ask Fran to bring in some tea. We don't need any more coffee now.

"By the way, Alex. What are you going to do once Stacey's company is sold? Do you have any irons in the fire?"

"Maybe I'll come and work for you?" I ask jokingly. "I have some thoughts. Nothing concrete yet. But don't worry, I'll manage."

"I'm sure. Any company would grab you with both hands. With your achievements and connections, I'm not worried at all. I just wondered if you'd already decided."

Frankly, I'm starting to feel itchy. I had a little time to look around and there aren't many jobs that I'd like to have. Not to mention being able to get. But there is enough time.

I hope.

"You know, Alex," he interrupts my thoughts, "if there is one thing that I don't like about my new job it's that I won't have you to turn to. No, don't stop me. I have wanted to tell you this for a long time, but it was somehow inappropriate. Now that it's apparent that I don't need to brown-nose you . . ."

"You still need. The contract is not signed yet."

"Will you shut up, please. As it is, this is not easy for me to say. I don't need your jokes on top of it."

"So don't say a thing. There is no need. I understand."

He sits quietly for a few seconds. "No. It should be said. Alex, I'm six years older than you. I reached where I am the hard way, nobody gave me any gifts. Especially not you. You made me sweat like no other boss. But in the past eight years I've gotten used to thinking about you as my father. Don't smile. I'm serious.

"I knew that you were there watching and caring about me. Not like a hen helping when it's not needed, but the opposite. Allowing me to grow, to make mistakes, but ready to guide me whenever I needed direction.

"I knew that no matter what happened, you would be there making sure that I found the way to put things back on track. You can't imagine what a good feeling it is to know it. Thank you, Alex.

"Okay, I said it. Please don't answer back."

What can I answer?

When the signing ceremony is over, Granby signals me to stay. People leave the boardroom one-by-one, or in small groups. Everybody is leaving in a good mood. It's a real win-win deal.

Finally, it is only Granby, Trumann, Doughty and me. Just the four of us in this large, luxurious room. We sit down in one corner. We all worked hard on this deal, it's as if we want this moment to last a little longer.

"Congratulations, Alex," Granby says. "I wanted to thank you personally. You turned a fiasco into a big victory. It's much easier to retire knowing that I'm leaving a solid company behind. Thank you, again."

"Hear, hear," they say.

After a little while Granby asks, "How is Pressure-Steam doing? When can we move on that deal?"

"It's too early to tell," I answer. "They are doing well, but as long as we don't understand the full impact, it's very difficult to construct a reasonable proposal."

They don't seem concerned. "Can you elaborate?" Brandon asks.

"Everything is moving according to plan, no real surprises. They've already got four major new accounts, and their proposals are being seriously considered by another dozen or so companies.

"The problem now is more controlling the process. It's a fine balance between getting more accounts and making sure that no bottlenecks pop up."

"I can imagine that everybody who uses pressure steam is watching those new accounts with a hawk's eye," Granby comments.

"More or less," I agree. "That's why it's so crucial to move prudently. Any serious slip-up and the competitors will blow it out of proportion. They aren't laughing at our approach any more. They're starting to panic."

"They should," Brandon says. "I still don't understand how you pulled it off. Yes, we went over all your trees. Forty-seven negative branches. Over one hundred obstacles. I've never seen such meticulous planning."

"What do you want? We didn't have time for mistakes. so we had to spend extra time planning!" I tease him. "Yes, I agree. Stacey and her people have done a remarkable job.

"I particularly admire how they timed the reduction in their regional spare parts' inventory with the increase in equipment they had to put on the new clients' sites. They didn't need even one cent from UniCo. It was a master-piece of synchronization."

"What impresses me the most," Granby comments, "is how they built their field maintenance force. Taking on board the best maintenance people of their clients as part of the deal was ingenious. It solved so many problems for everyone, in one fell swoop. Impressive."

I smile. Because of our hiring freeze, I had to fight Granby to the hilt on this exact point. He probably doesn't remember it anymore.

"So, when do you think we can resume negotiations?" Jim asks.

"I don't know, it's really too early to tell. At some point we'll have to decide, but not now, that's for sure."

"I think that about two months from now we should have a good idea what market share we can capture," Brandon speculates. "Maybe then?"

Granby turns to me, "Is that so?"

"Brandon is right. By that time Stacey will probably have exhausted all her spare capacity. Progress will be de-pendent on the rate she can train more engineers. Maybe we'll have to steal them from the competitors, but even then it will take them time to adjust to the way we operate. It's very different from what they are used to. Yes, two months might be about right."

"So it's two months, hmm." Granby doesn't sound too happy.

"Is there a problem?" Brandon politely inquires.

"Not really. It's only that I wanted to have some time

to clear my desk. I retire in three months and I wanted to devote my last month to visiting all our facilities. Brandon and Jim, I know that it's too much, you have already done more than your share, but can I ask you to handle this deal as well?"

"I have a better idea," Brandon says. "Alex is really the one who led the last two deals. He came up with the concept of what we are selling. He decided which of the prospects would be the best to contact. His presentations are what really made it possible. And let's face it, he was the one who almost dictated the selling price, first to us and then to the other side. Jim, don't you agree?"

"Facts are facts," he says.

"We'll help, of course. But Alex should formally lead the deal. Alex, don't you think so?"

"No, I don't."

"Come on, stop being modest. It doesn't suit you," Jim smiles at me.

"Nothing to do with modesty. I think I shouldn't lead the deal because I don't believe that there should be a deal."

"A typical Alex bomb," Brandon sighs. "Okay, what do you mean this time?"

"It's like that joke about Napoleon and the bells," I answer, knowing that it's the best way to demonstrate my point. Without allowing them time to object I proceed. "Once Napoleon came to a small village and they didn't ring the bells for him. Furious, he called the village head and demanded an explanation. 'We had three good reasons, the frightened man apologized. 'First is that we didn't know you were coming. Second, the bell man is sick, and third, we don't have bells.' "

"Nice joke," Jim enjoys it. "Now what's the point?"

"We shouldn't initiate any deal to sell Pressure-Steam because of three reasons. First, there is no more reason to sell. Second, there are no longer any good prospects to sell it to. And third, we need it badly ourselves."

"Alex, explain, please."

"What was the original reason for selling the diversified group's companies? It was the need to improve UniCo's credit rating. And how much did we expect to get from the sales of all three companies? Less than one hundred and fifty million dollars. And how much have we gotten so far? With today's deal, it's four hundred and thirty-eight. How much more do you want? Our credit rating is fine, and admit it, we don't yet know what we're going to do with the money we've already got. Do we?"

I don't bother to wait for an answer.

"The second reason is that the best deal we could get would be from Pressure-Steam's competitors. But how much money is it? They simply can't raise that much, no matter what. To sell it to anybody else would be a waste.

"Which brings me to the third reason. UniCo as a whole is quite a mediocre company. Sorry sir, but which company in UniCo can we point to as the best in its industry? How about in the top ten? None. We need an internal model. We need a catalyst, a company that will be the school for change. Pete's company was not appropriate; UniCo doesn't deal with anything remotely close to the printing industry. Bob's company was not appropriate for the same reason. But look to what extent Stacey's company is exactly what we need.

"Almost all our core business companies deal with some mixture of mechanical work and electronics. Almost all of them involve a lot of tailored engineering. They are actually very large job shops. Even if we looked everywhere for a model, Pressure-Steam comes out as the best choice. Gentlemen, we need that company if we want to bring UniCo once again to be the leader that it was. We need Pressure-Steam badly.

They think about what I've said. After a few minutes, Brandon turns to Granby, "Next week you are going to present the board with an investment plan. Can you tell us now what you're going to suggest we do with the money?"

"I decided not to submit any investment plan," he surprises them. "Bill Peach and Hilton Smyth worked very hard on it, but no matter what they came up with, I wasn't happy. Nothing was good enough to justify committing the new CEO to it. I decided to leave this headache for my successor."

"I see," Brandon doesn't seem too surprised. He turns to me, "Alex, what would you recommend as an investment plan?"

I know exactly what I would recommend, but it is not for me to say it.

"Come on, Alex, knowing you I'm sure you have some thoughts about it. Speak up," Jim urges me.

"I prefer not to."

"Alex, you are between friends here. Tell us your thoughts," he insists.

"Look, Jim, I don't think an investment plan can be discussed in isolation. An investment plan should be derived from a strategic direction. So what you are actually asking me is my opinion of the best strategic direction for UniCo. Don't start me on that, it will take me at least an hour.

"Excellent idea," Brandon says. "Let's meet for dinner, the four of us. We need to celebrate."

"Good," says Granby. "I'm all for it."

I'm not. I'm not anxious to ramble on about my unpolished work on how to develop a corporate strategy. But how can I refuse this dinner invitation?

It's a good thing Julie convinced me to prepare for a new job. Not knowing which company I'd end up at, I procrastinated by trying to figure out how one should devise a company's strategy. Now it will be handy. There are almost four hours before dinner. I can go over my tree and turn it into a nice presentation. Four hours should be sufficient.

But first, I have to take care of another issue. It's perfect timing.

I follow Granby into his office.

"What is it, Alex?" he asks me.

"I think that the time has come to talk about my next assignment. Now that I Cosmetics is sold and it looks like we might not be selling Pressure-Steam, I really don't have a job. Being in Stacey's way is not what I'd call productive."

Before he can brush my concerns aside with some empty words, I hurry to continue. I really don't want to spend the next few months twiddling my thumbs.

"I have been doing a lot of thinking. I have ideas on how to increase the productivity of our companies, all our companies. Not by small incremental improvements, but progressing by leaps and bounds. Like we've done in the diversified group. I think that we've perfected it into almost a science. I'll show it tonight, in some detail."

"That will be interesting," he says politely.

"So, what I'm suggesting is that I be nominated to a newly created position, executive vice-president of strategic planning."

He doesn't say a word.

"I can easily work with Bill Peach. He will be glad to let me in. What I don't know is how Hilton Smyth will react. But I think you can take care of that. What do you think?"

"I think that you should wait." He puts his hand on my shoulder. "Alex, what you are proposing has serious ramifications to the organizational structure of the company. I am in no position to make such a change three months before I leave. You'll have to wait for the new CEO."

30

As soon as we order cocktails, Jim Doughty gets to the point. "Alex, you promised to tell us your opinion of what is the best strategic direction for UniCo. We are, all ears."

"If you don't mind," I say, "I prefer not to talk about UniCo specifically."

"Alex, don't do it to us," Brandon puts both his hands on his heart. "I've heard so many presentations on how to choose a strategy. I can't stand it any more. Tell us something concrete. Please." Brandon is in one of his cheerful moods.

"Stop it, Brandon, it won't help you. As a matter of fact, I'm afraid that I'll have to start with even bigger generalities. Like the question, 'What is the goal of a company?' You've heard this question before."

"Yes, too many times."

"Fellows," I insist, "if you want to hear my opinion on what we should do with the money, you'll have to cooperate. So, what is the goal of a company? An industrial company like us."

"You promise that you'll reach it? Tonight?" Brandon pleads.

"The goal of our company," Jim cuts in, "is to make money now as well as in the future."

"If that's the case," I tease him, "then I have a very good strategy for you. Open a bank. Late at night."

When they finish laughing, I continue. "Choosing a goal is not so simple. We can't talk about a goal in isolation. We have to work within some frame of limitations. It's futile to define a goal without defining the boundaries within which we can attempt to reach it."

"A goal does not justify the means," Brandon agrees. "So what you're saying is that together with defining a goal, we also have to determine the necessary conditions that we are not allowed to violate. You are going to suggest such necessary conditions now?"

"Why don't you try?"

"Not tonight. There are too many of them."

"Brandon, do you remember our first conversation, almost nine months ago? The conversation that we had in the plane, flying to London?"

"You mean when you said you didn't have any clue how to increase sales?"

"Yes, you remember," I smile. "Do you also remember the cloud we wrote? The one that highlighted the perceived conflict between protecting the interests of shareholders and protecting the interests of employees?"

"How could he forget?" Jim says. "That cloud opened the world of the Thinking Processes for us. Carry on."

Jim is quite impatient tonight. I wonder why? I continue, "The goal of 'Making money now as well as in the future,' is how we protect the interests of the shareholders. What about the employees? We agreed that it's essential to protect their interests as well."

"I see." Brandon starts to cooperate. "That's where you take one of your necessary conditions. What are you suggesting?"

"Something like, 'Provide a secure and satisfying environment for employees now as well as in the future.' Make sense?"

"Quite demanding," Granby speaks up. "I don't think

that we have been too successful at that. But if you can do it, it certainly helps."

He doesn't get it, I think to myself, but what's the point of insulting him. It's not a matter of "it certainly helps." If you violate a necessary condition you can't reach your goal. That is the meaning of the words "necessary condition."

We at UniCo violated this necessary condition. We laid off thousands of dedicated employees, we didn't even think that it was our job to make sure that we provided a satisfying environment for our people. No wonder we didn't succeed in making money. How could we, with a demoralized workforce?

Aloud, I say, "There is another one. Remember what we deduced when we analyzed the current competitive market? We agreed that the market punishes companies that don't satisfy the market perception of value."

"You can fool a few customers for a long time," Brandon rehashes the old cliche. "You can mislead many customers for a short time. But you cannot mislead many, for long."

Cliche or not, it fits.

"Which means," I say, "that we have another necessary condition, 'Provide satisfaction to the market now as well as in the future.' That's it. We don't need any more necessary conditions."

"What do you mean, we don't need any more?" Jim doesn't agree. "You mean that there are no other necessary conditions besides the two you mentioned? What about obeying the rules of society? Your own example, about opening a bank 'late at night'?"

"That's already covered, 'Provide satisfaction to the market now as well as in the future.' Think about it Jim. All the moral code is covered by the two necessary conditions."

His expression shows that he doesn't agree yet. No wonder, for a long time we thought that business and social values were almost contradictory. They were. Not any-more.

To help him quickly digest it, I say, "Let me review what we have agreed on. We agreed that we should, 'Make money now as well as in the future,' 'Provide a secure and satisfying environment for employees now as well as in the future,' and 'Provide satisfaction to the market now as well as in the future.' The first one represents the traditional view of people who own companies. The second is the traditional view of the unions, the employees' representatives. And the third expresses the message that all new management methods are zealously advocating. We, as top managers, must make sure that our companies provide all of them."

"Easy to say," Granby sighs. "The problem is that so often there are conflicts between them."

"No, there aren't," I say. "There are modes of operations that apparently conflict with one of them. These same modes in the long run conflict with all of them."

"What you are telling us," Jim is trying hard to digest, "is that we have to realize that there is no conflict between them. That they don't contradict but in fact supplement each other."

"Precisely."

"Alex is probably right," Brandon joins me. "As people who believe in making money as the goal we are also awakened to the fact that the other two entities are absolutely necessary conditions for achieving our goal."

"The same awakening is happening in the other camps," I add. "Show me a union leader who believes that there is job security in a company that constantly loses money. Show me a quality zealot who thinks that a company can provide good service to the market while constantly losing money."

"So you claim that these three entities are actually important to the same degree?" Jim is on to it. "If that's the case, how come everyone is talking about making money as the goal?"

"Maybe in Wall Street circles, everyone is," I can't resist the opportunity. "But you have a point. Making money is much more tangible than the other two. It's the only one that can be measured."

"I knew that we were right," Brandon smiles.

"Don't fall into the trap that the first entity is more important," I warn him. "Making money can be measured just because of a coincidence. You see, somewhere in prehistory a genius invented a way to compare wheat to goats. He or she invented the abstract unit of money, a currency. No one yet has invented a unit of measure for security or satisfaction."

"I'm three-point-seven X secure, and Jim is fourteen and a half Y frustrated." Brandon demonstrates my point.

"I think that we'd better order dinner," Jim says. "This conversation is deteriorating.

While we wait for our appetizers, Jim presses on. "Alex, this is all very interesting, but you still haven't told us a thing either about strategy or how you suggest investing the money."

"I don't agree," I say. "I think that we have actually defined what makes a good or bad strategy."

"Maybe we did, but if so, it escaped me."

"Do you agree that strategy is the direction we take to reach our goal?"

"Naturally," he agrees.

"Do you also agree that if we violate any of the three entities that we outlined before, we are bound not to reach our goal? Remember, whichever of the three you choose as a goal, we agreed that the other two are necessary conditions to achieving it."

"So a good strategy must not clash with any of them," Brandon concludes. "How are you going to find a strategy that you know will not violate any of the three entities? And even if you find one, how do you know that it will work?"

"First of all, by not choosing a strategy that we know is bad. As you just said, any strategy that clashes with one of the three entities should be discarded. That trims out half of the strategies I've ever come across."

"More than half," Granby corrects me.

"You're probably right," I agree. "They are, by definition, not sensible strategies; at best they are panic-driven." Like the original decision to sell the diversified group, I almost add. "So if the only strategies that I can come up with clash with one of the three entities, I must keep on looking."

"Yes, but how?" Jim continues to urge me on.

I refuse to be urged. "I haven't finished telling you what I think should not be done. We shouldn't ever build a strategy based on a market forecast."

"That trims away all the remaining strategies that I've ever seen," Granby laughs. "But are you saying that we shouldn't start with a forecast of the market? To me that seems like the most natural point to start."

"No, because trying to forecast the market is like trying to capture the wind," I say. "For decades we've tried to forecast sales. Did we ever succeed? Is there something that we trust less than the accuracy of our companies' sales forecasts?" Hilton Smyth, I secretly answer my own question.

"For years we blamed the forecasting methods," Jim supports me. "Recently, I read that the chaos theory proved that accurate forecasting of the weather is not a matter of more sensors or bigger computers. It is theoretically an impossibility. Probably the same holds true for detailed market forecasts. So, Alex, what is your starting point?"

"I'd start with developing a decisive competitive edge. If the company doesn't have a unique technology, or outstanding products, I'd do the same as we have done in the companies of the diversified group. Concentrate on small changes that eliminate the negatives for the market."

"You call what you have done, small changes?" Granby almost chokes on his salad.

I wait a second to let him recover, and then explain, "We haven't changed the physical products at all. We have changed policies, on a large scale, but not the products. That's what I meant by small changes. I agree that the name is not appropriate, it's just a residual from when we developed the way to do it."

Brandon and Jim nod their heads.

"But I wouldn't stop there," I continue to explain. "Then I'd move immediately to find ways to segment the market."

"Did we do it?" Jim asks.

"We did it at Pressure-Steam, that was easy. When you have to substantially tailor the product for the client, there is no problem segmenting. We haven't for Bob and Pete's companies. But I made sure that they know how to take what they have done to the next level. You see, I believe that as long as you haven't established a decisive competitive edge in many segments of the market, you should feel exposed."

"Why?"

"Because the competitors will catch up," I explain. "There is no absolute competitive edge, it's just a window of opportunity, which will be closed."

"So what you're saying is that we must always be on the move," Jim concludes.

"Of course."

"When can we afford to relax?" Brandon asks jokingly.

"When we retire," is Granby's answer.

I hope much before that. There are ways to identify windows that will take a long time for the competitor to close. But if I mention it they will hold me here until morning. Better to not mention it.

Instead I say, "Having a decisive, competitive edge in many segments of the market is far from being enough."

"What more do you want?" Brandon is surprised. "Alex, Alex, do you ever say 'enough'?"

"Yes, when all necessary conditions are met."

"And you think that bringing a company to a position where it has a decisive competitive edge in a segmented market is not sufficient to be considered fulfillment of a CEO's duties?" Jim waits tentatively for my reaction.

"How can it be?" I'm amazed at them. "We agreed that the market cannot be accurately forecasted. You know better than I do that markets oscillate. Today it's booming, tomorrow a recession."

"You have to make enough money in good times to carry you through bad times," Granby confirms.

But that's not the point. I have to be more explicit. "What are you going to do when the market drops below your capacity? Fire your people, or let them twiddle their thumbs?"

It's Granby again, "In bad times you have to tighten the belt."

I know that's what he believes in. I went through what he calls tightening the belt.

It's not prudent for me to continue. I need these people. I need their active help in finding a new job and I worked hard to earn it.

"Did you already forget the second entity?" I hear myself say. " 'Provide a secure and satisfying environment to employees.' "

They don't say a word. What are they thinking about? Why are they looking at me like that?

"Alex," Jim is careful choosing his words, "are you against layoffs, no matter what the profit of the company is?"

"Yes."

It's funny. They probably think that they just uncovered a radical in disguise.

They don't smile. They look at each other in silence. The atmosphere becomes heavier and heavier.

Jim says, "I don't think that this is realistic."

Granby says, "It's dangerous."

That gets to me. Why can't they see the obvious? Just because it puts more responsibility on their shoulders? Let them think whatever they want. I'm sick and tired of top people who refuse to acknowledge the responsibility that they actually carry. Refuse to acknowledge it at the expense of the people around them.

Give me all the authority, none of the responsibility, that's probably their motto.

Good-bye connections.

Julie will understand. She will.

31

"So, what happened then?" Julie is not happy with me.

"Nothing for a while."

"And after that while? Alex, stop pulling my leg."

"I'm telling you exactly what happened," I say innocently.

"Listen, my dear husband. I've known you for many years. And I know you would not throw your career to the wind and then come home with a face like a cat who just swallowed a canary. So please stop these funny games and tell me what happened."

"You want just the bottom line? Without what I had to go through to get it? No way, darling. The entire story or nothing at all."

"Sorry, I'll be patient. Continue."

"So then Brandon asked if I am against laying off no matter what the situation. What a question! Of course when you have maneuvered your company into a cash crunch, you must lay off. Otherwise everybody will lose his job."

"Sorry, but I don't understand. If that's what you think, why did you put them off when Jim asked if you are against laying off when the company is not profitable?"

"Because I am. Not having cash and not having profits

are two different things. Listen, Julie. Seven, six, even five years ago, UniCo was firing like crazy. The company was not profitable enough, but at the same time it had hefty cash reserves. There was no reason to lay off. That was the easy way for top managers to try to improve their bottom line. Cut cost rather than finding ways to better satisfy the market. Of course it didn't help. We laid off and we continued to lose money, so we laid off again. It's a vicious cycle. That's what I'm against."

"I see now. So what was their reaction?"

"The same as yours. I had to explain the difference to them as well."

"And?"

"They were unhappy. Especially Granby. He said that not everyone can come up with new ways to take the market."

"He has a point."

"No, he doesn't. We were discussing what a good strategy is, and at that point in the conversation, we were discussing a company that had already achieved a competitive edge."

"You lost me. If it's the best company in its field, how can it lose money?"

"Let me remind you where we were. A company succeeds in developing for itself a dominant competitive edge, or as you call it, is the best in its field. Everybody is working, the company makes a lot of money, everybody is happy. Now the market goes down, the demand drops. As a result you have more people than you need. What do you do? That was the question."

"I understand. What can you do?"

"My answer is that if you are operating under a good strategy, it will never happen."

"Once again I don't understand. Look, Alex, companies and markets are not my fortè. I'm a marriage counselor. Why don't you just tell me what happened? Why are you so happy?"

"No, Julie, it won't help you. You understand no less than they did. It's common sense, you don't need to know much about industry. What you read in the newspapers is more than enough. So what don't you understand?"

"I don't remember. What were you talking about? Oh, yeah, you said that if you follow a good strategy, the market should never drop on you. What do you mean? When the market drops, it drops."

"Precisely what they didn't understand. Jim asked the same question, almost word for word."

"I'm glad that I'm not the only dummy around you."

"Jim is no dummy. Not at all. It's only that people are so used to blaming external circumstances that at the moment cannot be changed, rather than blaming themselves for not preparing in advance. It's like the cricket blaming the winter, while the ant is fed and warm."

"Bringing it to a childish level doesn't help me," she laughs. "How can you prevent the market from dropping."

"I cannot. But with a correct strategy, I can prevent the market of my company from dropping to the extent that there is not sufficient work for all of my employees."

"How can you achieve this miracle?"

"Simple. By creating enough flexibility. One precaution is to make sure that every employee is serving not just one segment of the market, but many segments. Do you agree that if I plan my actions carefully it's possible? For example, I can be careful to develop new products that require almost the same type of resources I already have."

"I think it's possible. But Alex, calm down, you don't have to shout."

"By the way, this is the opposite of what most companies are doing. To accomplish flexibility of the work force, you have to segment your market and not your work force. Do you know what they usually do? Even when the market naturally segments for them, a new market opens up, the idiots immediately open a new plant. They segment the resources. The exact opposite of what should be done under a sensible strategy."

"Now it's clear. But Alex, it's already one in the morning and I'm dying to know what really happened. Just give me a shorter version. I promise that some other time you can tell me all the details."

"Okay. Just the essence. I told them that there are two more things that a good strategy must be based on. One is that even in a market segment where we have a dominant competitive edge, we should not take the entire segment."

"But, why? Oops, sorry. I didn't say anything."

"It will be immediately clear. The other thing is that the company must be careful to enter into segments for which the probability of many of them dropping during the same time period is very small. This last concept has far-reaching ramifications."

"That I'll be happy to hear about some other time. Now, what happened?"

I give up. It's very difficult to tell somebody important things if she doesn't want to listen.

"The conclusion is obvious. If a company does everything that we said, then when a lucrative segment is up, the company shifts their focus away from some less lucrative segments. They can do it because their resources are flexible. When a market segment goes down, the company shifts focus to other segments. Segments that they didn't bother to fully exploit before.

"You see, the result for that company is that there is very rarely the need to lay off people. And all the three entities—the goal and the necessary conditions—are simultaneously satisfied."

"Interesting. But what happened then? Tell me."

"Oh, they were impressed. Much more than you are. Brandon even said I was full of good surprises. 'I expected to hear some coherent view of how to strengthen the core business, but this is certainly beyond my expectations,' he said. Did you hear that? . . . Beyond his expectations!"

"And what did Doughty say?"

"He just said, and I quote, 'Passed with flying colors.' "

"That's why you are so pleased? I thought that maybe you had done what you promised. That you asked them if they could help you find a good job."

"Yes. I did."

"And what did they say? Did they promise to help?"

"Not exactly. They looked at each other. Then Jim smiled and said that they definitely can help me find a good job. And Brandon said 'How about being the next CEO of UniCo?' "

For information about other books on the
Theory of Constraints (TOC)
please visit our web site at:
www.goldratt.gen.in

For more information on the
Theory of Constraints (TOC)
please visit
www.toc-goldratt.com
www.timencash.com
www.sisl.siemens.co.in